T0197947

Get the eBook FREE!
(PDF, ePub, Kindle, and liveBook all included)

We believe that once you buy a book from us, you should be able to read it in any format we have available. To get electronic versions of this book at no additional cost to you, purchase and then register this book at the Manning website.

Go to https://www.manning.com/freebook and follow the instructions to complete your pBook registration.

That's it!
Thanks from Manning!

Learn Cisco Network Administration in a Month of Lunches

BEN PIPER

MANNING
SHELTER ISLAND

For online information and ordering of this and other Manning books, please visit
www.manning.com. The publisher offers discounts on this book when ordered in quantity.
For more information, please contact

 Special Sales Department
 Manning Publications Co.
 20 Baldwin Road
 PO Box 761
 Shelter Island, NY 11964
 Email: orders@manning.com

Manning Publications Co.   Development editor: Helen Stergius
20 Baldwin Road   Review editor: Ivan Martinović
PO Box 761   Technical development editor: Richard Siddaway
Shelter Island, NY 11964   Copyeditor: Linda Recktenwald
                                         Proofreader: Melody Dolab
                     Technical proofreader: James Berkenbile
                                          Typesetter: Marija Tudor
                                     Cover designer: Leslie Haimes

ISBN 9781617293634
Printed in the United States of America

brief contents

1 ▪ Before you begin   1

2 ▪ What is a Cisco network?   8

3 ▪ A crash course on Cisco's Internetwork
Operating System   30

4 ▪ Managing switch ports   46

5 ▪ Securing ports by using the Port Security feature   59

6 ▪ Managing virtual LANs (VLANs)   75

7 ▪ Breaking the VLAN barrier by using switched
virtual interfaces   87

8 ▪ IP address assignment by using Dynamic Host
Configuration Protocol   99

9 ▪ Securing the network by using IP access control lists   115

10 ▪ Connecting switches using trunk links   132

11 ▪ Automatically configuring VLANs using the
VLAN Trunking Protocol   146

12 ▪ Protecting against bridging loops by using the
Spanning Tree Protocol   159

13 ▪ Optimizing network performance by using port
channels   171

14 ▪ Making the network scalable by connecting routers
and switches together   184

15 ▪ Manually directing traffic using the IP routing table   197

16 ▪ A dynamic routing protocols crash course   213

17 ▪ Tracking down devices   232

18 ▪ Securing Cisco devices   243

19 ▪ Facilitating troubleshooting using logging and
       debugging   252

20 ▪ Recovering from disaster   264

21 ▪ Performance and health checklist   273

22 ▪ Next steps   280

contents

preface xiii
acknowledgments xiv
about this book xv
about the author xvii

1 *Before you begin* 1

1.1 Is this book for you? 1

1.2 How to use this book 2

   *The main chapters 3 ▪ Hands-on labs 3 ▪ Further
   exploration 3 ▪ Above and beyond 3*

1.3 Lab considerations 3

   *Choosing your lab environment 3 ▪ Virtual lab considerations 4
   Practicing on a live, production network 5 ▪ My recommendation
   for your lab environment 5 ▪ Cisco Internetwork Operating System
   versions 6*

1.4 Online resources 6

1.5 A word on my recommendations 6

1.6 Being an immediately effective network administrator 7

2 *What is a Cisco network?* 8

2.1 The truth about routers and switches 9

2.2 MAC addresses 10

2.3   The Ethernet frame: a big envelope   12

      When everybody talks, nobody listens   13

2.4   Broadcast domains   14

      Closing the floodgates: the MAC address table   15 ▪ *Breaking
      up the broadcast domain   17* ▪ *Joining broadcast domains   18*
      Addressing devices across broadcast domains   18

2.5   Internet Protocol addresses   18

      Where are you?   18 ▪ *The IP vs. MAC dilemma   20*
      Address Resolution Protocol   20

2.6   Connecting broadcast domains using a router   21

      Where are you? Where am I?   23 ▪ *Understanding
      subnets   23*

2.7   Traversing broadcast domains using a default gateway   24

2.8   Managing routers and switches   29

2.9   Hands-on lab   29

3 *A crash course on Cisco's Internetwork Operating System   30*

3.1   What is IOS?   30

3.2   Logging into Cisco devices   31

3.3   The show command   32

      Filtering output   35

3.4   Identifying the IOS version and package   38

      Version numbers   38 ▪ *Packages   39*

3.5   Viewing the running configuration   39

3.6   Changing the running configuration   41

3.7   Saving the startup configuration   43

3.8   The no command   44

3.9   Commands in this chapter   45

3.10 Hands-on lab   45

4 *Managing switch ports   46*

4.1   Viewing port status   47

4.2   Enabling ports   49

      The interface range command   51

4.3   Disabling ports   52

      Finding unused interfaces   53

4.4   Changing the port speed and duplex   54

Speed   54 ▪ Duplex   55 ▪ Autonegotiation   55 ▪ Changing the port speed   56 ▪ Changing the duplex   57

4.5   Commands in this chapter   58

4.6   Hands-on lab   58

5   Securing ports by using the Port Security feature   59

5.1   The minimum Port Security configuration   60

Preventing MAC flood attacks   60 ▪ Violation modes   64

5.2   Testing Port Security   65

5.3   Handling device moves   66

Port Security never forgets!   66 ▪ Aging time   67

5.4   Preventing unauthorized devices   69

Making Port Security maximally secure   70 ▪ Sticky MAC addresses   70 ▪ Caveats about sticky MACs   73

5.5   Commands in this chapter   73

5.6   Hands-on lab   74

6   Managing virtual LANs (VLANs)   75

6.1   What is a VLAN?   75

6.2   Inventorying VLANs   76

The VLAN database   76 ▪ The default VLAN   78 ▪ How many VLANs should you create?   78 ▪ Planning a new VLAN   78

6.3   Creating VLANs   78

6.4   Assigning VLANs   80

Checking port configuration   81 ▪ Setting the access VLAN   81 Setting the access mode   83

6.5   Voice VLANs   84

6.6   Using your new VLANs   85

6.7   Commands in this chapter   86

6.8   Hands-on lab   86

7   Breaking the VLAN barrier by using switched virtual interfaces   87

7.1   Understanding the VLAN–subnet connection   88

7.2   Switches or routers?   91

Enabling IP routing   92

7.3 What are switched virtual interfaces? 93

Creating and configuring SVIs 93

7.4 Default gateways 95

Testing inter-VLAN connectivity 97

7.5 Commands in this chapter 98

7.6 Hands-on lab 98

8 IP address assignment by using Dynamic Host Configuration Protocol 99

8.1 To switch or not to switch? 99

8.2 Configuring a Cisco DHCP server 100

Scopes 101 ▪ Options 101 ▪ Lease time 102 ▪ Subnets and VLANs 102

8.3 Configuring a DHCP pool 103

8.4 Excluding addresses from assignment 104

8.5 Configuring devices to request DHCP addresses 106

8.6 Associating DHCP Pools with VLANs 108

8.7 Creating a second DHCP pool 109

8.8 Viewing DHCP leases 110

8.9 Using non-Cisco DHCP servers 111

Asking the switch for help using the ip helper-address command 112

8.10 Commands in this chapter 113

8.11 Hands-on lab 114

9 Securing the network by using IP access control lists 115

9.1 Blocking IP-to-IP traffic 116

Creating an access list 117

9.2 Applying an ACL to an interface 120

9.3 Blocking IP-to-subnet traffic 122

Wildcard masks 123 ▪ Replacing an ACL 124 Applying an access control list to a switched virtual interface 126

9.4 Blocking subnet-to-subnet traffic 127

9.5 Commands in this chapter 130

9.6 Hands-on lab 131

10 **Connecting switches using trunk links 132**

10.1 Connecting the new switch 133

10.2 Understanding VLAN trunk links 134

Configuring a trunk link 135 ▪ Configuring DTP to automatically negotiate a trunk 136

10.3 Configuring Switch2 138

Configuring VLANs on the new switch 139

10.4 Moving devices to the new switch 141

10.5 Changing the trunk encapsulation 142

10.6 Commands in this chapter 144

10.7 Hands-on lab 145

11 **Automatically configuring VLANs using the VLAN Trunking Protocol 146**

11.1 Two words of warning 147

11.2 Configuring Switch1 as a VTP server 148

11.3 Configuring Switch2 as a VTP client 149

11.4 Creating new VLANs on Switch1 150

11.5 Enabling VTP pruning 153

11.6 Commands in this chapter 157

11.7 Hands-on lab 158

12 **Protecting against bridging loops by using the Spanning Tree Protocol 159**

12.1 How Spanning Tree works 161

How Spanning Tree deals with link failures 163

12.2 Rapid Spanning Tree 166

12.3 PortFast 168

12.4 Commands in this chapter 170

12.5 Hands-on lab 170

13 **Optimizing network performance by using port channels 171**

13.1 Static or dynamic? 172

Static 172 ▪ Dynamic 173

13.2 Configuring a dynamic port channel using the Link Aggregation Control Protocol 173

13.3   Creating a static port channel   177

13.4   Load-balancing methods   179

13.5   Commands in this chapter   182

13.6   Hands-on lab   183

14 Making the network scalable by connecting routers and switches together   184

14.1   The router-on-a-stick configuration   185

14.2   Connecting Router1   186

14.3   Configuring subinterfaces   187

14.4   The IP routing table   192

14.5   Applying an ACL to a subinterface   194

14.6   Commands in this chapter   195

14.7   Hands-on lab   196

15 Manually directing traffic using the IP routing table   197

15.1   Connecting Router1 to Switch2   199

15.2   Configuring transit subnets   200

Assigning transit IP addresses directly to physical interfaces   201
Assigning transit IP addresses to subinterfaces and SVIs   202

15.3   Removing the trunk link between switches   203

15.4   Configuring default gateways   204

15.5   Creating a DHCP pool for the Executives subnet   205

15.6   Commands in this chapter   212

15.7   Hands-on lab   212

16 A dynamic routing protocols crash course   213

16.1   Understanding router IDs   214

Configuring loopback interfaces   215

16.2   Configuring EIGRP   216

*Choosing the best path   221 • Routing around failures   224
EIGRP recap   225*

16.3   Open Shortest Path First   225

16.4   Commands used in this chapter   230

16.5   Hands-on lab   231

17 **Tracking down devices 232**

17.1 Device-tracking scenarios 232

17.2 Steps to tracking down a device 233

*Get the IP address 233 ▪ Trace the device to the last hop 233
Get the MAC address 233*

17.3 Example 1—Tracking down a network printer 234

*Tracing to the last hop using traceroute 234 ▪ Cisco Discovery
Protocol 235 ▪ Obtaining the MAC address of the device 236
Viewing the MAC address table 236*

17.4 Example 2—Tracking down a server 238

*Tracing to the last hop using traceroute 238 ▪ Obtaining the MAC
address of the device 239 ▪ Viewing the MAC address table 239*

17.5 Commands used in this chapter 242

17.6 Hands-on lab 242

18 **Securing Cisco devices 243**

18.1 Creating a privileged user account 244

Testing the account 244

18.2 Reconfiguring the VTY lines 246

*Enabling SSH and disabling Telnet access 246 ▪ Restricting SSH
access using access lists 248*

18.3 Securing the console port 250

18.4 Commands used in this chapter 251

18.5 Hands-on lab 251

19 **Facilitating troubleshooting using logging and debugging 252**

19.1 Configuring the logging buffer 253

19.2 Debug commands 254

*Debugging Port Security 255 ▪ Debugging DHCP 256
Debugging the VLAN Trunking Protocol 257
Debugging IP routing 258*

19.3 Logging severity levels 259

19.4 Configuring syslogging 261

19.5 Commands used in this chapter 262

19.6 Hands-on lab 263

20 *Recovering from disaster 264*

   20.1 Narrow the scope to a subset of devices 265

   20.2 Reloading the device 265
         Scheduling a reload 266

   20.3 Deleting the startup configuration 267

   20.4 Resetting the password 269
         Resetting the password on a router 269 ▪ Resetting the password on a switch 271

   20.5 Commands used in this chapter 272

21 *Performance and health checklist 273*

   21.1 Is the CPU being overloaded? 274

   21.2 What's the system uptime? 275

   21.3 Is there a damaged network cable or jack? 276

   21.4 Are ping times unusually high or inconsistent? 276

   21.5 Are routes flapping? 277

   21.6 Commands in this chapter 278

   21.7 Hands-on lab 279

22 *Next steps 280*

   22.1 Certification resources 280

   22.2 Cisco's Virtual Internet Routing Lab 281

   22.3 Troubleshooting end-user connectivity 281

   22.4 Never the end 281

         index 283

preface

Computer networks are one of the most difficult concepts for IT professionals to fully grasp. A network isn't a discrete thing like a piece of software, a printer, or a motherboard. It's a vast, sometimes nebulous collection of hardware and software all working together to move bits from one place to another. The level of complexity in a network is overwhelming, which is one reason so many brilliant and dedicated IT professionals tend to stay away from it. It often seems unapproachable.

If you've tried to read other networking books, you've probably found that they're far too academic and dripping with theory. They steep you in a brew of counterintuitive concepts and terms without tying them to practical, hands-on skills. My goal in writing this book is to make the network accessible to you—the IT professional who loves technology and loves to learn, but has found learning networking too intimidating or time-consuming. You won't be cramming years' worth of theory and concepts into a month-long boot camp. Instead, you'll start with a big-picture view of how networks operate, and then you'll dive right into practical, hands-on tasks that you can start using today. You'll pick up the concepts as you go, and they'll make sense because you'll be able to tie them in with day-to-day administration tasks. Best of all, you'll be able to *prove* your skills while simultaneously being able to explain *why* networks work the way they do.

Give me a part of your lunch break every weekday for a month, and by the time you're done, you'll have a shiny new set of marketable networking skills you can show off to your boss, your friends, and maybe even a future employer.

Let's get started!

acknowledgments

Thanks to Eric for his feedback on the early chapters. Also thanks to Bill, Brad, Kevin, Myles, and Miranda for supporting me in various ways throughout the process.

Thanks to all the reviewers whose comments helped make this a better book: Benoit Benedetti, Chad McAuley, David Kerns, Kent R. Spillner, Luis Moux, Mark Furman, Mikael Dautrey, Roy Legaard, Jr., Sau Fai Fong, and Shawn Bolan. A special note of appreciation goes to James Berkenbile, the technical proofreader who meticulously reviewed the manuscript.

Last but not least, thanks to the folks at Manning, especially Marjan Bace, Helen Stergius, Greg Wild, and Don Jones. Everyone who worked with me in editorial, production, and promotion, both directly and behind the scenes, helped to make this book possible.

about this book

For server administrators and desktop support technicians, the network has long been a mysterious labyrinth of boxes and wires. This book takes the existing networking knowledge and skills you already have from working on computers and expands on it by giving you practical, hands-on exercises that you'll be able to use on the job almost immediately.

Most of what you'll need to get started with this book is covered in chapter 1, but there are some things I want to mention here.

First, to complete the hands-on exercises, you'll need access to a physical or virtual Cisco lab. I cover lab options in more detail in chapter 1. Just be prepared to spend some time setting up your lab if you don't already have one.

Second, I've organized this book so that you begin with the most common tasks of a network administrator. These common tasks are fundamental and provide the foundation for the later chapters. Read the chapters in order, and don't skip any.

Third, there are some conventions I use throughout the book to make it easier to digest. `Fixed-width fonts` indicate commands you'll type in or output you should expect to see. *Italics* indicate important networking terms and concepts you should commit to memory. Not surprisingly, you'll see a lot more commands than terms!

About the code

This book contains many examples of Cisco commands and output in line with normal text. This is formatted in a `fixed-width font like this` to separate it from ordinary text. The solutions for the Hands-on Labs and guidelines for a virtual lab set-up are available for download under the Source Code link on the publisher's website at https://www.manning.com/books/learn-cisco-network-administration-in-a-month-of-lunches.

Author Online

The purchase of *Learn Cisco Network Administration in a Month of Lunches* includes access to a private forum run by Manning Publications where you can make comments about the book, ask technical questions, and receive help from the author and other users. To access and subscribe to the forum, browse to https://www.manning.com /books/learn-cisco-network-administration-in-a-month-of-lunches and click the Book Forum link. This page provides information on how to get on the forum once you are registered, what kind of help is available, and the rules of conduct on the forum. Manning's commitment to our readers is to provide a venue where a meaningful dialogue between individual readers and between readers and the author can take place. It's not a commitment to any specific amount of participation on the part of the author, whose contribution to the book's forum remains voluntary (and unpaid). The Author Online forum and the archives of previous discussions will be accessible from the publisher's website as long as the book is in print.

about the author

 BEN PIPER (benpiper.com) is a hands-on IT consultant who holds numerous Cisco, Citrix, and Microsoft certifications, including the Cisco CCNA and CCNP. He has over 17 Pluralsight courses covering networking, Cisco CCNP certification, Puppet, and Windows Server Administration.

Before you begin 1

The majority of business networks rely on Cisco hardware, specifically routers and switches. The thing about hardware is that it has a long shelf life, and even when it's time to replace it, it's easier to stick with the tried and true. Hence, large corporations, small businesses, and everybody in between depends on the proper care and feeding of their Cisco gear to stay in business. Networks are not "set it and forget it." They're in continual flux. Whenever an organization hires or fires an employee, or whenever an employee moves desks or departments, someone has to make a change to the network. When a business adds more heads (and more computers), it may have to expand its network by adding more Cisco devices. This book will teach you how to configure Cisco routers and switches to accommodate these types of moves, additions, and changes.

1.1 Is this book for you?

Let's start off by making sure this book is right for you. If you're interested in becoming a Cisco Certified Network Administrator (CCNA) or Cisco Certified Entry Networking Technician (CCENT), consider this book a foundational prerequisite. Although this book alone doesn't aim to make you a CCNA or CCENT, it *does* give you a solid foundation that will save you a lot of time and effort later on should you decide to pursue certification. In addition to giving you a clear conceptual understanding of routers and switches that many certification books lack, this book will also teach you how to maintain a Cisco network, expand it to accommodate organizational growth, and perform a little bit of troubleshooting.

Large organizations often have the luxury of hiring one or more network adminis-trators. These folks may hold an advanced Cisco certification and spend their days doing nothing but working on the network. But surprisingly, even some large organizations have only a handful of full-time network administrators. Small to midsize organizations often can't afford even one full-time network administrator, so the task of managing the network usually falls on one of the people in charge of handling the workstations, servers, and applications. At first blush, this seems to be a match made in heaven. This person who knows the ins and outs of the company's critical servers and applications is in a prime position to see how those components fit in with the rest of the network. They have a holistic view of the IT landscape and are well suited to the task.

But more and more organizations are finding this arrangement to be problematic. What if the person who normally does all the "network stuff" is on vacation and a new user in a remote office needs network access? What if that person is out sick and a user needs to move departments? What if the business wants to expand the network into a new suite but has to wait for that person to do all the work of expanding the network? Hiring a full-time network administrator is overkill. The problem isn't that they're lazy or don't care. The problem isn't that they don't want anyone else to do it instead (they probably wish someone else would!). The problem is that they're the only one who *knows* how to administer the network!

In the absence of the de facto network administrator, you have two choices: wait for them to return or attempt to do it yourself. *This book is for those who can't wait and must take the reins.* I'll show you how to perform the most common network administration tasks. I'll show you how to get new users set up on the network, how to handle moves and changes, how to secure the network using IP access lists, and even how to increase its capacity to accommodate growth using VLAN trunks and IP routing. I'll share enough nerdy networking theory to help you understand why networks work the way they do and to give you a practical foundation should you decide to delve deeper into networking later on.

I've met a lot of IT professionals for whom the network is a mysterious web of cables and boxes that somehow connects together all the computers, servers, and applications they're so familiar with. But the one thing that remains a mystery to them is the network. They *want* to learn it, but they don't know where to even begin. They have some network knowledge, but they don't know what they don't know. This book is for any IT professional who wants (or needs) to become proficient with Cisco networks over the next 30 days.

1.2   *How to use this book*

Try to focus on one chapter a day. Each chapter should take about 30 minutes to read and 30 minutes to practice. Read this book sequentially. Although you can use it as a desk reference later on, it's important that you start at the beginning and give each chapter time to soak in.

1.2.1 *The main chapters*

Chapters 2 through 22 represent the meat of the book, so you can expect to finish in about a month. Resist the temptation to jump straight to a particular chapter because it covers something you've recently encountered or are specifically interested in. I've organized the chapters with the most common and foundational configuration tasks first, and you should start with those so you'll have plenty of time to repeat them and build proficiency.

1.2.2 *Hands-on labs*

The majority of chapters contain a lab for you to complete. Each lab includes a set of tasks for you to complete and maybe even a set of questions to answer to test your practical and conceptual understanding of what you learned in that chapter. The answers are not in the book, but you can find them under the Source Code link at https://www.manning.com/books/learn-cisco-network-administration-in-a-month-of-lunches. Just remember that you'll learn much better by figuring out the answers for yourself.

1.2.3 *Further exploration*

Cisco networks use a plethora of technologies, many of them quite complex. This book gives you a gentle introduction to the most commonly used technologies, just enough to get your feet wet and become proficient at configuring them on a real network. If you find yourself needing more information as you gain experience, I'll point you to additional resources that you can use to expand your skill set.

1.2.4 *Above and beyond*

Sometimes you need just a little more information to understand the more esoteric aspects of networking. The "Above and beyond" sidebars provide this sort of additional information that you may find helpful when learning a more difficult topic. If you're feeling rushed, feel free to skip these and come back to them later.

1.3 *Lab considerations*

The only way to learn Cisco network administration is to perform the same tasks you would when administering a real network, which is exactly why this book provides the hands-on labs just described. In order to complete the labs, you must have an appropriate lab setup. Let's start with the bare minimum requirements.

For starters, you'll need a laptop computer with a network interface card (NIC). It can be Windows or Mac OS X, but regardless of the operating system, you'll need to have administrator or root access. You'll also need to decide whether you want to practice on an existing network or set up your own lab. The next few sections offer guidance on choosing your lab environment.

1.3.1 *Choosing your lab environment*

The best way to learn how to administer a real Cisco network is to practice on one. The ideal way to do this is to build or borrow a lab using genuine Cisco routers and switches. Your organization may already have one available, but my experience tells me that most places don't maintain a separate network lab. They do, however, often have some extra gear lying around. When it comes to building your own lab, you can either get hold of used Cisco gear or set up a virtual lab using software that simulates real Cisco equipment. Let's go through the advantages and disadvantages of each.

Building a lab with physical Cisco equipment gives you a better understanding of what a network looks like. When you can see an Ethernet cable going from one switch to another, you know how and where switches are connected. The connections between various devices are easy to visualize and consequently easier to remember. You also get the satisfaction of hearing an Ethernet cable snap into place and connecting a console cable to the back of the switch to reset the switch's password. These are real, valuable network administration skills that only a physical lab can provide.

If you have a friend or employer who is willing to loan you their Cisco gear, this is your cheapest option. If you can't beg or borrow, your other option is to purchase it. Used Cisco gear is inexpensive, but it's not free.

Table 1.1 lists the Cisco equipment I recommend for your lab along with rough price estimates. You'll need two layer-3 Catalyst switches and one router. For administering your lab network, your computer must have one free USB or RS-232 serial port. You'll also need a blue Cisco rollover cable, sometimes called a console cable. If you don't have an RS-232 serial port, you'll need a serial-to-USB adapter.

Table 1.1   Minimum physical lab requirements

Device	Quantity	Model	Price estimate (USD)
Catalyst 3560 (layer-3 switch)	2	WS-C3560-24TS-S	$120
1841 Integrated Services Router	1	CISCO1841-SEC/K9	$60
Console/rollover cable	1	72-3383-01	$10

TIP   When you acquire your switches and router, you can probably get the seller to throw in a rollover cable for free. At the very least, you may be able to purchase one at a reduced cost.

1.3.2   *Virtual lab considerations*

The advantages and disadvantages of a virtual lab are essentially the inverse of those of the physical lab. A virtual lab doesn't require the commitment of purchasing or borrowing physical equipment. But understand that a virtual lab can't provide the same administration experience or help you develop the same skills that hands-on access to physical Cisco gear can. Connecting a real computer to a virtual lab network is very different than connecting one to a physical network. If you decide to go the virtual route, the lab set-up guide under the Source Code link at https://www.manning.com/books/learn-cisco-network-administration-in-a-month-of-lunches has up-to-date information on virtual lab options.

My goal is not to teach you how to configure a virtual lab environment from scratch; it's to teach you how to maintain a real, fully functional Cisco network like you would find in an organizational environment. There are significant differences between a virtual lab and a real network, and I'm not going to point them out because you aren't going to encounter them on a real production network.

One of the more popular virtual lab environments is GNS3. GNS3 is a powerful network virtualization platform, but that power comes with some trade-offs. For starters, it's more complicated to set up than a physical lab. Second, you have to obtain a copy of Cisco's Internetwork Operating System (IOS), which is proprietary, copyrighted Cisco software that's available only to individuals and organizations that have a support agreement with Cisco. This means if you want to use GNS3, you'll need to find and download a compatible IOS image.

Another option is to use the Cisco Virtual Internet Routing Lab (VIRL). VIRL is not free, but it's not terribly expensive either. The personal edition is about $200 per year. The advantage of VIRL is that it's blessed by Cisco, and they offer technical support and keep it up to date with bug fixes and new features. The disadvantage is that, like GNS3, it's complicated to set up.

1.3.3 *Practicing on a live, production network*

If using your own physical or virtual lab is out of the question, a possible alternative is to practice on a live, production network. This will give you most of the advantages that a physical lab offers, but you won't be able to complete all of the hands-on labs. Also, practicing on a live network is not without its risks. If you choose to practice on a production network, you'll need the blessing of the network administrator or team responsible for the network. You'll need what's called a privileged account to administer routers and switches, and you'll also need physical access to those devices.

1.3.4 *My recommendation for your lab environment*

Although you can perform some of the hands-on labs on a production network, I prefer that you make every effort to get access to a physical lab. If you can't get access to a physical lab, then I recommend that you use a virtual lab. Both VIRL and GNS3 will require some horsepower. You'll need a Windows 7 or later machine with 8 GB of RAM and 60 GB of available disk space. For VIRL, you'll also need an Intel processor that supports virtualization extensions (VT-x) with extended page tables (EPT). Let's summarize:

- *Good: privileged access to Cisco devices on a live network*—You won't be able to complete all of the labs, and you'll have to get permission from the person in charge of the network before performing the labs to ensure they don't disrupt normal operations. You'll need a Windows 7 or Mac OS X laptop with an RS-232 serial port or a USB port and a USB-to-serial adapter. You'll also need a blue Cisco rollover cable.
- *Better: a virtual lab using GNS3, VIRL, or other virtualization platform*—You'll have to invest some extra time and possibly some money, but you'll still be able to

complete most of the labs in the book. The online appendix at www.manning .com/books/learn-cisco-network-administration-in-a-month-of-lunches will give you up-to-date information on setting up a virtual lab.

- *Best: a homebrew lab with two layer-3 switches and one router*—This will give you a feel for what a real network looks like, but with the freedom to break it and experiment as much as you want without risk. You won't have to ask permission to make changes, and if something goes wrong, you can pull the plug and start over. You'll need a Windows 7 or later laptop with an RS-232 serial port or a USB port and a USB-to-serial adapter. You'll also need a blue Cisco rollover cable.

1.3.5 *Cisco Internetwork Operating System versions*

Cisco's Internetwork Operating System is the software that controls Cisco routers and switches. It's what you're really interacting with when you configure a Cisco device. I wrote this book for IOS version 15, and everything in it should be accurate for that version. If you build a lab from used equipment, you're likely to run into an older version. That's probably not going to be a problem, because the tasks you'll be performing are fundamental, and the configuration specifics haven't changed much over the years. Cisco equipment has a long shelf life, and some organizations keep their Cisco networking equipment around for a long time. You're likely to run into an older IOS version sooner or later, so don't fret if you don't have the latest and greatest IOS.

Many organizations have a mix of old and new Cisco equipment. The newer equipment will have at a minimum IOS version 15, whereas older equipment could have IOS version 12 or even earlier. Generally, different IOS versions are compatible, so a switch running IOS 12.4 can interoperate with a switch running IOS 15.0 without much hassle. Again, because you'll be performing fundamental configuration tasks, you'll find that what works on a brand-new Cisco switch running IOS 15 also works on a dirty, banged-up switch running IOS 12.4. But my focus is on IOS 15. If you use a different version, just understand that some commands may be a little bit different, and I'm not going to point out those differences.

1.4 *Online resources*

Visit the Source Code link at https://www.manning.com/books/learn-cisco-network-administration-in-a-month-of-lunches for complete instructions on setting up your lab. If along the way you have any questions or run into any problems, be sure to visit the official forum for this book on the book's web page.

1.5 *A word on my recommendations*

Some organizations vigilantly keep all of their Cisco equipment up to date with the latest IOS versions. Others happily will keep the same router around for 10 years, and when it fails, the network administrator will go to an online garage sale site to find an identical replacement. You never know what you're going to encounter, and that's why I strive to be as version-neutral as possible. Nearly everything you'll learn applies to every Cisco router and switch you're likely to encounter, whether you're working on your lab or in an organizational environment.

If you decide to do your own research on Cisco equipment and software versions, you'll quickly become inundated with massive amounts of marketing lingo and details about Cisco's wide variety of offerings. Cisco creates products to serve organizations of every size, from small mom-and-pop shops to large international organizations. You should understand that this book covers only a small sliver of the Cisco ecosystem. Although this book *will* make you an immediately effective Cisco network administrator, it won't turn you into a master of every device and application that has the word *Cisco* on it. In an organizational environment, you may run into Cisco switches that run the Nexus Operating System (NX-OS) instead of IOS. Although NX-OS has some significant architectural differences from IOS, the command-line configuration is mostly the same for the tasks you'll perform in this book. The skills you'll learn in the coming chapters will translate easily to NX-OS, so don't be rattled by anyone who tells you you're missing out on the next big thing by sticking with IOS. You're not. In fact, the opposite is true. You're learning fundamental skills that you will use day after day regardless of which platform or software version you're working on.

1.6　*Being an immediately effective network administrator*

At this point you're probably ready to dive right into the practical, hands-on chapters. First, though, there are two questions that bug a lot of newcomers to networking:

- What do switches and routers actually do?
- Why do devices have both a MAC address and an IP address?

In the next chapter, I clearly answer both of these questions by giving you the big picture of how Cisco networks operate. If you've tried to grasp networking concepts before and found them difficult or confusing, the next chapter is going to be a pleasant surprise.

I've designed the rest of this book so that each chapter teaches you something you can use immediately in a real production environment. That means I'll often skip over or give light treatment to some of the theoretical underpinnings. You don't need a deep theoretical understanding of networking concepts in order to be an immediately effective network administrator. When necessary, I'll cover the theory after you've practiced enough that you can clearly visualize how the theory relates to specific network administration tasks. When given the choice between telling you something and showing you something, I'll almost always choose to show you first. That doesn't mean I won't cover theory at all. I will, but only to the extent that you can take that theory and apply it to real-world scenarios and configuration tasks. Remember, this book is a starting point, and you can spend years (as many do) studying the details of how and why networks work the way they do. But you have to learn to crawl before you can run. Again, my goal for this book is to make you an immediately effective network administrator, not an eventually effective one. So without further delay, let's get started on your first lesson.

What is a Cisco network?

Every organization's most valuable traffic passes through two types of networking devices: routers and switches. Cisco makes some of the most popular, dependable routers and switches around, so most organizations standardize on Cisco for these devices. For other networking devices like firewalls and wireless access points, they may go with Cisco or they may choose a different brand altogether. But as long as the network uses Cisco routers and switches, you can consider it a Cisco network.

There's no requirement that you must use Cisco-branded routers and switches. You can use a Cisco switch with a Juniper router, and they'll work together just fine. You can use a Cisco router with a Juniper switch, and that will work fine too. But there are a couple of disadvantages to doing this.

First, the steps to configure a Cisco device are substantially different from the steps to configure a Juniper device. The commands, terminology, and order in which you do things are different. Administering a mixed network requires knowing how to configure both platforms and getting them to interoperate. This book addresses only the Cisco side of things.

Second, if you have a problem on your network and aren't sure whether it's the router or switch, you have to open support tickets with both companies. In the worst case, you get a lot of finger-pointing between the companies. In the best case, you get a delayed resolution.

Mixing different brands of routers and switches isn't a good idea. That's why the vast majority of organizations use Cisco for both. It's just easier. But if you have a mixed environment, you can still use this book to learn how to administer the Cisco

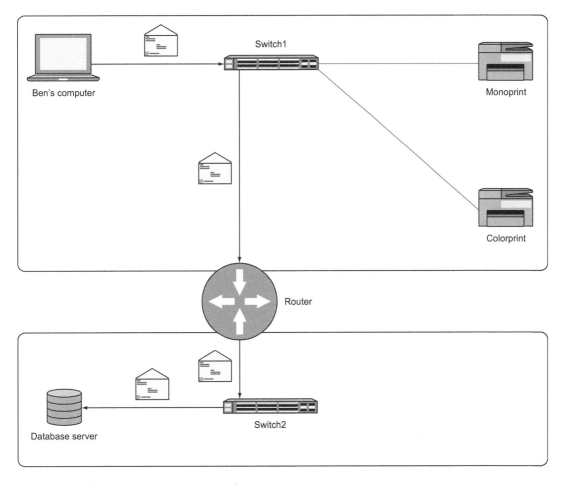

Figure 2.1   Switches and a router in a network

routers or switches on your network. Just be aware that for the purposes of this book, a Cisco network *always* consists of Cisco routers and switches.

In figure 2.1, my computer needs to send an "envelope" containing some data to the database server. In this chapter, you're going to learn how the switches and router ensure the data gets to its destination in the most efficient way possible.

2.1   The truth about routers and switches

Newcomers to networking often have two questions:

- What do routers and switches actually do?
- Why do devices have both MAC and IP addresses?

These seemingly simple questions don't have a straightforward answer. I've seen many attempts to answer these questions in a few sentences, and all such attempts invariably cause more confusion than they clear up.

The truth is that routers and switches were born out of necessity rather than practicality. In principle, neither device is particularly elegant or clever, although Cisco has done some clever things to make them perform better. Like most technologies, routers and switches came about because of questionable decisions that were made decades ago.

Later technology is usually built on earlier technology. For instance, e-books borrow concepts such as *pages* and *bookmarks* from traditional printed books. Imagine explaining the page concept to someone who is used to reading scrolls but has never seen a traditional printed book. How would you do it? Before you can explain what a page is, you have to explain why pages exist in the first place.

Similarly, before I can explain what a router or a switch is, I have to briefly explain what problems each was designed to solve. Once you understand that, everything else will fall into place more easily, and you'll be administering your own Cisco network in no time.

2.2   MAC addresses

A long time ago, some folks decided that all network devices would uniquely identify each other using something called a media access control (MAC) address. A MAC address is 48 bits long and is represented as a string of hexadecimal numbers, like this: 0800.2700.EC26. You've probably seen a few of these.

Here's the interesting part: the manufacturer of each network device assigns it a unique MAC address at the time of manufacture. The rationale behind this is to make it possible to simply plug a device into a network and have it communicate with other devices without having to manually configure anything. That sounds noble, but there's a rub: because the manufacturer assigns the MAC address, it has no relationship to where the device will physically end up. In that sense, it's not really an address because it can't help you locate the device.

> **Try it now**
>
> Open a Windows command shell and type `ipconfig /all`. Your computer's MAC address is listed next to `Physical Address`. If you have multiple network interface cards (NICs), you'll see multiple MAC addresses.

A MAC address works like a person's full name. It's assigned at birth and makes it easy to identify someone, get their attention in a crowd of people, and even send them a message by calling out their name. If we're in a large crowd of people, and you need to communicate a message to me but have no idea where I am, you could get on a bullhorn and yell, "Ben Piper, where are you?" If I'm in that crowd, I'll receive your message.

Network devices communicate with each other in a similar fashion, but instead of using full names, they use MAC addresses. Suppose that my computer has a MAC address of 0800.2700.EC26, and it needs to print to a network printer named Monoprint with the MAC address 0020.3500.CE26. My computer and the printer have a physical connection to a device called a switch, as illustrated in figure 2.2. Specifically, my computer and the printer are *physically* connected to individual Ethernet ports on the switch. Note that unlike a wireless access point, connections to a switch are *always* physical connections. In this sense, a switch is like a gathering place for network devices. Just as you and I might gather together with others in a crowded outdoor marketplace, network devices gather together on a switch. This collection of connected devices is called a local area network (LAN).

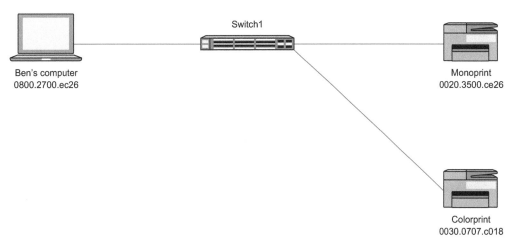

Figure 2.2   Computer and two printers connected to a switch

But here's the problem: my computer doesn't know where Monoprint is or if it's even a part of the LAN—the "crowd" of devices connecting to the switch. *MAC addresses, like full names, make good identifiers, but they're lousy at telling you exactly where a device is.* Because of this, my computer has to get on its "bullhorn" and call out to Monoprint using its MAC address.

Above and beyond

Each device manufacturer has an organizationally unique identifier (OUI), which is a string of six hexadecimal numbers. The OUI makes up the leftmost part of every MAC address the manufacturer assigns. You can think of the OUI as a person's surname. Even though it's assigned "at birth," devices from the same manufacturer share the same OUI. The rest of the MAC address is assigned sequentially. This is how manufacturers ensure each device's MAC address is unique.

2.3   *The Ethernet frame: a big envelope*

My computer creates an *Ethernet frame* containing its own MAC address as the source and the printer's MAC address as the destination. Think of the Ethernet frame as the big envelope in figure 2.3 with a return address and a destination address.

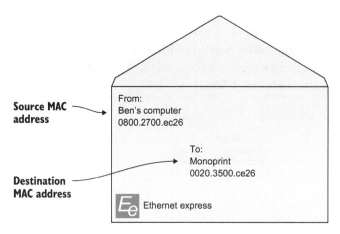

Figure 2.3   An Ethernet frame contains source and destination MAC addresses.

My computer places the data it wants to send—in this case, a print job—inside the "big envelope" and sends it to the switch. The switch receives the frame and looks at the destination printer's MAC address. Initially, the switch has no idea which switch port the printer is connected to, so it sends the frame to every other device plugged into the switch in order to get it to the one device that needs it, the printer. This is called *flooding*.

In step 1 in figure 2.4, my computer sends an Ethernet frame addressed to Monoprint's MAC address (0020.3500.ce26). In step 2, the switch floods this frame to all other connected devices.

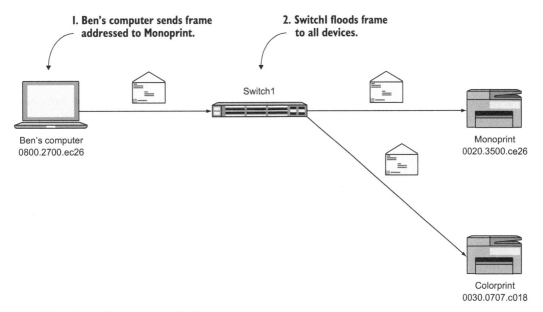

Figure 2.4 Ethernet frame flooding

2.3.1 *When everybody talks, nobody listens*

Flooding has an effect similar to that of blasting a bullhorn into a large crowd. Everyone hears you, but for that moment, people in the crowd can't hear each other. You effectively stop their communication, at least momentarily. Even after you stop bellowing into your bullhorn, it takes a bit of time for the people in the crowd to process your message and realize that they were not the intended recipient. The same thing happens when a switch floods or sends a message to all devices. Those devices won't be able to "hear" any other devices until the flood is over. And even then, they must process the message to determine whether they need to do anything with it. This phenomenon is called an *interrupt*.

Although a few flooded frames and interrupts here and there might seem negligible, consider what would happen in a crowd of, say, 1,000 people who each have a bullhorn. Just as you're ready to get on your bullhorn and send a message to me, someone right next to you gets on their bullhorn and yells out to someone else. After your ears stop ringing, you raise your bullhorn again, only to be once again interrupted by someone else. Eventually, you might get enough of a break to get your message out. But that's the problem. You're competing with others for the use of a shared medium, the air. This one-to-many communication method makes it difficult to relay a message to a specific person in a timely manner. And the larger the crowd, the worse the problem becomes.

On a LAN with a few devices, flooding isn't a problem. On a LAN with hundreds or thousands of devices, it is. But that raises another problem. A network that can't connect thousands of devices is virtually useless.

2.4   Broadcast domains

Suppose you add another switch named Switch2 to the network topology and connect a database server to it, as shown in figure 2.5. When my computer sends a frame to the server's MAC address, Switch1 will flood (and interrupt) every device connected to its ports, including Switch2! Switch2 in turn will flood the frame to every other device. In this case, the database server is the only other device connected to Switch2.

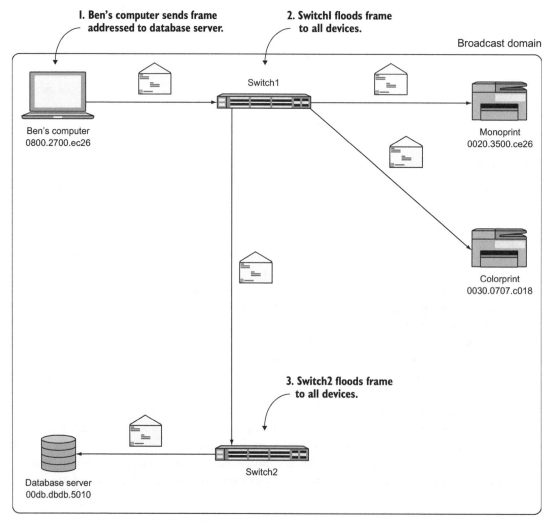

Figure 2.5   Second switch extending the broadcast domain

In step 1, my computer sends a frame addressed to the database server's MAC address (00db.dbdb.5010). In step 2, Switch1 floods this frame to all of its connected devices. Finally, in step 3, Switch2 floods the frame to the database server.

All of these devices that receive the frame are members of the same *broadcast domain*. A broadcast domain isn't a thing or a directly configurable setting but rather an emergent property of a network. To better understand this, consider the following analogy.

When you stand alone in the middle of a street, you're not a crowd. But as a few people gather around you, you become part of a small crowd. As more people gather around you, you become part of a larger crowd. You don't change, but you become part of a crowd by virtue of how many others gather around you. Similarly, a device becomes part of a broadcast domain by virtue of which devices it receives flooded frames from.

2.4.1 Closing the floodgates: the MAC address table

Flooding is an inevitable side effect of using MAC addresses. Fortunately, switches use a neat little trick to mitigate unnecessary flooding. Whenever a switch receives a frame, it looks at the source MAC address and the switch port it came in on. It uses this information to build a *MAC address table*.

> **Above and beyond**
>
> Cisco sometimes refers to the MAC address table as a content addressable memory (CAM) table, but they're the same thing.

When Switch1 receives a frame from my computer, it takes note of the source MAC address—0800.2700.ec26—as well as the switch port the frame came in on—FastEthernet0/1. It adds this information to its MAC address table, as shown in table 2.1.

Table 2.1 Switch1's MAC address table

Device	MAC address	Switch port
Ben's computer	0800.2700.ec26	FastEthernet0/1

Now suppose the database server sends a frame addressed to my computer's MAC address. The frame reaches Switch2, which in turn forwards it to Switch1. But this time, instead of blindly flooding the frame to all other devices, Switch1 checks its MAC address table.

It sees that the destination MAC address—0800.2700.ec26—is on FastEthernet0/1, so it sends that frame *only* out of that specific port; see figure 2.6. This works similarly to an old telephone switchboard, which is where the term *switch* comes from.

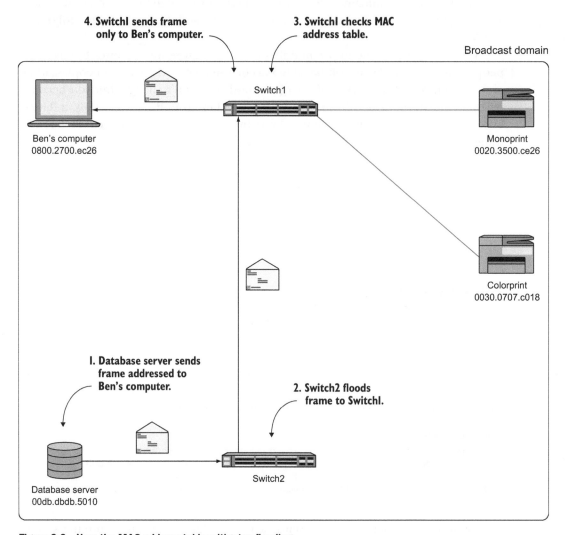

Figure 2.6   How the MAC address table mitigates flooding

In step 1, the database server sends a frame to my computer's MAC address (0800.2700.ec26). In step 2, Switch2 floods the frame to Switch1. In step 3, Switch1 consults its MAC address table and finds a corresponding entry for the destination MAC. In step 4, Switch1 sends the frame only to my computer instead of flooding it to all devices.

2.4.2   *Breaking up the broadcast domain*

As the size of the broadcast domain grows, communication becomes more difficult. Consequently, a broadcast domain containing hundreds of devices performs poorly. But modern organizations require network connectivity among thousands of devices. And just having connectivity isn't good enough. The network still has to be fast and reliable.

The solution is to limit the size of the broadcast domain. This means breaking it into multiple, small broadcast domains that somehow can still communicate with each other.

Going back to our example, the simplest way to split the broadcast domain is to remove the Ethernet cable connecting Switch1 and Switch2, as shown in figure 2.7. Note that the switches aren't connected in any way. That's the easy part. Here's the hard part: My computer and the database server reside on two separate broadcast domains. There's no way my computer and the server can communicate. What do you do? You can't just plug the switches back together because that would re-create the original, single broadcast domain.

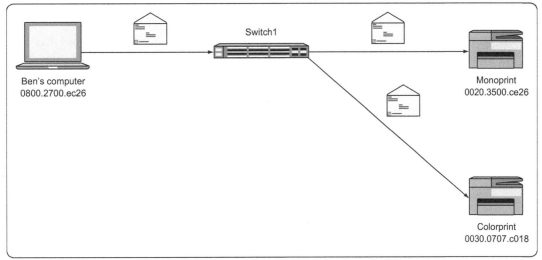

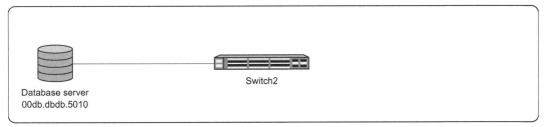

Figure 2.7   Two broadcast domains

2.4.3   *Joining broadcast domains*

In order to join two broadcast domains together without encountering that nasty flooding problem, two things must happen: First, because both broadcast domains are physically disconnected, you need a special device to physically connect them in such a way that flooded frames can't cross the broadcast domain boundary. Because frames contain source and destination MAC addresses, this device will effectively hide the MAC addresses in one broadcast domain from the MAC addresses in the other.

Second, because MAC addresses in one broadcast domain will be hidden from those in another, you need a different scheme to address devices across multiple broadcast domains. This new addressing scheme, unlike MAC addresses, must not only be able to uniquely identify devices across broadcast domains, but it must also provide some clues as to which broadcast domain each device resides in. Let's start with the latter.

2.4.4   *Addressing devices across broadcast domains*

The addressing scheme has to meet some requirements: First, the addresses have to be unique across broadcast domains. A device in one broadcast domain can't have the same address as another device. Second, the address has to tell us all by itself which broadcast domain it's a part of. *The address should be able to not only uniquely identify a device but also tell other devices which broadcast domain it resides in.* This is to avoid that ugly flooding problem. Third, the addresses can't be "assigned at birth" like MAC addresses. They have to be configurable by you, the network administrator.

Fortunately, you don't have to look very far. Such an addressing scheme already exists, and you're already using it.

2.5   *Internet Protocol addresses*

You already know what an IP address looks like. One of the most common IP addresses is 192.168.1.1. It's a series of four *octets* separated by dots, and each octet can range from 0 to 255.

You've probably seen these 192.168.x.x addresses pop up in a variety of places. That's because 192.168.x.x addresses are reserved for use on private networks like your home or business. They're not globally unique because they're not reachable via the public internet. But you can still use them to address devices on your own internal networks.

Unlike a MAC address, you can assign any IP address to whatever device you like. You can create your own addressing scheme based on where devices are, not just what they are. Let's look at an example.

2.5.1   *Where are you?*

Devices connected to Switch1 are in broadcast domain 1 and devices connected to Switch2 are in broadcast domain 2. You could, then, assign a 192.168.1.x address to all devices connected to Switch1 and a 192.168.2.x address to devices connected to Switch2. Even without looking at figure 2.8, just knowing the IP addresses makes it painfully obvious which broadcast domain each device resides in.

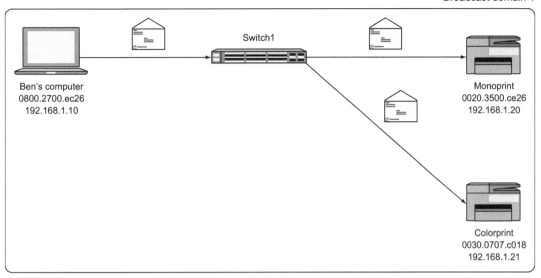

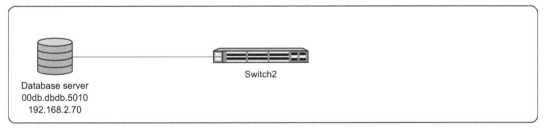

Figure 2.8 **Each device has an IP address that corresponds to its broadcast domain.**

Above and beyond

Note that if you wanted to add a third broadcast domain, you could assign 192.168.3.x addresses to the devices in that domain. The nice thing about using IP addresses is that there's no practical limit to the number of separate broadcast domains you can address with them.

But at this point, there's still no connectivity between the two broadcast domains, so it's only possible for devices to communicate within the same broadcast domain. But that raises this question: Now that each device has both an IP and MAC address, which one will it use to communicate *within* its broadcast domain?

2.5.2   *The IP vs. MAC dilemma*

"Why don't we just use IP addresses instead of MAC addresses?" is a common refrain among IT professionals trying to learn networking. It's a good question.

After all, MAC addresses aren't very friendly. They're hard to remember, mostly meaningless, and difficult (if not impossible) to change. IP addresses, on the other hand, are easy to remember, easy to change, and can be very meaningful with regard to location and function. The winner here is obvious.

So why don't we just use IP addresses and get rid of MAC addresses altogether? The answer is simple but a bit disturbing.

Network devices within a broadcast domain still have to communicate using MAC addresses. This is a requirement of the Ethernet standard that's been around for decades. Assigning IP addresses doesn't change that. Sure, someone could come along and create a new standard that makes MAC addresses unnecessary, but that would require replacing every single device on your network.

In short, MAC addresses are here to stay. That's the bad news. The good news is that you don't have to think about them, at least not very often.

2.5.3   *Address Resolution Protocol*

Remembering both the MAC and IP address of a device is inefficient and wasteful. That's why almost all networked applications use the IP address and completely ignore the MAC address. The *Address Resolution Protocol (ARP)* makes this possible.

ARP provides a clever way to map or resolve IP addresses to MAC addresses. The advantage of ARP is that it lets you use human-friendly IP addresses without even having to think about MAC addresses. All network devices made since the mid-1980s use ARP by default, so you don't need to manually configure it.

Suppose that my computer needs to send another print job to Monoprint. Both devices are in the same broadcast domain, so they're still going to talk using their MAC addresses. But you, as a network administrator, don't want to even think about MAC addresses. So you configure my computer to print to Monoprint's IP address: 192.168.1.20.

Figure 2.9 illustrates how ARP works. My computer sends an *ARP request* to figure out Monoprint's MAC address. The request says, "This is 192.168.1.10 and my MAC address is 0800.2700.EC26. Who has 192.168.1.20?" My computer stuffs this ARP request inside an Ethernet frame and sends it to a special *broadcast MAC address*, FFFF.FFFF.FFFF, as shown in figure 2.9.

Remember that all network devices *must* use MAC addresses to communicate. In order for my computer to get the ARP request to all devices on the network, it has to address the Ethernet frame to *some* MAC address. It can't send it to a blank address. So it sends the ARP request to the broadcast MAC address. Each device listens for the broadcast address in addition to listening for its own MAC address. This ensures that every device on the network pays attention to every ARP request.

In step 1, my computer sends an ARP request to the broadcast MAC address (FFFF.FFFF.FFFF). In step 2, Monoprint sends back an ARP reply containing its IP

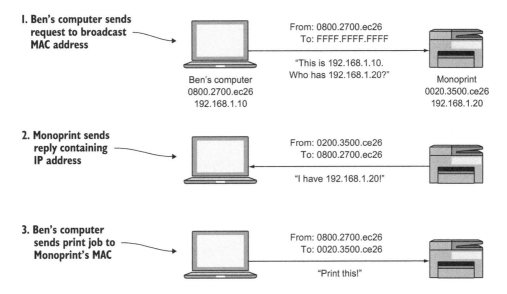

1. Ben's computer sends request to broadcast MAC address

From: 0800.2700.ec26
To: FFFF.FFFF.FFFF

"This is 192.168.1.10. Who has 192.168.1.20?"

Ben's computer
0800.2700.ec26
192.168.1.10

Monoprint
0020.3500.ce26
192.168.1.20

2. Monoprint sends reply containing IP address

From: 0200.3500.ce26
To: 0800.2700.ec26

"I have 192.168.1.20!"

3. Ben's computer sends print job to Monoprint's MAC

From: 0800.2700.ec26
To: 0020.3500.ce26

"Print this!"

Figure 2.9   Address Resolution Protocol request and reply

address (192.168.1.20). Finally, in step 3, my computer sends the print job to Monoprint's MAC address.

The switch floods this frame out all ports, including the port Monoprint is connected to. Monoprint receives the frame, peeks inside, and sees the ARP request. Monoprint sees the query "Who has 192.168.1.20?" and thinks, "Oh, that's my IP address!" Monoprint then sends an ARP reply back to my computer: "This is 192.168.1.20. My MAC address is 0020.3500.CE26." Bingo. My computer now knows Monoprint's MAC address and will communicate with it using that.

ARP is the secret sauce that rescues you from having to think about MAC addresses very much. It frees you up to think in terms of friendly, meaningful IP addresses the vast majority of the time.

2.6   *Connecting broadcast domains using a router*

Now that you're free to think in terms of IP addresses, it's time to learn how devices use them to communicate across broadcast domains.

At this point you have two separate broadcast domains with no connectivity between them. In order to join the two broadcast domains together without re-creating a single broadcast domain, you need a special device called a *router*. A router physically connects broadcast domains in such a way that frames can't cross the broadcast domain boundary. Because frames are what contain source and destination MAC addresses, the router effectively hides the MAC addresses in one broadcast domain from the MAC addresses in the other.

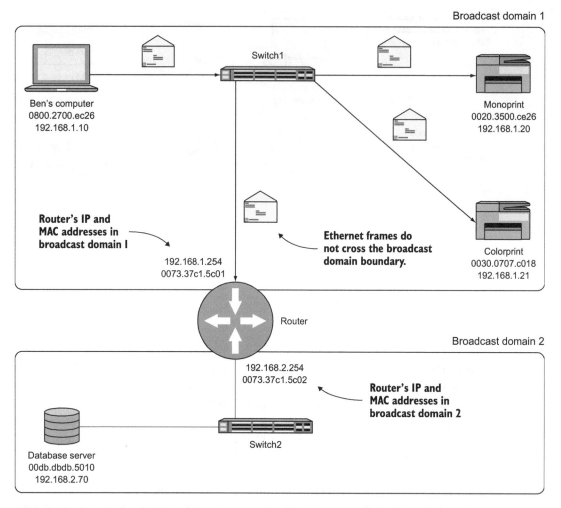

Figure 2.10   A router connecting two broadcast domains. The router has a unique IP and MAC address for each broadcast domain. Notice that Ethernet frames do not traverse the broadcast domain boundary.

In figure 2.10, the router physically sits on both broadcast domains. It has at least two ports or interfaces, one to connect to each broadcast domain. Each network interface on a router has its own unique MAC address. Keep in mind that each interface on the router has a unique MAC address only for the purpose of being compatible with the Ethernet standard that all the other devices on the network use. Just like e-books still use "pages," routers use MAC addresses for backward compatibility. Not only does the router have two MAC addresses, but it also has two IP addresses. On the interface connecting to Switch1, the router has an IP address of 192.168.1.254. On the interface connecting to Switch2, the router has an IP address of 192.168.2.254. Again, these are unique IP addresses, and the third octet (1 or 2) corresponds to the broadcast domain.

2.6.1 *Where are you? Where am I?*

My computer has an IP address of 192.168.1.10 and resides in broadcast domain 1. A database server with an IP address of 192.168.2.70 resides in broadcast domain 2. The significance of these addresses is obvious to a person. Devices with 192.168.1.x addresses are in broadcast domain 1, and those with 192.168.2.x addresses are in broadcast domain 2.

But my computer doesn't know that. Computers are, after all, just dumb machines that do what we tell them. So my computer needs some way to know which broadcast domain it's in. Once it knows that, it will be able to figure out whether another device is in the same broadcast domain or a different one.

2.6.2 *Understanding subnets*

In reality, broadcast domains aren't given numbers because they're not real things. But associating a set of IP addresses with a broadcast domain makes the abstract idea of a broadcast domain a lot easier to think about and work with. The set of addresses that corresponds to a broadcast domain is called a subnetwork, or *subnet* for short.

Take the 192.168.1.x subnet, for example. When you think about it, there's nothing about this address that says, "All addresses from 192.168.1.1 to 192.168.1.255 are in the same broadcast domain!" Even if you were already thinking that, you probably got that idea from this chapter and not just from looking at the address. But my computer can't read and comprehend as humans can, so you need a more explicit way of telling it which broadcast domain it's in.

To do this, you use a *subnet mask*. The subnet mask is an additional quartet of octets, formatted like an IP address, that indicates which IP addresses are inside the broadcast domain and which are outside.

As you can see in figure 2.11, my computer has an IP address of 192.168.1.10 and a subnet mask of 255.255.255.0. Line the two up as shown in table 2.2 and compare

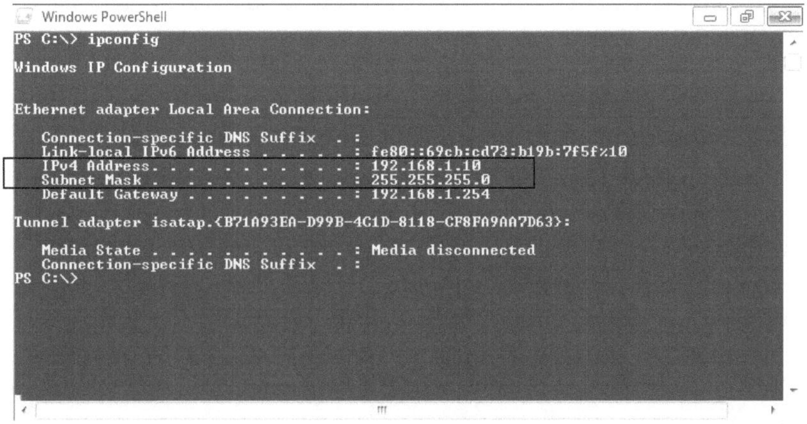

Figure 2.11 Output from `ipconfig` **showing my computer's IP information**

each octet. A 255 in the subnet mask indicates that another IP with the same octet is in the same broadcast domain. A 0 in the subnet mask indicates that the corresponding octet has no bearing on the broadcast domain.

Table 2.2   Determining the broadcast domain based on the IP address and subnet mask

My computer's IP address	192	168	1	10
Subnet mask	255	255	255	0

My computer's IP address and subnet mask are useless by themselves. The question at hand is whether 192.168.2.70 is in the same broadcast domain as my computer. Let's plug in that IP address and find out, as shown in table 2.3.

Table 2.3   The database server's IP address is in a different subnet than my computer's IP address.

My computer's IP address	192	168	1	10
Subnet mask	255	255	255	0
Database server's IP address	192	168	2	70

The first two octets match, but the third octet is different. And because the subnet mask for that octet is 255, my computer knows that the database server is in a different broadcast domain. So in order to get across to the database server, it has to traverse the router. But before it can use the router, it has to know that the router exists and how to reach it.

> **Try it now**
> Open a Windows command shell and type `ipconfig`. Note the IP address and subnet mask. Think of a different IP address that you know your organization uses. Determine whether it's in the same broadcast domain as your machine.

2.7   *Traversing broadcast domains using a default gateway*

Now that my computer has done the hard work of figuring out that the database server is on a different broadcast domain, it needs to know which router to use to connect to the database server. For this, it checks its default gateway address.

My computer has a default gateway address of 192.168.1.254. This corresponds to the IP address of the router's interface that sits in broadcast domain 1. Based on the default gateway address, my computer knows that when it needs to send anything to an IP address outside its own broadcast domain, it must relay that message through the router.

> ### Above and beyond
>
> Note that my computer's IP address—192.168.1.10—and the default gateway IP address are in the same subnet. This is really important. If a device isn't on the same broadcast domain and subnet as its router, that device can't reach any devices outside its broadcast domain.

My computer sends an ARP request for 192.168.1.254, and the router responds with its own MAC address of 0073.37c1.5c01. My computer puts together an Ethernet frame addressed to the router's MAC address. But this time it also puts together a smaller envelope called an IP packet. If an Ethernet frame is a large envelope with MAC addresses, an IP packet is a smaller envelope with source and destination IP addresses.

The IP packet contains my computer's IP address, 192.168.1.10, as the source and the server's address, 192.168.2.70, as the destination. Figure 2.12 illustrates my computer stuffing this smaller envelope—the IP packet—into the larger envelope—the Ethernet frame, which, again, has the router's MAC address as the destination. This process of "stuffing the Ethernet envelope" is called *encapsulation*.

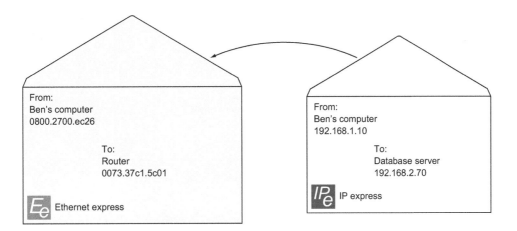

Figure 2.12   IP packet being encapsulated in an Ethernet frame

My computer sends the Ethernet frame containing the IP packet off to the router. The router receives the Ethernet frame, pulls out the IP packet, and sees the IP packet's destination—192.168.2.70. The router recognizes that 192.168.2.70 is in the same broadcast domain as the interface connected to broadcast domain 2.

The router then sends an ARP request for the server's IP address, 192.168.2.70. The ARP request says, "This is 192.168.2.254. Who has 192.168.2.70?" The server responds

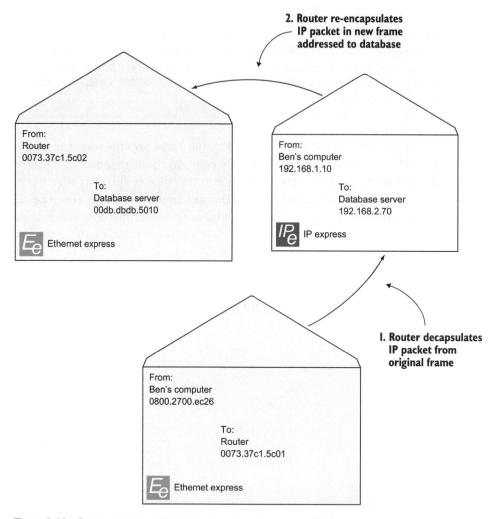

Figure 2.13   Router re-encapsulating the IP packet from my computer

with its MAC address, and the router takes the IP packet and tucks it inside a new Ethernet frame addressed to the server's MAC address, as shown in figure 2.13.

In step 1, the router removes (decapsulates) the IP packet from the original frame. In step 2, the router re-encapsulates the packet in a new frame addressed to the database server.

Notice that the IP packet itself never changes during this process. The router preserves both the source and destination IP addresses but changes only the MAC addresses on the Ethernet frames. The router then sends this new Ethernet frame to the server. The server receives it, takes out the IP packet, and says, "Hey! I'm 192.168.2.70! This packet is meant for me."

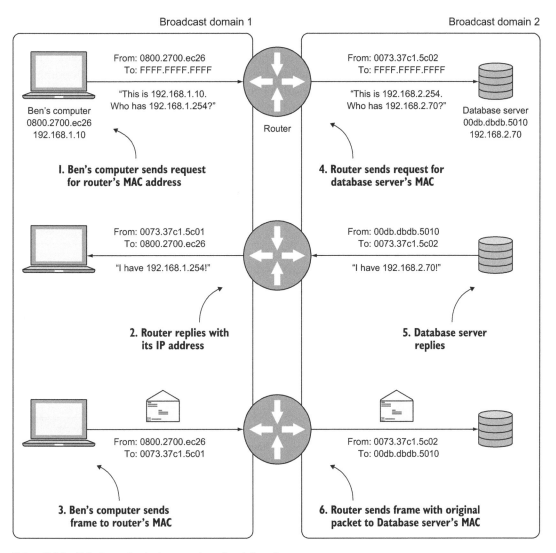

Figure 2.14   Using a router to traverse broadcast domains

Figure 2.14 illustrates how the router gets the IP packet across the broadcast domain boundary while hiding the MAC addresses in one broadcast domain from the devices in the other. This process is called *IP routing*.

In step 1, my computer sends an ARP request to get the router's MAC address. In step 2, the router sends an ARP reply containing its IP address. In step 3, my computer sends a frame addressed to the router's MAC address (0073.37c1.5c01). The frame contains an IP packet addressed to the database server (192.168.2.70). In step 4, the router sends an ARP request to get the database server's MAC address. In step 5, the database server sends an ARP reply. Finally, in step 6, the router sends a frame addressed to the database server's MAC address (00db.dbdb.5010) containing the original IP packet.

Now it's time to put it all together. Figure 2.15 shows how the IP packet from my computer gets all the way to the database server without any unnecessary flooding.

In step 1, my computer encapsulates an IP packet in a frame addressed to the router. It sends the frame to Switch1, which forwards it to Switch2. In step 2, the router removes the IP packet, looks at the destination IP address, and re-encapsulates it in a new frame addressed to the database server. In step 3, the router sends the new frame to Switch2, which forwards it to the database server.

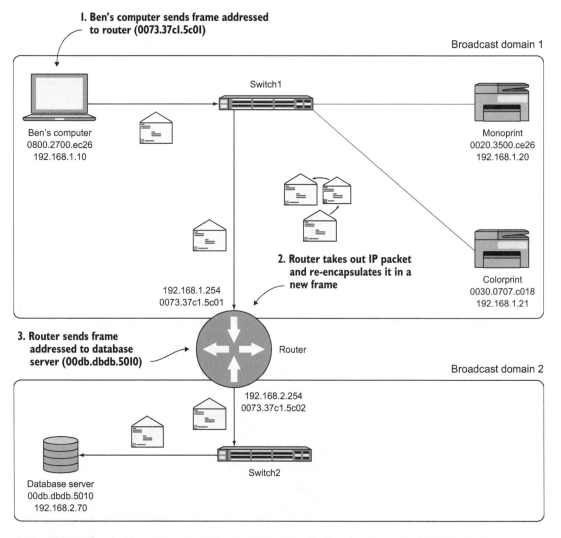

Figure 2.15   Using routing and switching to get an IP packet from one broadcast domain to another without unnecessary flooding

2.8   *Managing routers and switches*

At this point, you should have a basic understanding of the roles routers and switches play. You're probably anxious to get your hands on these devices and start poking around and configuring them. But before you can do that, you need to actually get access to them.

Routers have their own IP addresses, but switches can have them too. You'll typically find a special management IP address assigned to each router and switch on a network. The management IP address allows you to administer these devices remotely without having to physically walk up to the device and plug into the serial console port. Your organization's routers and switches are likely locked in a closet or data center facility somewhere, and even if you have physical access to them, configuring them in person is a pain. That's why you need to obtain the management IP addresses and login credentials for each device you might need to administer. Be sure to do this before tomorrow's lesson.

2.9   *Hands-on lab*

Download the inventory worksheet from the Source Code link at https://www.manning .com/books/learn-cisco-network-administration-in-a-month-of-lunches. Obtain the management IP addresses of all routers and switches on your network (or lab) and record them. Also obtain the login credentials (usernames and passwords) for logging into each of these devices.

On your computer, open an administrative command prompt or terminal. Get the MAC address, IP address, and default gateway of your computer with `ipconfig /all`. Type `arp -a` and get the MAC address of the default gateway. Record this information in the inventory worksheet.

A crash course on Cisco's Internetwork Operating System

If you're used to using a graphical user interface (GUI) for system administration, administering a Cisco network will take some getting used to. Although Cisco has made a modest effort at point-and-click configuration utilities, the command-line interface (CLI) has always been available. It's powerful, efficient, and mostly unambiguous. When you type configuration commands into a switch or router, you're generally going to have a pretty good idea about what that command will do. Unlike a GUI, which hides a lot of things behind colorful buttons and user-friendly messages, the CLI is black and white.

If you're not used to using the command line on other platforms like Windows or Linux, don't worry. In many ways, the IOS CLI is easier because it provides inline help, which I'll show you how to access in a moment.

3.1   What is IOS?

The vast majority of Cisco routers and switches run the Cisco Internetwork Operating System (IOS). IOS controls every aspect of a device's operation, including who can log into it, what traffic is allowed or blocked, whether an interface is enabled or disabled, and so on.

IOS provides a command-line interface to configure Cisco devices. You'll perform all of the configuration tasks in this book at the IOS command line, so it's important that you understand how to navigate it. In this chapter, you'll learn how to access the IOS CLI and how to use it to view, change, and save device configurations.

IOS is powerful—so powerful you can easily bring down an entire network by accidentally typing in the wrong command. The commands you'll learn in this chapter are fairly innocuous, and you can safely execute all of them in a production environment—with permission, of course. Just be aware that typing in random commands can be catastrophic, so don't get into the habit of doing it. If you have a lab that you can break, feel free to experiment, but don't jump around in the book. You still need to go through it chapter by chapter.

Above and beyond

IOS-XE is another Cisco operating system that runs regular IOS under the hood. IOS and IOS-XE use different software architectures, but the commands are almost identical. All of the commands used in this book should work fine on IOS-XE.

3.2 *Logging into Cisco devices*

Whether you're connecting to a Cisco router or switch, the process is mostly the same. First, you need to have a terminal client that supports both Telnet and Secure Shell (SSH). For Windows, I recommend PuTTY, which you can download from http://www.chiark.greenend.org.uk/~sgtatham/putty/download.html. If you're a Mac OS X or Linux aficionado, you can use the `telnet` or `ssh` commands from your terminal. I use Windows and PuTTY for the examples in this book, but just know that once you're connected to a Cisco device, your operating system and terminal client make little difference. The configuration commands you'll use to configure the devices are exactly the same.

Open your terminal client of choice and connect to one of the switches in your environment. I'm going to connect to my lab switch by typing its management IP address in the Host Name (or IP address) field, selecting Telnet, and clicking Open, as shown in figure 3.1. If you can't connect via Telnet, try SSH instead. PuTTY's interface hasn't changed much over the years, but if it ever does, the basic settings should still be the same.

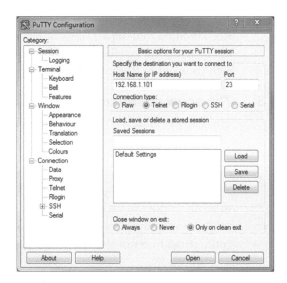

Figure 3.1   The PuTTY configuration window. In the Host Name (or IP address) field, type the IP address of the device you want to connect to. Select Telnet or SSH, and then click Open.

When prompted, enter the username and password of a privileged user. You should see the switch hostname followed by either a hash (#) or a greater-than sign (>):

```
User Access Verification

Username: admin            | Type "enable" to get into
Password:                  | privileged EXEC mode.
Switch1>enable        ←────┘
Password:                      | The hash sign indicates you're
Switch1#                   ←───┘ in privileged EXEC mode.
```

If you don't see the hash sign, type `enable` and press Enter. You may be prompted for another password called the enable password. If you log in successfully, you should see a prompt with a hash (#) sign. Cisco calls this privileged EXEC mode, but many people call it enable mode. Enable mode is like root or administrator mode in the sense that it lets you view more detailed information on the switch and make configuration changes.

Try it now

Go ahead and log into one of your layer-3 switches. Make sure that you can get to enable mode. If you can't, don't continue past this chapter. You must be able to get into enable mode on all devices, or else you can't administer your network. The biggest obstacle to getting into enable mode is not having the correct enable password. Make sure you type it correctly!

Keep in mind that depending on the switch's individual setting, you may get kicked out after a period of inactivity. This is a security setting and doesn't indicate anything wrong with your setup. If this happens, just log back in and go back to where you left off.

3.3   *The show command*

The `show` command is the one command you're going to use more than any other. It can show you almost any information about the device you're logged into. Type `show ?` at the prompt. The inline help should fill your screen with an intimidating list of commands that can tell you about different aspects of the device. This list is multiple screens long, and each screen is followed by a `--More--` prompt. Press the spacebar to scroll to the next screen. And the next. And the next. Keep pressing the spacebar until the switch drops you back to the prompt. Alternatively, you can press any key (other than Enter or the spacebar) to exit the inline help and get back to the prompt:

```
Switch1#show ?
  aaa                Show AAA values
  access-expression  List access expression
  access-lists       List access lists
  adjacency          Adjacent nodes
  aliases            Display alias commands
  ...
```

```
vtp                      VTP information
wsma                     Show Web Services Management Agents information
xdr                      Show details about XDR
xos                      Cross-OS Library Information and Traces
xsd-format               Show the ODM XSD for the command
Switch1#show
```

Notice that there are two columns. The left column contains the actual commands, whereas the right column has a brief description of what kind of information the command provides.

Most show commands require one or more subcommands. For example, if you type show ip and press Enter, you'll get an error:

```
Switch1#show ip
% Incomplete command.

Switch1#
```

This indicates that a subcommand is required to view IP-related information. Considering the large number of show commands, it's unreasonable to expect you to remember all or even most of them. Fortunately, you don't have to. If you type show ip ?, another not-as-long list of subcommands should pop up. Notice that this list is different from the last one. It's shorter and it contains only IP-related subcommands:

```
Switch1#show ip ?
  access-lists          List IP access lists
  accounting            The active IP accounting database
  admission             Network Admission Control information
  aliases               IP alias table
  arp                   IP ARP table
  as-path-access-list   List AS path access lists
  auth-proxy            Authentication Proxy information
  bgp                   BGP information
  cache                 IP fast-switching route cache
  cef                   Cisco Express Forwarding
  community-list        List community-list
  device                Show IP Tracking Hosts
  dhcp                  Show items in the DHCP database
  eigrp                 Show IPv4 EIGRP
  extcommunity-list     List extended-community list
  flow                  NetFlow switching
  host                  IP host information
  http                  HTTP information
  igmp                  IGMP information
  interface             IP interface status and configuration
  irdp                  ICMP Router Discovery Protocol
  local                 IP local options
--More--
```

If you thought the first list of show commands was bad, the *total* number of possible show commands is much, much worse. Fortunately, there are only a handful of commands you actually need to remember. Let's look at one of them.

On the first list of show ip subcommands, about halfway down the page, you should see interface followed by IP interface status and configuration.

Type interface ? so that the full command reads show ip interface ?. Now you get a much shorter list consisting mostly of interface types such as FastEthernet and GigabitEthernet, followed by an option for brief:

```
Switch1#show ip interface ?
  Async              Async interface
  Auto-Template      Auto-Template interface
  BVI                Bridge-Group Virtual Interface
  CTunnel            CTunnel interface
  Dialer             Dialer interface
  FastEthernet       FastEthernet IEEE 802.3
  Filter             Filter interface
  Filtergroup        Filter Group interface
  GigabitEthernet    GigabitEthernet IEEE 802.3z
  GroupVI            Group Virtual interface
  Lex                Lex interface
  Loopback           Loopback interface
  Null               Null interface
  Port-channel       Ethernet Channel of interfaces
  Portgroup          Portgroup interface
  Pos-channel        POS Channel of interfaces
  Tunnel             Tunnel interface
  Vif                PGM Multicast Host interface
  Virtual-Template   Virtual Template interface
  Virtual-TokenRing  Virtual TokenRing
  Vlan               Catalyst Vlans
  brief              Brief summary of IP status and configuration
 --More-
```

Type brief ? and you should get a list almost identical to the last one:

```
Switch1#show ip interface brief ?
  Async              Async interface
  Auto-Template      Auto-Template interface
  BVI                Bridge-Group Virtual Interface
  CTunnel            CTunnel interface
  Dialer             Dialer interface
  FastEthernet       FastEthernet IEEE 802.3
  Filter             Filter interface
  Filtergroup        Filter Group interface
  GigabitEthernet    GigabitEthernet IEEE 802.3z
  GroupVI            Group Virtual interface
  Lex                Lex interface
  Loopback           Loopback interface
  Null               Null interface
  Port-channel       Ethernet Channel of interfaces
  Portgroup          Portgroup interface
  Pos-channel        POS Channel of interfaces
  Tunnel             Tunnel interface
  Vif                PGM Multicast Host interface
  Virtual-Template   Virtual Template interface
  Virtual-TokenRing  Virtual TokenRing
  Vlan               Catalyst Vlans
```

```
fcpa                     Fiber Channel
|                        Output modifiers
<cr>
```

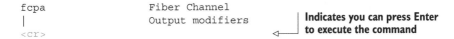

Indicates you can press Enter to execute the command

Look toward the bottom at the very last line that says `<cr>`. This means "carriage return," which is a fancy term for the Enter key. The `<cr>` indicates that you can press Enter without adding any additional subcommands. This is a good clue that the `show` command you've entered is probably going to work without any errors. If you don't see a `<cr>` at the bottom of the list, it means you have to specify more subcommands before pressing Enter. Go ahead and press Enter on the `show ip interface brief` command.

You should see a list of all the interfaces on the switch along with any assigned IPs. Your Vlan1 interface has an assigned IP address of 192.168.1.101. That should look familiar. It's the IP address you're connected to!

```
Switch1#show ip interface brief
Interface              IP-Address      OK? Method Status   Protocol
Vlan1                  192.168.1.101   YES NVRAM  up       up
FastEthernet0/1        unassigned      YES unset  up       up
FastEthernet0/2        unassigned      YES unset  down     down
FastEthernet0/3        unassigned      YES unset  down     down
FastEthernet0/4        unassigned      YES unset  down     down
FastEthernet0/5        unassigned      YES unset  down     down
FastEthernet0/6        unassigned      YES unset  down     down
FastEthernet0/7        unassigned      YES unset  down     down
FastEthernet0/8        unassigned      YES unset  down     down
FastEthernet0/9        unassigned      YES unset  down     down
FastEthernet0/10       unassigned      YES unset  down     down
FastEthernet0/11       unassigned      YES unset  down     down
FastEthernet0/12       unassigned      YES unset  down     down
FastEthernet0/13       unassigned      YES unset  down     down
FastEthernet0/14       unassigned      YES unset  down     down
FastEthernet0/15       unassigned      YES unset  down     down
FastEthernet0/16       unassigned      YES unset  down     down
FastEthernet0/17       unassigned      YES unset  down     down
FastEthernet0/18       unassigned      YES unset  down     down
FastEthernet0/19       unassigned      YES unset  down     down
FastEthernet0/20       unassigned      YES unset  down     down
 --More—
```

This is the interface and IP address I'm connected to.

Try it now

Run `show ip interface brief`. Locate the interface and IP address that you used to connect to the switch.

3.3.1 Filtering output

The `show` commands can produce a lot of output, and if you're looking for just one or two lines in a screen full of data, it can become pretty time-consuming. The `include` and `exclude` commands are two parsing commands that let you filter `show` command output to display only the lines you want to see.

INCLUDING LINES

Type another show ip interface brief ?. On the second-to-last line you should see a pipe character (|) listed as the output modifier. The pipe character is commonly used in scripts and batch files to pipe or redirect output from one command to another. In IOS, the pipe command has a similar function—to pipe the output to one of IOS's built-in parsing functions:

```
Switch1#show ip interface brief ?
  Async              Async interface
  Auto-Template      Auto-Template interface
  BVI                Bridge-Group Virtual Interface
  CTunnel            CTunnel interface
  Dialer             Dialer interface
  FastEthernet       FastEthernet IEEE 802.3
  Filter             Filter interface
  Filtergroup        Filter Group interface
  GigabitEthernet    GigabitEthernet IEEE 802.3z
  GroupVI            Group Virtual interface
  Lex                Lex interface
  Loopback           Loopback interface
  Null               Null interface
  Port-channel       Ethernet Channel of interfaces
  Portgroup          Portgroup interface
  Pos-channel        POS Channel of interfaces
  Tunnel             Tunnel interface
  Vif                PGM Multicast Host interface
  Virtual-Template   Virtual Template interface
  Virtual-TokenRing  Virtual TokenRing
  Vlan               Catalyst Vlans
  fcpa               Fiber Channel
  |                  Output modifiers
  <cr>
```

Redirects show output to another command

Go ahead and press Enter on the show ip interface brief command:

```
Switch1#show ip interface brief
Interface          IP-Address      OK? Method Status    Protocol
Vlan1              192.168.1.101   YES NVRAM  up        up
FastEthernet0/1    unassigned      YES unset  up        up
FastEthernet0/2    unassigned      YES unset  down      down
FastEthernet0/3    unassigned      YES unset  down      down
FastEthernet0/4    unassigned      YES unset  down      down
FastEthernet0/5    unassigned      YES unset  down      down
FastEthernet0/6    unassigned      YES unset  down      down
FastEthernet0/7    unassigned      YES unset  down      down
FastEthernet0/8    unassigned      YES unset  down      down
FastEthernet0/9    unassigned      YES unset  down      down
FastEthernet0/10   unassigned      YES unset  down      down
FastEthernet0/11   unassigned      YES unset  down      down
FastEthernet0/12   unassigned      YES unset  down      down
FastEthernet0/13   unassigned      YES unset  down      down
FastEthernet0/14   unassigned      YES unset  down      down
FastEthernet0/15   unassigned      YES unset  down      down
FastEthernet0/16   unassigned      YES unset  down      down
FastEthernet0/17   unassigned      YES unset  down      down
```

```
FastEthernet0/18         unassigned      YES unset   down       down
FastEthernet0/19         unassigned      YES unset   down       down
FastEthernet0/20         unassigned      YES unset   down       down
FastEthernet0/21         unassigned      YES unset   down       down
FastEthernet0/22         unassigned      YES unset   down       down
FastEthernet0/23         unassigned      YES unset   down       down
FastEthernet0/24         unassigned      YES unset   down       down
GigabitEthernet0/1       unassigned      YES unset   down       down
GigabitEthernet0/2       unassigned      YES unset   down       down
```

You should see a lot of FastEthernet interfaces and a couple of GigabitEthernet interfaces, but you're not interested in those. You just want to see the Vlan1 interface. If you don't want to scan through 28 lines of output, you can include only the lines with the search term `Vlan` in them using the command `show ip interface brief | include Vlan`:

```
Switch1#show ip interface brief | include Vlan
Vlan1                    192.168.1.101   YES NVRAM   up         up
Switch1#
```

Notice that instead of 28 lines, you get one containing the exact information you want.

> **NOTE** The command includes the word `Vlan` with a capital *V*. When it comes to filtering, IOS is case-sensitive. The command `show ip interface brief | include vlan` won't show anything because `vlan` with a lowercase *v* doesn't appear anywhere in the output.

EXCLUDING LINES

Suppose that you want to see IP information on all of your interfaces except the FastEthernet ones. For this you can use the `exclude` keyword to leave out any lines that contain the search term `Fast`.

Type `show ip interface brief | exclude Fast` and press Enter. Now you get only four lines of output showing you all interfaces except the FastEthernet ones:

```
Switch1#show ip interface brief | exclude Fast
Interface                IP-Address      OK? Method Status    Protocol
Vlan1                    192.168.1.101   YES NVRAM  up        up
GigabitEthernet0/1       unassigned      YES unset  down      down
GigabitEthernet0/2       unassigned      YES unset  down      down

Switch1#
```

Above and beyond

IOS supports using regular expressions (regexes) in search terms. Regexes provide a way to specify complex search strings. If you want to specify multiple search terms simultaneously, you can include a pipe character between them. For example, if you want to view all lines with "Fast" or "Giga," you could type `show ip interface brief | include Fast|Gig`.

Try it now

Practice filtering output using the following `show ip` commands. These commands are safe and will not interfere with any switch functionality:

```
show ip interface | include up|Internet
show ip interface brief | exclude down
```

Also, try to find the command that would show you detailed information on all inter-faces, but filter the output to include only lines with the term "address."

3.4   *Identifying the IOS version and package*

Although network folks colloquially refer to Cisco IOS as a single operating system, there are actually many different IOS *images*. You don't need to know all the differences between them, but you do need to be able to determine which image your switch or router is running so you can determine which features and functionality are available.

Cisco IOS images vary by platform, version, and package. You can view this information in one fell swoop with the `show version | include IOS` command:

```
Switch1#show version | include IOS
Cisco IOS Software, C3560 Software (C3560-IPSERVICESK9-M), Version
    15.0(2)SE5, RELEASE SOFTWARE (fc1)
Switch1#
```

The platform C3560 describes the hardware this IOS image is designed for. In my case, it's for a Catalyst 3560 switch. The platform isn't going to come as much of a surprise to you because you already know whether you're connected to a router or a switch. Let's look at the more interesting parts of this output: the version and package.

3.4.1   *Version numbers*

My switch is running version 15.0(2)SE5. The 15 is the major release, .0 is the minor release, and (2) is the feature release. You don't need to know the differences between these, but if you ever deal with Cisco technical support and the tech asks, "What feature release are you on?" it's helpful to know.

SE indicates the platform/family identifier, and 5 is the maintenance rebuild number. The SE indicates that the IOS version is for Cisco Catalyst switches. This might seem redundant because the C3560 is a dead giveaway.

Releases 12 and 15 are the most common major releases as of this writing. Cisco skipped 13 and 14 because they consider those numbers unlucky. As far as minor releases go, it's not unusual to see something as early as 12.1. I recently logged into a switch running 12.1 that had been up continuously for almost seven years!

You're not likely to see anything earlier than 12.0, although it's possible. Anything prior to that is ancient by technological standards. If you're working in an environment that's running anything earlier than 12.0, I suggest getting out of there!

Above and beyond

Upgrading IOS is beyond the scope of this book because it's not an everyday administrative task. If you ever find the need to upgrade, you're better off letting a qualified network consultant take care of it. Upgrading the IOS image on production equipment can be a harrowing experience even for Cisco-certified professionals.

3.4.2 Packages

Packages are also known as feature sets because they determine what specific features are available. There are three common packages you may run into:

- IP Base (IPBASE)
- Advanced IP Services (IPSERVICES)
- Advanced Enterprise Services (ADVENTERPRISE)

Let's take another look at the package I'm running:

```
Cisco IOS Software, C3560 Software (C3560-IPSERVICESK9-M), Version
    15.0(2)SE5, RELEASE SOFTWARE (fc1)
```

Although it's buried a little, the `C3560-IPSERVICESK9-M` in parentheses indicates I'm running the Advanced IP Services package. Advanced IP Services contains more functionality than IP Base, and Advanced Enterprise Services contains all possible features.

Try it now

Type `show version` to view the IOS version on each of your switches. Verify that you have at least the Advanced IP Services feature set. You don't need IOS version 15, but the higher the version, the better.

3.5 *Viewing the running configuration*

During normal operation, Cisco devices store most configuration settings in random access memory (RAM). This is called the *running configuration.* The running configuration is what IOS looks at in real time. Hence, any changes you make to the running configuration take effect almost immediately. For example, if you change the management IP address of a switch, that change gets stored in the running configuration and becomes effective immediately.

The running configuration is a long string of text—essentially a text file—split up into various sections that control different aspects of the device. As you get to know your network and begin to make changes to it in the coming chapters, you need to know how to locate and view each of these sections. To view the entire running configuration, type `show running-config`:

```
Switch1#show running-config
Building configuration...
```

```
Current configuration : 3069 bytes
!
version 15.0
no service pad
service timestamps debug datetime msec
service timestamps log datetime msec
no service password-encryption
!
hostname Switch1
!
boot-start-marker
boot-end-marker
!
!
!
username admin privilege 15 secret 5 $1$r/gI$sNjAw2i0L1Syobws.5tzT1
no aaa new-model
system mtu routing 1500
vtp domain cisco
vtp mode transparent
!
!
 --More--
```

NOTE   You can abbreviate IOS commands to avoid typing out the entire thing. For example, you can type sh run instead of show running-config and it will do the same thing. The inline help doesn't give you a list of abbreviations, but as long as what you type isn't ambiguous, IOS will figure out what you mean.

Your configuration may be verbose or just a few screens long. Keep pressing the spacebar until you get to the part that lists the interfaces:

```
!
interface FastEthernet0/20
!
interface FastEthernet0/21
!
interface FastEthernet0/22
!
interface FastEthernet0/23
!
interface FastEthernet0/24
!
interface GigabitEthernet0/1
!
interface GigabitEthernet0/2
!
interface Vlan1
 ip address 192.168.1.101 255.255.255.0
!
ip http server
ip http secure-server
!
!
!
 --More--
```

Near the end of your switch's configuration, you should have a section called `inter-face Vlan1`. Notice that the next line containing the IP address is indented by one space, indicating it's part of this section. You can view only this section using the command `show run | section Vlan1`:

```
Switch1#show run | section Vlan1
interface Vlan1
 ip address 192.168.1.101 255.255.255.0
Switch1#
```

The `section` keyword is another filter you can use to select specific sections of the running configuration for viewing. You can also use the `include` and `exclude` keywords if you like.

> **Try it now**
> View the running configuration of your switch. Pick a section of the configuration and use an output filter to view only that section.

3.6   *Changing the running configuration*

You can change the running configuration on the fly. There's no need to reboot or otherwise commit your changes. In many cases, as soon as you type a command, it takes effect.

You'll be configuring your Cisco devices from the command line, what Cisco calls the *terminal*. To make configuration changes, you need to enter a special mode called *global configuration mode*. Get into global configuration mode by typing `configure terminal`:

```
Switch1#configure terminal
Enter configuration commands, one per line.  End with CNTL/Z.
Switch1(config)#
```

The prompt changes to `Switch1(config)#`, indicating that you're in global configuration mode. The inline help works here too. If you type a question mark (?), you get a long list of commands, similar to those `show` commands earlier:

```
Switch1(config)#?
Configure commands:
  aaa                 Authentication, Authorization and Accounting.
  access-list         Add an access list entry
  access-session      Access Session Global Configuration Commands
  alias               Create command alias
  archive             Archive the configuration
  arp                 Set a static ARP entry
  authentication      Auth Manager Global Configuration Commands
  auto                Configure Automation
  banner              Define a login banner
  beep                Configure BEEP (Blocks Extensible Exchange Protocol)
  boot                Modify system boot parameters
```

This command isn't very descriptive, but the inline help can provide more info.

```
bridge                 Bridge Group.
buffers                Adjust system buffer pool parameters
call-home              Enter call-home configuration mode
cdp                    Global CDP configuration subcommands
cef                    Cisco Express Forwarding
cisp                   Set CISP parameters
class-map              Configure CPL Class Map
clns                   Global CLNS configuration subcommands
clock                  Configure time-of-day clock
--More--
```

Just to demonstrate how the configuration cadence works, suppose you want to change the login banner, which is a string of text that IOS displays when you log in. But you're not sure how the banner command works. If you type banner ?, you'll get a list of banner subcommands:

```
Switch1(config)#banner ?
  LINE            c banner-text c, where 'c' is a delimiting character
  config-save     Set message for saving configuration
  exec            Set EXEC process creation banner
  incoming        Set incoming terminal line banner
  login           Set login banner
  motd            Set Message of the Day banner
  prompt-timeout  Set Message for login authentication timeout
  slip-ppp        Set Message for SLIP/PPP
```

This is the command you're looking for!

You're still not sure what to do, so you type banner login ? and get a little more information:

```
Switch1(config)#banner login ?
  LINE  c banner-text c, where 'c' is a delimiting character
```

This is where you have to pay close attention to the inline help. It indicates you need to enter a delimiting character that specifies the end of the message, followed by the message itself, and then the delimiting character again. Type the hash (#) sign and press Enter:

```
Switch1(config)#banner login #
Enter TEXT message.  End with the character '#'.
Welcome to Switch1!#
Switch1(config)#
```

This is the login banner message followed by the delimiting character.

Now that you've finished, type exit to get out of global configuration mode. The change you just made is effective immediately. Now log out of the switch by typing exit again. If you're using PuTTY, your session should close.

Open PuTTY back up and reconnect to the switch. This time, you should see the login banner!

```
Welcome to Switch1!
User Access Verification

Username:
```

Login banner

Try it now
Get into global configuration mode and change the login banner. Log out of the switch and reconnect to it. Do you see the banner?

Although the configuration is stored in running configuration, it's not permanent. The running configuration is stored in RAM, which gets cleared when the switch gets powered off or rebooted. In order to make your change permanent, you have to save the running configuration to the startup configuration. *This is a vitally important step to ensure any configuration changes you made don't get inadvertently reversed later on.*

3.7 *Saving the startup configuration*

When a Cisco device boots, IOS reads the *startup configuration*, which is stored in the aptly named startup-config file. This file is stored permanently in non-volatile RAM (NVRAM), which is a special type of memory that persists even when the switch reboots or loses power. You can think of NVRAM as like a hard disk. The data stays there whether the device is on or off. IOS then copies the contents of the startup-config file into RAM, and that becomes the running configuration.

When you make a change to the running configuration—like changing the login banner—you usually want to make it permanent by saving the running configuration to the startup-config file.

The surefire way to do this is with the command `copy running-config startup-config`. When you type this command and press Enter, IOS prompts you for the filename, which shows up in brackets, indicating you can press Enter to accept the given filename:

```
Switch1#copy running-config startup-config
Destination filename [startup-config]?
Building configuration...
[OK]
Switch1#
```

After about a second, the switch saves the startup-config file. Now when you reboot the switch, the change you made to the login banner will persist.

Try it now
Save the running configuration on your switch. If you have permission and can do so safely, reboot your switch using the `reload` command. See if your new login banner is still there.

OI 880 1899

Above and beyond

I like to use a shorter command to save the startup configuration. `write memory` (which you can abbreviate `wr me`) does something similar to `copy run start`, except it doesn't prompt you for the filename of the destination file. Keep in mind that the abbreviated command doesn't work on all Cisco devices.

3.8   *The no command*

Most configuration commands can be negated using the `no` command. Putting `no` before a command removes it from the running configuration.

You'll use the `no` command to remove the login banner you just created. First, check the running configuration for the exact command:

```
Switch1#show run | include banner
banner login ^C
```

The configuration looks a bit different than what you typed. You didn't ever type `^C` in global configuration mode, yet there it is. This isn't a cause for concern because IOS sometimes changes or reorders the commands you type. Also notice that the message `Welcome to Switch1!` doesn't show up either. It's on a separate line in the configuration, so it doesn't show up in the output. But that's not a problem because you just need to remove the `banner login` command.

To do this, go back into global configuration mode and place a `no` before the command:

```
Switch1#configure terminal
Enter configuration commands, one per line.  End with CNTL/Z.
Switch1(config)#no banner login ^C           ◁──┐ The "no" command removes this
Switch1(config)#exit                              │ from the running configuration.
```

Now you need to verify that IOS actually removed the configuration command:

```
Switch1#show run | include banner
Switch1#
```

You get no output, so you know that IOS did your bidding and removed that command from the running configuration. But the command still exists in the startup configuration:

```
Switch1#show startup-config | include banner
banner login ^C
Switch1#
```

To make the removal permanent, you have to save the running configuration again, overwriting the existing startup-config:

```
Switch1#write memory
Building configuration...
```

```
[OK]
Switch1#show startup-config | include banner
Switch1#
```

| The banner login command is no longer in the startup configuration.

IOS overwrites the existing startup configuration with the running configuration, and you're finished!

> **Try it now**
> Remove the login banner from your switch's running configuration. Compare the running configuration with the startup configuration. Do you notice any difference? Save the startup configuration to make the change permanent.

3.9 Commands in this chapter

IOS is context-sensitive, so you can't just type any command anywhere and expect great things to happen. But there are some commands that you'll use over and over again, so it's important that you understand what they do. Table 3.1 lists some common commands and their descriptions.

Table 3.1 Commands used in this chapter

Command	Description
show ?	Displays subcommands that show information about the device
show version	Displays the device platform, IOS version, and package
show running-config	Displays the current running configuration
configure terminal	Enters global configuration mode
no	In global configuration mode, removes the specified command from the running configuration
show startup-config	Displays the startup configuration in NVRAM
copy running-config startup-config	Overwrites the startup configuration with the current running configuration
reload	Reboots the device

3.10 Hands-on lab

Practice everything you learned in this chapter. Make sure you can log in to all of the devices in your environment and can view the running configuration. There's no need to make additional configuration changes yet. What's important is that you can get into the IOS CLI, navigate it, view the running configuration, and get into global configuration mode.

Managing switch ports 4

A network can consist of many different kinds of devices: PCs, IP phones, printers, servers, wireless access points, and even other switches. The one thing these devices all have in common is that they physically connect to a switch, specifically, the *Ethernet port* of a switch.

Although Cisco *sometimes* refers to ports as *interfaces*, I'm going to call them ports because that's how most people know them. Although plugging a device into a switch port is a trivial task, the magic behind how data gets transferred between a device and a switch is anything but trivial.

See if any part of this story sounds familiar: I used to work for a company that had offices scattered around the country. Each office had a few switches, a firewall, and a router, but no IT people to manage it hands-on. Whenever an employee moved desks, or a new employee came on board, a non-IT person (usually a manager) would plug the employee's IP phone into the network jack in their cubicle. To their surprise, the phone would often not even turn on. Other times, it would turn on but wouldn't work. Or maybe the phone would work, but the computer (which was plugged into the phone) would not be able to access the network.

Even the simplest networks are not plug-and-play. When someone plugs a device into a switch and that device doesn't work as expected, you need to be able to understand why. You start by logging into the switch and investigating at the port level. Maybe the port is disabled or misconfigured. Sometimes it isn't a port configuration problem. Maybe it's a cabling or computer problem, but IOS can help you determine that as well.

In this chapter, you're going to learn what causes these all-too-common issues and how to troubleshoot them.

4.1 *Viewing port status*

Suppose a user tells you they just moved desks and now their computer can't get on the network. You go to their desk, make a note of the network jack their computer is plugged into, and walk back to the network closet. You find the port on the patch panel and trace it back to port FastEthernet0/2 on the switch. You notice that the link light on the switch isn't lit. The network cable is connected, but the network connectivity isn't there. Why? Did you trace the cable wrong? Did a rat chew through the cable somewhere up in the ceiling? Is there a problem with the network interface card (NIC) on the computer? Is there a problem with the switch port?

Investigating each of these possibilities independently is inconvenient and time-consuming. And if the problem occurs in an office 800 miles away, you're at an even greater disadvantage when it comes to troubleshooting. What you need is a set of commands to give you the status of each switch port. The show interfaces status command gives you just that. Not only is the command intuitive, but its output is as well. Let's see what I mean.

> **Try it now**
>
> Log in to one of your switches, get into enable mode, and type show interfaces status.

You should see something like this:

```
Switch1#show interfaces status

Port      Name    Status      Vlan    Duplex    Speed    Type
Fa0/2             disabled    1       auto      auto     10/100BaseTX    ◁───  Port is
Fa0/3             connected   1       a-full    a-100    10/100BaseTX          disabled
Fa0/4             connected   1       a-half    a-10     10/100BaseTX
Fa0/5             notconnect  1       auto      auto     10/100BaseTX
Fa0/6             disabled    1       auto      auto     10/100BaseTX
Fa0/7             connected   1       a-full    a-100    10/100BaseTX
```

The first thing you'll notice is that there are several columns here, but what you're interested in right now are the Port and Status columns.

> **NOTE** It's interesting to note that even though the command uses the term *interfaces*, the output calls them *ports*. As you get more experienced with IOS, you'll start to notice that Cisco tends to use different terms to describe the same thing.

Notice that the ports have a mix of three statuses: notconnect, disabled, and connected. It doesn't take a network nerd to figure out what these mean. As I said, the command output is quite intuitive. Notice that FastEthernet0/2 is disabled. That might explain why the user can't get on the network! But why is it disabled? Let's find out.

As useful as the `show interfaces status` command is, its output is limited. To get more detail on a particular interface, in this case FastEthernet0/2, you can use the `show interface FastEthernet0/2` command. As you learned in chapter 2, you can abbreviate IOS commands. But you can also abbreviate interface names.

> **Try it now**
>
> If you have a disabled port in your `show interfaces status` output, run the command `show interface [interface]` command against it. Otherwise, run `show interface fa0/2`.

You should see something similar to the following:

```
Switch1#show interface fa0/2
FastEthernet0/2 is administratively down, line protocol is down (disabled)  ◄─┐
 Hardware is Fast Ethernet, address is 0023.ab40.8e04 (bia 0023.ab40.8e04)    │
 MTU 1500 bytes, BW 10000 Kbit/sec, DLY 1000 usec,                            │
 reliability 255/255, txload 1/255, rxload 1/255                 This is a dead
 Encapsulation ARPA, loopback not set                          giveaway that
 Keepalive set (10 sec)                                            somebody
 Auto-duplex, Auto-speed, media type is 10/100BaseTX              disabled
 input flow-control is off, output flow-control is unsupported   this port.
 ARP type: ARPA, ARP Timeout 04:00:00
 Last input never, output never, output hang never
 Last clearing of "show interface" counters never
 Input queue: 0/75/0/0 (size/max/drops/flushes); Total output drops: 0
 Queueing strategy: fifo
 Output queue: 0/40 (size/max)
 5 minute input rate 0 bits/sec, 0 packets/sec
 5 minute output rate 0 bits/sec, 0 packets/sec
 0 packets input, 0 bytes, 0 no buffer
 Received 0 broadcasts (0 multicasts)
 0 runts, 0 giants, 0 throttles
 0 input errors, 0 CRC, 0 frame, 0 overrun, 0 ignored
 0 watchdog, 0 multicast, 0 pause input
 0 input packets with dribble condition detected
 0 packets output, 0 bytes, 0 underruns
 0 output errors, 0 collisions, 1 interface resets
 0 unknown protocol drops
 0 babbles, 0 late collision, 0 deferred
 0 lost carrier, 0 no carrier, 0 pause output
 0 output buffer failures, 0 output buffers swapped out
```

Don't be overwhelmed by the amount of output. Most of the time, the information you need is near the top. In this case, the very first line of output gives it away. It says that the port is administratively down, meaning that somebody disabled this port.

When a port is disabled, it's almost as if nothing is plugged into it. The switch doesn't do anything with a disabled port. When a port is disabled, it won't even provide electrical power to an IP phone if one happens to be plugged into it. It's effectively dead, and you need to revive it.

4.2 Enabling ports

A disabled port is said to be in the *shutdown* state. In case you're keeping track, that makes three different terms Cisco uses to describe a disabled port: *disabled*, *administratively down*, and *shutdown*. All of these terms mean the same thing.

Now suppose that your manager starts getting a lot of complaints about people's computers not being able to get on the network. You're asked to check all the ports on the switch and make sure none of them are disabled. You should use the show interfaces status command from earlier, but to make the output more readable, you can also filter the output to include only ports in a disabled state.

> **Try it now**
>
> Use the command show interfaces status | include disabled to display only disabled ports.

All you should see are disabled ports, if there are any:

```
Fa0/2   disabled 1 auto auto 10/100BaseTX
Fa0/6   disabled 1 auto auto 10/100BaseTX
Fa0/13  disabled 1 auto auto 10/100BaseTX
Fa0/14  disabled 1 auto auto 10/100BaseTX
Fa0/18  disabled 1 auto auto 10/100BaseTX
Fa0/23  disabled 1 auto auto 10/100BaseTX
```

Notice that the column headings are missing. This would be a good time to practice a little more output filtering to also include those.

> **Try it now**
>
> Type show interfaces status | i disabled|Status to display only disabled interfaces and the column headings.

Again, if you don't have any disabled interfaces on your switch, you should still at least see the headings:

```
Switch1#show interfaces status | i disabled|Status          Headings
Port      Name   Status      Vlan    Duplex    Speed   Type  ◄───┘ included
Fa0/2            disabled    1       auto      auto    10/100BaseTX
Fa0/6            disabled    1       auto      auto    10/100BaseTX
Fa0/13           disabled    1       auto      auto    10/100BaseTX
Fa0/14           disabled    1       auto      auto    10/100BaseTX
Fa0/18           disabled    1       auto      auto    10/100BaseTX
Fa0/23           disabled    1       auto      auto    10/100BaseTX
```

Recall from chapter 3 that the IOS running configuration controls what the switch is doing *right now.* That means that IOS has disabled these ports because of a command in the running configuration. Let's take FastEthernet0/2 again and see what command is disabling this port.

> **Try it now**
>
> Execute `show run interface FastEthernet0/2` to see the interface configuration.

Your output may differ, but you should at least see the section of the running configuration that controls port FastEthernet0/2:

```
Switch1#show run interface FastEthernet0/2
Building configuration...

Current configuration : 43 bytes
!
interface FastEthernet0/2              Port is disabled
  Shutdown                  ←─────┘
End                                    Indicates the end of the
                          ←──────────┘ port configuration section
```

This little slice of the running configuration is called the interface or port configuration section. The `shutdown` command is an *interface command* that disables the port. Notice how the command is indented, indicating that it's within the port's own configuration section. The `end` keyword signifies the end of the section.

Enabling FastEthernet0/2 involves removing the `shutdown` command. You should remember from the last chapter that putting a no in front of a command is usually sufficient to remove that command or at least undo it. Let's try that.

> **Try it now**
>
> The first step is to get into global configuration mode by typing `configure terminal`.
>
> Next, because you need to make a change to one specific interface, FastEthernet0/2, type `interface fa0/2`.

You should see the following:

```
Switch1#configure terminal
Enter configuration commands, one per line. End with CNTL/Z.
Switch1(config)#interface fa0/2
Switch1(config-if)#
```

Notice that the prompt changes from `config` to `config-if`, indicating you're in interface configuration mode (the `if` is short for *interface*). Now you're ready to negate the `shutdown` command, which will enable the interface.

> ### Try it now
> While still in interface configuration mode, type no shutdown and press Enter.

After entering the command, you should see two messages indicating the port is up:

```
Switch1(config-if)#no shutdown
Switch1(config-if)#
*Mar  1 06:49:27.824: %LINK-3-UPDOWN: Interface FastEthernet0/2, changed
    state to up
*Mar  1 06:49:28.831: %LINEPROTO-5-UPDOWN: Line protocol on Interface
    FastEthernet0/2, changed state to up
```

It's always a good idea to verify your changes, so do that with a show interfaces status | i Fa0/2 |Status :

```
Port      Name    Status     Vlan   Duplex   Speed   Type
Fa0/2             connected  1      a-full   a-100   10/100BaseTX
```

Port FastEthernet0/2 is now in the connected state. This is a good start, but your manager wants all of the ports enabled. If there are more than a few ports disabled, manually enabling them one by one is a time-consuming hassle. You need a way to enable all the ports in one fell swoop with a couple of commands.

4.2.1 The interface range command

Earlier you got into interface configuration mode by typing interface fa0/2 while in global configuration mode. Any changes you make in interface configuration mode affect only the port you specify in the command. In other words, you've selected only one port. But there's a way to select and configure multiple ports at once.

The interface range command lets you specify a range of interfaces separated by a dash. Because you need to enable all the ports on your switch, you can specify the entire range of ports on the switch and then issue the no shutdown command against them all at once.

> ### Try it now
> Get into global configuration mode and type the following to enable ports Fast-Ethernet 0/1 through 0/24:
>
> ```
> Interface range fa0/1-24
> no shutdown
> ```
>
> If your switch has 48 ports instead of 24, you can specify 48 instead. Regardless of how many ports are on your switch, you must specify a starting port and an ending port.

You should see output similar to the following:

Selects interfaces FastEthernet0/l
through 0/24 inclusive

```
Switch1(config)#interface range fa0/1-24
Switch1(config-if-range)#no shutdown
Switch1(config-if-range)#
*Mar  1 14:40:53.438: %LINK-3-UPDOWN: Interface FastEthernet0/6, changed
    state to down
*Mar  1 14:40:53.455: %LINK-3-UPDOWN: Interface FastEthernet0/13, changed
    state to down
*Mar  1 14:40:53.463: %LINK-3-UPDOWN: Interface FastEthernet0/14, changed
    state to down
*Mar  1 14:40:53.480: %LINK-3-UPDOWN: Interface FastEthernet0/18, changed
    state to down
*Mar  1 14:40:53.496: %LINK-3-UPDOWN: Interface FastEthernet0/23, changed
    state to down
```

The prompt indicates interface range configuration mode.

The output indicates that some of the interfaces changed their state to down. That might seem a bit odd, considering you just enabled the interface. But all this means is that there are no active devices on those ports. A spot check with a show inter-faces status | i Fa0/6|Status should confirm this:

```
Port    Name    Status      Vlan    Duplex    Speed Type
Fa0/6           notconnect  1       auto      auto 10/100BaseTX
```

And indeed FastEthernet0/6 is in the notconnect state, which means that it is enabled, but either there's no device connected to it or the connected device is not turned on. What's important is that with all of the switch ports enabled, you should be able to plug a working device into any port and get it to a connected state.

4.3   Disabling ports

You just learned how to enable ports, so you should already have a pretty good idea of how to disable them. But you might be wondering why anyone would disable a port to begin with. Why not leave them all enabled? It's certainly more convenient to patch an Ethernet cable into a switch and have everything work. But in some environments, security policies dictate that unused ports should be disabled. Although such a policy might sound like the brainchild of a bureaucratic busybody, there are some good reasons to disable unused ports.

Suppose that every weekend a salesperson comes into the office, sits down at an empty desk, and plugs their personal laptop into the network. Their laptop, unbeknown to them, is infected with a nasty virus. One Monday morning, you find out that all of the computers on the network are infected with a crippling virus. It turns out that the salesperson's personal laptop infected all of the other computers over the weekend when they plugged it into the network. Had the switch port they were using been disabled, their laptop wouldn't have been able to get on the network. That would have led them to enlist the help of an IT person who might have found the virus before it infected other machines.

There are many other good reasons to disable an unused switch port, too many to discuss during lunch. Just look at it as a cheap and easy way to avoid a lot of headaches.

4.3.1 *Finding unused interfaces*

Disabling ports because you *think* they're unused is a bad idea—really bad. In a live environment, you can wreak some real havoc by doing this. It's vital that you first verify that the ports you're going to disable are, in fact, not being used. You can do this by looking for ports that are in a `notconnect` state.

> **Try it now**
> List all interfaces with a `notconnect` status:
>
> `show interfaces status | i notconnect`

If any port has no devices plugged in, or plugged in and not turned on, it will show up in the output as follows:

```
Switch1#show interfaces status | i notconnect
Fa0/5           notconnect   1     auto    auto 10/100BaseTX
Fa0/6           notconnect   1     auto    auto 10/100BaseTX
Fa0/8           notconnect   1     auto    auto 10/100BaseTX
Fa0/9           notconnect   1     auto    auto 10/100BaseTX
Fa0/10          notconnect   1     auto    auto 10/100BaseTX
Fa0/11          notconnect   1     auto    auto 10/100BaseTX
Fa0/13          notconnect   1     auto    auto 10/100BaseTX
Fa0/14          notconnect   1     auto    auto 10/100BaseTX
Fa0/15          notconnect   1     auto    auto 10/100BaseTX
Fa0/16          notconnect   1     auto    auto 10/100BaseTX
Fa0/17          notconnect   1     auto    auto 10/100BaseTX
Fa0/18          notconnect   1     auto    auto 10/100BaseTX
Fa0/19          notconnect   1     auto    auto 10/100BaseTX
Fa0/20          notconnect   1     auto    auto 10/100BaseTX
Fa0/21          notconnect   1     auto    auto 10/100BaseTX
Fa0/22          notconnect   1     auto    auto 10/100BaseTX
Fa0/23          notconnect   1     auto    auto 10/100BaseTX
Fa0/24          notconnect   1     auto    auto 10/100BaseTX
```

The idea is to get all of these ports into a disabled state. As you can see, there are a lot of them. Because ports FastEthernet0/13 through 0/24 are consecutive, you can disable all of them at once by getting into interface range configuration mode and shutting them down. You can do that with the following commands:

```
Configure terminal
interface range fa0/13-24
Shutdown
```

This still leaves a handful of interfaces that need to be disabled: FastEthernet0/5, 0/6, and 0/8 through 0/11. Fortunately, you can also disable these using the `interface` range command. But this time, in addition to specifying a range, you'll specify individual interfaces separately, separating each with a comma:

```
Interface range fa0/5,fa0/6,fa0/8-11
shutdown
```

Now run the `show interfaces status | i notconnect` command again:

```
Switch1#show interfaces status | i notconnect|Status
Port       Name            Status        Vlan       Duplex  Speed Type
```

This time, you get no interfaces listed, implying that all the unused interfaces are now disabled.

Try it now

Find all of the unused interfaces on your switch:

```
show interfaces status | i notconnect
```

If you have any that are unused, disable them using the `shutdown` command.

A WORD OF WARNING

Just because an interface is in the `notconnect` state doesn't mean someone won't *try* to use it. If a user goes home sick for the day and turns their computer off, the port their computer is connected to may be in the `notconnect` state. If you disable the port, when they come back the following workday, their computer won't have network connectivity, and you'll have to re-enable the port. Before disabling an unused port, it's *always* a good idea to verify that it isn't going to be needed in the very near future.

4.4   *Changing the port speed and duplex*

At the beginning of the chapter I said that networks are not plug-and-play. Just because a port shows `connected` doesn't mean that everything is working correctly. The switch port and the device on the other end have to operate at the same speed and duplex in order for data to flow smoothly. The port speed and duplex are concepts you're already familiar with, but they have special implications for switch port configuration. Let's briefly cover speed and duplex.

4.4.1   *Speed*

The port speed is another term for the bandwidth—how fast data can travel between a device and the switch. Although 100 megabits per second (Mbps) is a common speed, you may occasionally see the slower 10 Mbps speed. There is no one right speed, but most devices should be operating at *at least* 100 Mbps. Some older devices may not be capable of this and operate at 10 Mbps instead. The point is that if you see a device operating at 10 Mbps, it warrants further investigation but doesn't necessarily indicate a problem.

The command `show interfaces status | i connected|Status` gives you a summary of the operating speed of each port:

```
Switch1#show interfaces status | i connected|Status
Port      Name      Status        Vlan      Duplex  Speed  Type
Fa0/1               connected     1         a-full  a-100  10/100BaseTX
Fa0/2               connected     1         a-full  a-100  10/100BaseTX
Fa0/3               connected     1         a-full  a-100  10/100BaseTX
Fa0/4               connected     1         a-half  a-10   10/100BaseTX
Fa0/7               connected     1         a-full  a-100  10/100BaseTX
Fa0/12              connected     1         a-full  a-100  10/100BaseTX
```

Operating at 100 Mbps, full duplex

Operating at 10 Mbps, half duplex

The relevant column heading here is the one labeled `Speed`. Take a look at the row for FastEthernet0/1. The `a-100` indicates the port is operating at 100 Mbps, and the switch and the device have automatically negotiated that speed. This is called *autonegotiation*, and it's enabled by default on all ports. The switch and device attempt to negotiate the highest speed they both support, which in this case is 100 Mbps.

4.4.2 *Duplex*

Duplex describes simultaneous two-way communication between a switch port and a device. The terminology around duplex gets a bit awkward. *Full duplex* means that both the device and the switch can transmit data at the same time without stepping on each other. *Half duplex* means that only one device can transmit at a time. If the switch port is sending data, for example, the computer on the other end has to wait for the switch to stop before it can start transmitting.

Take a look at the `Duplex` column. All of the ports show `a-full` except for FastEthernet0/4, which shows `a-half`. Like with speed, the `a` indicates the duplex is autonegotiated. Most modern devices will autonegotiate to full duplex.

4.4.3 *Autonegotiation*

In the late 1990s and early 2000s, it was common practice to disable speed and duplex autonegotiation on all switch ports because it was unreliable. Those days are long gone, and you shouldn't disable autonegotiation unless you have a specific reason to do so.

Disabling autonegotiation isn't something you do explicitly. It's a side effect of *hardcoding* the speed or duplex of a port. For example, when you hardcode a port to 10 Mbps, half duplex, you're telling the switch to allow that port to operate *only* at that speed and duplex *all the time*. Hardcoding is the opposite of autonegotiation.

Although you shouldn't hardcode speed and duplex for most ports, there are times when it's a good idea. Some devices like older HP JetDirect print servers and Cisco Analog Telephone Adapters want to operate at 10 Mbps, half duplex. Although even older devices *support* autonegotiation, many are from that era when autonegotiation wasn't reliable.

Moving into more modern territory, devices like IP cameras and security systems are themselves often hardcoded to a specific speed and duplex, and your switch port configuration has to match that. Sometimes a device manufacturer will require a hardcoded speed and duplex for no good reason, but you have to comply or else you can't get support when things go south.

The bottom line is that although changing the port speed and duplex isn't something you want to do every day, it's likely that you already have at least one device in your environment that will mandate it.

4.4.4   *Changing the port speed*

Let's take another look at the status of the connected interfaces:

```
Switch1#show interfaces status | i connected|Status
Port      Name    Status       Vlan   Duplex    Speed   Type
Fa0/1             connected    1      a-full    a-100   10/100BaseTX
Fa0/2             connected    1      a-full    a-100   10/100BaseTX
Fa0/3             connected    1      a-full    a-100   10/100BaseTX
Fa0/4             connected    1      a-half    a-10    10/100BaseTX
Fa0/7             connected    1      a-full    a-100   10/100BaseTX
Fa0/12            connected    1      a-full    a-100   10/100BaseTX
```

My computer is plugged into FastEthernet0/1, and it has negotiated a speed and duplex of 100 Mbps, full duplex with the switch. Let's see what happens when I change the speed and duplex to 10 Mbps:

```
Switch1(config)#interface fa0/1
Switch1(config-if)#speed 10
Switch1(config-if)#
*Mar  2 03:33:25.235: %LINEPROTO-5-UPDOWN: Line protocol on Interface
     FastEthernet0/1, changed state to down
*Mar  2 03:33:27.248: %LINEPROTO-5-UPDOWN: Line protocol on Interface
     FastEthernet0/1, changed state to up
```

Notice that the port momentarily goes into a down state and then comes back up. Network folks call this *flapping* or *bouncing*. The fact that the port came back up indicates my computer does in fact support a speed of 10 Mbps. If my computer didn't support 10 Mbps, the interface wouldn't have come back up. Let's check that port again:

```
Switch1#show interfaces status | i Fa0/1 |Status
Port      Name    Status       Vlan   Duplex    Speed   Type
Fa0/1             connected    1      a-full    10      10/100BaseTX
```

This time, the speed shows 10. But not only that, the a is missing as well, indicating the speed wasn't autonegotiated.

Try it now

Locate a port in the connected state that you know isn't being used and try to change the speed to 10 or 10 Mbps. Use the IOS inline help to guide you. If you're not sure of what to type, type ? and IOS will show you your options.

When you've finished, enable autonegotiate by using the `speed  auto` interface command.

By the way, network folks use shorthand to refer to speed and duplex combinations. For example, they'll refer to a 100 Mbps, full duplex combination as simply *100/full*. I'll refer to speed and duplex this way throughout the rest of the book.

4.4.5 *Changing the duplex*

We saw earlier that FastEthernet0/4 is operating at half duplex. Let's take a closer look at that port:

```
Switch1#show interfaces status | i Fa0/4|Status
Port      Name    Status      Vlan    Duplex  Speed   Type
Fa0/4             connected   1       a-half  a-10    10/100BaseTX
```

It's operating at 10/half, and both of those parameters are autonegotiated. If you ever see this on a live network, you definitely want to investigate it. At worst, it could indicate a cabling or other problem. At best, it could lead you to an interesting device. Chances are anything operating at 10/half is neither a desktop computer nor a server.

Notice that the speed and duplex were autonegotiated. Let's try to change the duplex to full:

```
Enter configuration commands, one per line.  End with CNTL/Z.
Switch1(config)#interface fa0/4
Switch1(config-if)#duplex full
Switch1(config-if)#
*Mar  2 04:39:12.755: %LINEPROTO-5-UPDOWN: Line protocol on Interface
    FastEthernet0/4, changed state to down
*Mar  2 04:39:13.761: %LINK-3-UPDOWN: Interface FastEthernet0/4, changed
    state to down
```

The port goes down and stays down. Whatever is on the other end certainly doesn't support full duplex communication. It's also possible, though less likely, that there's a damaged Ethernet cable. This is exactly why you always want to investigate any port with a speed and duplex that's out of the ordinary.

Let's look at that port again:

```
Switch1#show interfaces status | i Fa0/4|Status
Port      Name    Status      Vlan    Duplex  Speed   Type
Fa0/4             notconnect  1       full    auto    10/100BaseTX
```

Interesting! The port is now in the notconnect state. I didn't unplug anything, but the mismatched duplex makes it look like nothing is plugged into the port at all. This illustrates why it's a good idea to let autonegotiation do its work unless you have a really compelling reason not to.

> **Try it now**
> Locate a port in the connected state that isn't being used and try to change the duplex to half or full. What happens? When you've finished, set it back to autonegotiate with the duplex auto interface command.

4.5   *Commands in this chapter*

In this chapter, you learned how to manipulate individual ports in interface configuration mode. When working with the IOS command line, you need to be able to distinguish between *global configuration mode* commands and *interface configuration mode* commands. Table 4.1 differentiates these commands and also lists some of the show commands used in this chapter.

Table 4.1   Commands used in this chapter

Command	Configuration mode	Description
show interfaces status	N/A	Concisely displays the state, speed, and duplex of all ports
show run interface fa0/2	N/A	Displays detailed information about FastEthernet0/2
interface range fa0/5,fa0/6,fa0/8-11	Global	Selects a range of ports for configuration
speed 10/100/auto	Interface	Hardcodes the speed of a port or enables speed autonegotiation
duplex full/half/auto	Interface	Hardcodes the duplex of a port or enables duplex autonegotiation
(no) shutdown	Interface	Disables or enables a port

4.6   *Hands-on lab*

Practice everything you learned in this chapter if you haven't already. If you have, go ahead and perform the lab:

1 Display only the ports that aren't connected.
2 Select a range of unused ports and disable them.
3 Try selecting a range of ports that falls outside the number of ports on your switch. What error do you get?
4 Using the show commands, see if you can find any interesting devices operating at 10 Mbps or half duplex.
5 Select a port operating at 100/full. Change the speed to 10 Mbps. What happens?
6 What happens when you set it back to 100 Mbps?
7 Change the duplex of the port to half duplex. What happens now?
8 Change the duplex back to full. If it doesn't come back up, try shutting down the port and then enabling it.
9 When you've finished, remember to save your running configuration using the copy run start or write memory command.

Securing ports by using the Port Security feature

In the last chapter you learned how to secure unused ports by disabling them. Disabling unused ports can stop a bad guy from plugging a malicious device into an unused port and getting unauthorized access to the network. It can also help train users—especially those in remote offices—to call IT *before* moving things around. After a few go-rounds of plugging a computer into an empty port and having it not work, most people will take the hint that they need to call IT first.

But although disabling ports is the most secure option for dealing with unused ports, it does nothing to secure in-use ports. And in a live environment, the majority of switch ports *will* be in use.

Port Security is a versatile feature that can mitigate attacks against the network and prevent unauthorized moves, adds, and changes by limiting the number of unique media access control (MAC) addresses that can use a given port. Recall that every device on the network has a unique MAC address that it uses to communicate with other devices in the same broadcast domain. Versatility is crucial because security is not a one-size-fits-all proposition. Some organizations prefer a minimal level of security, whereas others require a level of security that borders on paranoia. Rather than tell you how secure you need to make your network, in this chapter I lay out the specific risks Port Security can mitigate so you can decide for yourself how lax or restrictive you need it to be. Then I'll show you how to configure Port Security to accommodate your requirements.

I'm not going to show you every possible way you can configure Port Security. Instead, I'm going to teach you how to configure it for minimum and maximum levels of security, as shown in table 5.1.

Table 5.1 Port Security levels

Protection level	Attacks mitigated
Minimum	MAC flood attack, denial-of-service attack, traffic sniffing
Maximum	All of the above, plus unauthorized device access and spread of malware

Table 5.1 lists which attacks each level of Port Security can help mitigate. Let's start with the minimum level.

5.1   *The minimum Port Security configuration*

Although I can't tell you how secure to make your network, I can tell you that you definitely want to enable a minimum Port Security configuration on all end-user ports.

Security is always a tradeoff. You have to consider whether it's worth the time, money, and effort to defend against a particular risk. Port Security is already included in IOS, so there's no additional cost. And the time and effort it takes to configure Port Security to a minimum level is negligible. But what you get in return is peace of mind and protection against a potentially debilitating and costly attack called a MAC flood attack.

5.1.1   *Preventing MAC flood attacks*

Recall from chapter 2 that a switch maintains a MAC address table containing the MAC address of each device and the port it's connected to. Table 5.2 is an example of the type of information you'd find in a MAC address table. By keeping track of where each device is, the switch avoids flooding every frame to every device.

Table 5.2 Sample MAC address table

Device	MAC address	Switch port
Ben's computer	0800.2700.ec26	FastEthernet0/1

In a MAC flooding attack, a malicious program continually sends frames with fake or spoofed MAC addresses as the source address. Because each frame appears to come from a different MAC address, the switch's MAC address table fills up with these fake addresses, and the switch has no choice but to send every frame to every port. The net effect of this is that the computer running the malicious program effectively becomes a network sniffer that's in a position to capture every frame on the network. Figure 5.1 illustrates how an attacker can use a MAC flooding attack to capture traffic.

In step 1, an attacker sends thousands of frames with bogus source MAC addresses to Switch1. In step 2, Switch1's MAC address table fills up. In step 3, the database

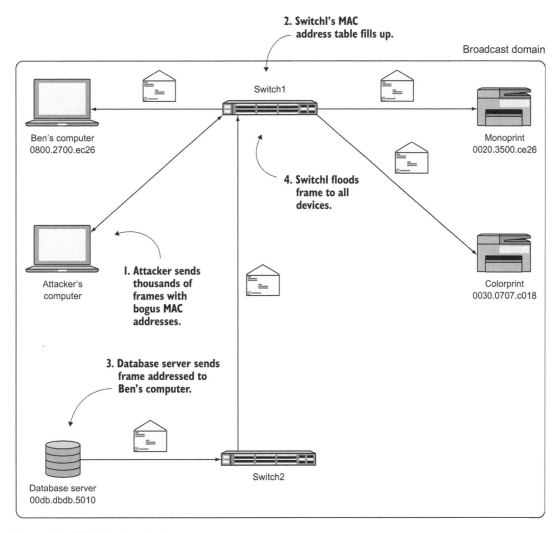

Figure 5.1   **MAC flooding attack**

server sends a frame addressed to my computer. Switch2 forwards this frame to Switch1. Finally, in step 4, Switch1 floods the frame out all ports, including the one connected to the attacker's computer.

But it's worse than that. A MAC flood can effectively result in a denial of service for all users. Remember the saying from chapter 2: "When everybody talks, nobody listens." MAC flooding severely diminishes network performance to the point of making the network practically unusable. Imagine dozens of customer calls getting dropped all at once because Voice over IP traffic can't traverse the network. Port Security can help ensure that you, as a network administrator, are never put in the unnerving position of having to deal with such an event. Just one unprotected port is all it takes for a MAC flooding attack to take down your network, which is why it's so important to configure Port Security on every port.

> **NOTE** You can protect against MAC flooding attacks with antivirus software on your PCs and servers and by making sure end users don't have administrative access on their machines. But these methods aren't 100% foolproof. Port Security is the most reliable way to prevent a MAC flood attack even if other security measures fail.

Normally, the switch doesn't care how many different MAC addresses are on the same port. It allows the traffic anyway, regardless of the source MAC address. Remember that MAC addresses were invented to make it possible to plug a device into the network and have it work. But this plug-and-play behavior is the very thing that makes a MAC flooding attack possible.

The obvious solution is to limit the number of source MAC addresses that can simultaneously be associated with a given port. This is exactly what Port Security does. You configure it to permit a specified number of simultaneous MAC addresses, and it allows access on a first-come, first-served basis. Let's look at an example.

Suppose that you have a user with two devices—a PC and a Cisco IP phone—connected to the same port. The phone is physically connected to the switch, and the PC is physically connected to the phone and communicates through it. Table 5.3 shows roughly how they would look in the MAC address table.

Table 5.3   MAC address table

Device	MAC address	Port
PC	0123.4567.8901	FastEthernet0/23
IP phone	0123.4598.7654	FastEthernet0/23

These two devices represent two unique MAC addresses, so you want to limit the maximum number of MAC addresses to two using the `switchport port-security maximum 2` interface command.

Try it now

Locate a port with two devices plugged into it. If you have a PC plugged in behind an IP phone, that's perfect. If you don't, you can still perform the exercise; just change the command to allow only one MAC address.

Issue the following commands to configure the maximum number of allowed MAC addresses on the port to two:

```
interface fa0/1
switchport mode access
switchport port-security maximum 2
```

At this point, nothing should happen. That's because this command doesn't actually enable Port Security. You might find that counterintuitive, but it's actually a blessing. Port Security has the ability to effectively render a port unusable if misconfigured. It's vital that you find out how many MAC addresses should be living on each port *before* enabling Port Security.

If you're not sure about the number of MAC addresses, you can set the number to something high like 10 and then go back and adjust it later. That way, if your boss has a secret workgroup switch under his desk with eight different MACs hanging off it, you'll find out from IOS instead of him.

Try it now

Once you have the maximum number of MAC address set properly, enable Port Security using the `switchport port-security` interface command.

Now verify your configuration with the command `show port-security`.

You should see something similar to the following:

```
Switch1#show port-security
Secure Port    MaxSecureAddr   CurrentAddr   SecurityViolation   Security Action
               (Count)         (Count)       (Count)
-------------------------------------------------------------------------------
    Fa0/1          2               2              0                 Shutdown
-------------------------------------------------------------------------------
Total Addresses in System (excluding one mac per port)    : 1
Max Addresses limit in System (excluding one mac per port) : 6144
```

The output doesn't provide much detail, but it's enough to figure out what's going on. When you enable Port Security on a port, it notes the MAC addresses that are talking on the port at that time and remembers them, up to the maximum value you specified. That's what the `MaxSecureAddr` column indicates. In this output, the maximum number of MAC addresses allowed on Fa0/1 is 2.

The `CurrentAddr` column indicates how many MAC addresses the switch has seen on the port since you enabled Port Security. In this output, the number is also 2 because there are only two devices attached.

The `SecurityViolation` column tells you how many times the switch has detected an additional MAC address on the port beyond the allowed maximum. As you might expect, that number is 0.

The last column, labeled `Security Action`, is arguably the most important one. It lists the action Port Security will take when it detects a *violation*—an additional MAC address beyond the configured maximum. This action is what Cisco calls the *violation mode*.

5.1.2   *Violation modes*

You're going to configure two violation modes: shutdown and restrict.

SHUTDOWN

In the output, the violation mode is shutdown. This means just what it sounds like. If Port Security detects a security violation—that is, an additional MAC address beyond the maximum two—it shuts down the port altogether. Without warning. No questions asked.

The shutdown behavior is the default. I suspect it's Cisco's way of preventing people from accidentally configuring Port Security and then wondering why things aren't working. When an in-use port abruptly shuts down right after you enable Port Security, it can be pretty dramatic and hard to miss.

RESTRICT

The alternative violation mode—restrict—is a bit more subtle. In this mode, when a violation occurs, Port Security keeps the port up but prevents the new MAC addresses from communicating. In a sense, it's like a dynamic access list that denies MAC addresses beyond the maximum.

You probably don't want Port Security to shut down the port altogether when it detects a violation. In that case, you must manually set the violation mode to restrict using the interface configuration command `switchport port-security violation restrict`.

Try it now

Change the violation mode to restrict using the following command:

```
switchport port-security violation restrict
```

As always, verify using the `show port-security` command.

You should see the violation mode in the last column change from `Shutdown` to `Restrict`. Everything else will stay the same:

```
Switch1#show port-security
Secure Port   MaxSecureAddr   CurrentAddr   SecurityViolation   Security Action
              (Count)         (Count)       (Count)
----------------------------------------------------------------------------
    Fa0/1          2               2             0                Restrict
----------------------------------------------------------------------------
Total Addresses in System (excluding one mac per port)    : 1
Max Addresses limit in System (excluding one mac per port) : 6144
```

Now when Port Security detects a violation, it won't shut down the port or otherwise affect the first two MAC addresses. They'll continue to communicate normally, and only subsequent addresses will get blocked.

Above and beyond

You may want to use the shutdown violation mode to prevent someone from setting up a rogue wireless access point that uses Power over Ethernet (PoE). When IOS shuts down a port on a PoE switch, it cuts power to whatever device is plugged in. That's also why you don't want to use the shutdown violation mode on ports with IP phones.

5.2   *Testing Port Security*

One of the most fun aspects of Port Security is testing it. You don't have to launch your very own MAC flooding attack to do this. All you have to do is get one additional MAC address to show up on the same port. There are a couple of ways to do this.

If you're dealing with a PC and IP phone, unplug the PC from the phone and plug in a laptop. Once the switch sees the laptop's MAC address, Port Security will log a security violation and prevent the laptop's MAC address from communicating.

If you just have a single PC, plug a small workgroup switch in between the Cisco switch and the PC. Get a couple of laptops or IP phones and plug those into the workgroup switch. This will give you three MAC addresses on the same port—enough to trigger a Port Security violation.

Try it now

It's important that you keep a close eye on things while you're testing Port Security. IOS can show you real-time information about what Port Security is doing. Just issue the `terminal monitor` command at the enable prompt.

Next, use one of the methods I just listed to test Port Security.

After connecting a third device, you should see a message similar to this:

```
%PORT_SECURITY-2-PSECURE_VIOLATION: Security violation occurred, caused by
    MAC address 0800.27ba.dbad on port FastEthernet0/1.
```

The console message leaves little room for interpretation. It gives you the port the violation occurred on and the MAC address that triggered it—good information to know when testing.

Now if you execute another `show port-security` command, you should see the `SecurityViolation` count increase:

```
Switch1#sh port-security
Secure Port   MaxSecureAddr   CurrentAddr   SecurityViolation   Security Action
              (Count)         (Count)       (Count)
-----------------------------------------------------------------------------
   Fa0/1         2               2             18              Restrict
-----------------------------------------------------------------------------
Total Addresses in System (excluding one mac per port)    : 1
Max Addresses limit in System (excluding one mac per port) : 6144
```

The number 18 may seem a bit unexpected considering Port Security should be blocking only one MAC address. The `SecurityViolation` counter increments every time an unauthorized MAC address tries to send a frame. If you've configured the maximum number of MAC addresses correctly, this number shouldn't get very high. If it does, it's a clue that you need to investigate the devices on that port.

Above and beyond

You can reset the `SecurityViolation` counter by shutting down the port and re-enabling it. As of this writing, there's no command to clear the counters directly.

5.3   Handling device moves

I mentioned earlier that Port Security is first come, first served. When you physically disconnect a device from a secured port, Port Security forgets all the MAC addresses it saw on that port. That way, if you plug a different device into the same port, Port Security will still allow it. This works well in cases when moving devices always entails physically unplugging something from the switch. For example, when a user moves desks, someone will physically unplug their PC and IP phone from the switch.

But there's another possibility. Suppose that an IT system administrator has a need to simultaneously connect five brand-new computers to the network in order to install software, download updates, and so on to get them ready for new users. But there's a problem: in the office where they're working, there's only one network jack. In order to stay efficient and get the PCs out on time, they plug a small, eight-port workgroup switch into the jack and plugs all the new PCs into that.

5.3.1   Port Security never forgets!

In the network closet, the jack is patched into port FastEthernet0/12 on the switch. You've done your homework, and you know that there should never be more than five simultaneous MAC addresses on the port that the workgroup switch is connected to. So you configure Port Security to allow a maximum of five MACs.

Try it now

It's okay if you don't actually have a small switch plugged in. This is just for practice. Use the following commands to configure Port Security to allow up to five simultaneous MAC addresses on FastEthernet0/12:

```
interface fa0/12
switchport port-security maximum 5
switchport port-security violation restrict
switchport port-security
```

After the system administrator boots up the five computers, each one begins sending traffic with its unique MAC address. Everything works as expected, and the computers can communicate with the network normally. A show port-security confirms Port Security is enabled and not blocking anything:

```
Switch1#show port-security
Secure Port    MaxSecureAddr   CurrentAddr    SecurityViolation   Security Action
               (Count)         (Count)        (Count)

--------------------------------------------------------------------------------
    Fa0/1        2                0                0               Restrict
    Fa0/12       5                5                0               Restrict
--------------------------------------------------------------------------------
Total Addresses in System (excluding one mac per port)     : 4
Max Addresses limit in System (excluding one mac per port) : 6144
```

When the administrator is finished, they shut down the machines and plug five new ones into the workgroup switch to get them set up. But now there's another problem. None of the machines can get on the network at all. You check Port Security again, and see the following:

```
Switch1#show port-security
Secure Port    MaxSecureAddr   CurrentAddr    SecurityViolation   Security Action
               (Count)         (Count)        (Count)

--------------------------------------------------------------------------------
    Fa0/1        2                0                0               Restrict
    Fa0/12       5                5                30              Restrict       <----
--------------------------------------------------------------------------------
Total Addresses in System (excluding one mac per port)     : 4              **MAC addresses**
Max Addresses limit in System (excluding one mac per port) : 6144           **getting blocked**
```

Port Security hasn't let go of the original five MAC addresses. It still remembers them and consequently doesn't allow the new PCs to communicate.

It's important to understand why this is happening. Port Security has no way of knowing that the original five PCs were unplugged from the network. The eight-port workgroup switch hides that. All Port Security knows is that it saw five unique MAC addresses, and then later on it saw five new ones. In keeping with the configuration, Port Security allowed only the first five MAC addresses and blocked the subsequent ones.

You could tell the system administrator to just unplug or reboot the workgroup switch every time they go through a round of computers, but that's impractical and annoying and would prematurely wear out the switch. You need another way to force Port Security to forget those MAC addresses without any manual intervention.

5.3.2   Aging time

The aging time is a parameter you can set to cause Port Security to periodically forget the MAC addresses it has learned.

After the system administrator finishes up one set of five computers, it takes about 10 minutes to unplug them, move them, and then plug in a new set. During this time, you want the MAC addresses from the first set to age out so that by the time they get around to the second set, Port Security will have forgotten about the first five.

> **Try it now**
>
> The aging time, like all other Port Security options, is set on a per-port basis. Use the following commands to set the aging time to 10 minutes:
>
> ```
> interface fa0/12
> switchport port-security aging time 10
> ```
>
> Use the following command to verify your configuration:
>
> ```
> show port-security interface fa0/12
> ```

Here's an example of what you should see:

```
Switch1#show port-security interface fa0/12
Port Security               : Enabled
Port Status                 : Secure-up
Violation Mode          `   : Restrict
Aging Time                  : 10 mins          ←⎤ Aging time set
Aging Type                  : Absolute          ⎦ to 10 minutes
SecureStatic Address Aging  : Disabled
Maximum MAC Addresses       : 5
Total MAC Addresses         : 5
Configured MAC Addresses    : 0
Sticky MAC Addresses        : 0
Last Source Address:Vlan    : 0800.271c.0b57:1
Security Violation Count    : 30
```

On the fourth line of the output, you can see the Aging Time in minutes. Port Security ages each MAC address *independently* based on when it first saw the address. You can see this with a show port-security address command:

```
Switch1#show port-security address
            Secure Mac Address Table
-------------------------------------------------------------------
Vlan   Mac Address     Type          Ports     Remaining Age
                                                  (mins)
----   -----------     ----          -----     -------------
   1   0800.2742.aab8  SecureDynamic Fa0/12         6
   1   0800.2782.4c93  SecureDynamic Fa0/12         6
   1   0800.27b8.b488  SecureDynamic Fa0/12         6
   1   0800.27e4.bb01  SecureDynamic Fa0/12         6
   1   0800.7200.3131  SecureDynamic Fa0/12         6
-------------------------------------------------------------------
Total Addresses in System (excluding one mac per port)    : 4
Max Addresses limit in System (excluding one mac per port) : 6144
```

Notice that each MAC address has the same Remaining Age time. This isn't surprising because the system administrator booted each of the five computers at the same time.

Now suppose that they're finished with four of the five computers and shut them down. They still have one left that's giving them trouble, so they leave it plugged in. They bring in four new computers, plug them in, and turn them on. They report that everything still seems to be working.

You run another `show port-security address`:

```
Switch1#show port-security address
           Secure Mac Address Table
------------------------------------------------------------------
Vlan   Mac Address      Type           Ports     Remaining Age
                                                  (mins)
----   -----------      ----           -----     -------------
   1   0800.2708.e69b   SecureDynamic  Fa0/12         9
   1   0800.27b6.b091   SecureDynamic  Fa0/12         9
   1   0800.27c1.5607   SecureDynamic  Fa0/12         9
   1   0800.27f4.803e   SecureDynamic  Fa0/12         9
   1   0800.7200.3131   SecureDynamic  Fa0/12         8
------------------------------------------------------------------
Total Addresses in System (excluding one mac per port)    : 4
Max Addresses limit in System (excluding one mac per port) : 6144
```

This device wasn't swapped out and ages independently of the other addresses.

Notice that the first four MAC addresses are different, and their remaining aging time is 9 minutes. The last address, which belongs to the computer that they did *not* unplug, hasn't changed and has a remaining aging time of 8 minutes. Because the MAC address of this computer was already in the list of allowed MAC addresses, it will still be able to access the network even after the timer expires. Once the timer reaches zero, it will reset to 10 minutes.

Now that you've configured the aging time, you probably won't ever have to mess with Port Security on this particular port. If the system administrator ever has a problem with connectivity, all they have to do is wait a few minutes and try again.

You'll likely have to go through some trial and error to get the aging time just right. If you find that newly connected devices are unable to access the network, you may want to decrease the aging time. Keep the needs of the user in mind, and don't feel like you have to set a long aging time. Even if you set a very short aging time, say 1 minute, the port is still protected against a MAC flood attack. Setting a longer time doesn't buy you any additional security. But if you do require more stringent security, Port Security can give you that as well.

5.4 Preventing unauthorized devices

So far, you've learned how to configure Port Security to prevent a MAC flooding attack without disrupting legitimate user traffic. With some research and maybe a little bit of trial and error, you can configure Port Security on all end-user ports without anyone knowing it's even there.

But although a minimum Port Security configuration may be great for end-user productivity, not all organizations are so lucky. Some have strict security requirements that prohibit non-company devices from connecting to the network. For them, it's not sufficient to limit the number of MAC addresses on a port; you have to limit which *specific* MAC addresses can use the port. That sounds like a cumbersome task, but as you'll see, Port Security makes it surprisingly easy.

Even if your organization doesn't require such a burdensome level of security, I still strongly suggest reading this section. Here's why: In chapter 4, you learned that one of the reasons for disabling unused ports is to prevent someone from walking in off the street with an infected laptop and plugging it in at an empty desk. But even if you faithfully check and disable unused ports once a day and twice on Sunday, that doesn't stop them from unplugging a work computer and plugging in the infected laptop.

You can probably think of other reasons to restrict a port to a single device. At the beginning of the chapter, I said I'd tell you how to configure Port Security for maximum security. Now that you have some rationale for when you might want to do this, I'm going to teach you how you'd do it.

> **Above and beyond**
> Security is all about having layers of protection. Although any organization with an ounce of sense will take measures to physically prevent people from walking in off the street with a malicious device, that doesn't negate the need to take technical measures to protect the network. All security can be broken; the best you can hope for is to slow an attacker down enough that they give up and move on to an easier target. Port Security is one technology that can make an attacker's life more difficult.

5.4.1   *Making Port Security maximally secure*

Recall that when you enable Port Security, it remembers and allows MAC addresses as it sees them, up to the configured maximum. When the device physically connected to the port gets unplugged, Port Security forgets those MACs. If you have aging configured for, say, 5 minutes, Port Security forgets each MAC address 5 minutes after it first sees it.

In a highly secure environment, you want Port Security to operate a bit differently. First, you want it to allow and remember the specific MAC addresses of the devices that are supposed to be connected. Second, you never want it to forget those MAC addresses—*ever*! Even if someone shuts down the port, disconnects the device, or reboots the switch, you want those MACs to stick to the port like glue as the only MAC addresses authorized to use that port. You can achieve this using what Cisco calls *sticky MAC addresses*.

5.4.2   *Sticky MAC addresses*

A sticky MAC address is one stored permanently in the startup configuration, under the interface configuration section. The reason it's called *sticky* is that you don't have to manually configure the MAC address. Instead, you let Port Security discover it in the usual way, and IOS will automatically write the MAC address into the running configuration. It's a clever way to achieve a high level of security with a little bit of effort.

Let's say your organization has a PC that sits in a semi-public area, like a lobby or reception area. You want to prevent someone from coming in after hours and plugging a malicious device into the same port. Because only one MAC address should ever be seen on that port, you configure the maximum number of MACs to one. Then you tell Port Security to permanently remember the MAC address using the command `switchport port-security mac-address sticky`.

Try it now

Select a port with only one device connected and configure Port Security to allow one sticky MAC address:

```
interface fa0/1
switchport port-security maximum 1
switchport port-security mac-address sticky
```

This is where the magic happens. As soon as Port Security sees the MAC address, it writes it to the running configuration. You can verify this with a `show run interface fa0/1`:

```
Switch1#show run interface fa0/1
Building configuration...

Current configuration : 233 bytes
!
interface FastEthernet0/1
 switchport mode access
 switchport port-security
 switchport port-security violation restrict
 switchport port-security mac-address sticky           ← You issued this command.
 switchport port-security mac-address sticky 0800.7200.3131   ← Port Security added this sticky MAC address.
End
```

Notice that the last two lines of the interface configuration are almost identical except for the MAC address. The first command is the one you issued, and the second is the one Port Security added.

Above and beyond

You may notice that the `switchport port-security maximum 1` command doesn't show up in the configuration. This isn't a mistake, and it doesn't mean you did anything wrong. Sometimes IOS changes or removes certain configuration commands if they're redundant or unnecessary. Port Security defaults to allowing only one MAC address per port, so explicitly setting the maximum to `1` is unnecessary.

Now do a show port-security address to compare:

```
Switch1#sh port-security address
          Secure Mac Address Table
-------------------------------------------------------------------
Vlan   Mac Address     Type             Ports       Remaining Age
                                                       (mins)
----   -----------     ----             -----       ------------
  1    0800.7200.3131  SecureSticky     Fa0/1           -
-------------------------------------------------------------------
Total Addresses in System (excluding one mac per port)    : 0
Max Addresses limit in System (excluding one mac per port) : 6144
```

Notice the type is SecureSticky and there is no aging time.

The same address shows up here, and the Remaining Age column is blank because the entry will never expire. Until you manually remove the configuration Port Security added, it will remember that MAC.

Try it now

Physically disconnect the PC from the port on which you configured a sticky MAC address and plug in a different device. What happens?

You should see a pattern similar to the following:

```
%LINEPROTO-5-UPDOWN: Line protocol on Interface FastEthernet0/1,
    changed state to down
%LINK-3-UPDOWN: Interface FastEthernet0/1, changed state to down
%LINK-3-UPDOWN: Interface FastEthernet0/1, changed state to up
%LINEPROTO-5-UPDOWN: Line protocol on Interface FastEthernet0/1,
    changed state to up
%PORT_SECURITY-2-PSECURE_VIOLATION: Security violation occurred,
    caused by MAC address 2c27.d737.9ad1 on port FastEthernet0/1.
```

Disconnect legitimate PC

Connect an unauthorized device.

Port Security blocks the unauthorized device's MAC.

In a real hacking attempt, an intruder might spend a few minutes trying to figure out why they can't get access to the network. They may try tweaking their network settings, rebooting, or connecting to a different port. The important thing is that Port Security thwarts their plug-and-play attempt to gain unauthorized access.

But as good as this configuration is, there's one shortcoming.

Above and beyond

MAC addresses can be spoofed quite easily. A sophisticated attacker can find out the MAC address of the authorized PC and clone it. But that still takes time. Remember, the goal isn't to rely on Port Security as the be-all and end-all of security. Its only job is to make it harder for an attacker to cause trouble.

5.4.3 *Caveats about sticky MACs*

The additional security of sticky MACs comes with a tradeoff. If you ever need to replace a device, you'll have to manually edit the port configuration to remove the old MAC address so that the new one can take its place. In the earlier example, Port Security added the following line to the running configuration:

```
switchport port-security mac-address sticky 0800.7200.3131
```

The way you'd remove this is to first ensure that that particular MAC address is no longer using that port. Next, you'd enter interface configuration mode and prepend the command with a no.

> **Try it now**
>
> Unplug the PC from FastEthernet0/1, or just shut down the port. Then issue the following commands to remove the sticky MAC address. Be sure to change the MAC address to match your particular configuration:
>
> ```
> int fa0/1
> no switchport port-security mac-address sticky 0800.7200.3131
> ```
>
> Do another show run int fa0/1, and the sticky MAC address should be gone.

That's it! Port Security will automatically add the next MAC address it sees as a sticky MAC to the running configuration. Another thing to keep in mind is that after Port Security writes the sticky MAC addresses to the running configuration, you still have to manually save the startup configuration in order for the addresses to persist across switch reboots.

5.5 *Commands in this chapter*

As you review the list of commands in table 5.4, keep in mind that two ports can be configured with completely different Port Security settings. This makes Port Security versatile, but it also means you have to individually check the port configuration when troubleshooting an issue.

Table 5.4 Commands used in this chapter

Command	Configuration mode	Description
switchport port-security maximum 5	Interface	Allows up to five MAC addresses
switchport port-security violation restrict	Interface	All MACs beyond the maximum are blocked
switchport port-security violation shutdown	Interface	Any MAC beyond the maximum triggers a port shutdown

Table 5.4   Commands used in this chapter *(continued)*

Command	Configuration mode	Description
`switchport port-security`	Interface	Enables Port Security
`switchport port-security mac-address sticky`	Interface	Writes allowed MAC address(es) to the running configuration
`show port-security`	N/A	Displays which ports Port Security is enabled on
`show port-security interface fa0/1`	N/A	Displays detailed Port Security configuration information for a port
`show port-security address`	N/A	Displays the allowed MAC addresses by port
`show run interface fa0/1`	N/A	Displays all interface-level configuration for FastEthernet0/1

5.6   *Hands-on lab*

Now that you've gotten some practice configuring Port Security on a couple of ports, you're ready to enable Port Security on all end-user ports. Just one unprotected port is all it takes for a MAC flooding attack to take down your network.

As you follow these steps to complete the lab, remember to use the `interface range` command to simultaneously apply the configuration to multiple ports:

1 Start by configuring the maximum number of MAC addresses for each port. If you already have a good handle on how many MAC addresses should be on each port, go ahead and set it using the `switchport port-security maximum` command. Otherwise, if you're not sure, play it safe and set it to a high number like 50. The maximum number of MAC addresses allowed per port is 3,072.

2 Next, set the violation mode on all ports to restrict using the `switchport port-security violation restrict` command. You can go back later and change it to shutdown if you require it, but don't start out with that.

3 Finally, enable Port Security using the `switchport port-security` interface command. If you've done everything correctly, nothing dramatic should happen (unless you're in the middle of a MAC flood attack). Use the `show` commands you learned in this chapter to verify your configuration.

Managing virtual LANs (VLANs)

Recall from chapter 2 that you need to keep broadcast domains small to avoid network performance problems like flooding and interrupts. On a large network, this brings with it the nasty side effect of having to split devices into separate broadcast domains.

But separating broadcast domains isn't just about necessity, nor is it a concern for only large networks. Many organizations—even small ones—want to maintain separate broadcast domains for security. For example, a company may want to keep computers in the Human Resources department in a separate broadcast domain from computers in the Marketing department.

In chapter 2, I illustrated one way to achieve such a configuration using two separate, disconnected switches. Although this is certainly a valid approach, it's not very efficient. Having at a minimum one switch per broadcast domain costs more money, takes up more space, and requires more management overhead than putting all devices into one big broadcast domain.

So what do you do? At first it may seem you're stuck choosing between two bad options. Do you ensure a reliable network, or do you try to keep costs down? Fortunately, there's a third option that gives you both: use *virtual LANs (VLANs)*.

6.1   What is a VLAN?

A VLAN is nothing more than a broadcast domain. The thing that makes a VLAN unique is that it's a broadcast domain that you arbitrarily define by assigning individual switch ports to it. Figure 6.1 illustrates two computers connected to the same switch but in different VLANs.

Using VLANs, you can configure multiple broadcast domains on a single switch. There's no need to have a separate switch for each broadcast domain. Each switch port can be a member of a different broadcast domain—a different VLAN. This allows you to arbitrarily place devices into different broadcast domains with a few simple configuration commands.

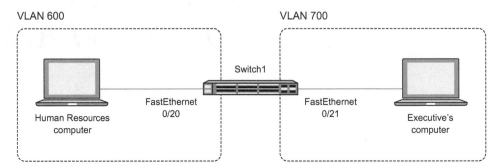

Figure 6.1 Computers in separate VLANs. Although both computers are connected to the same switch, they are in separate broadcast domains.

6.2   *Inventorying VLANs*

As usual, you need to start out by getting a handle on what VLANs currently exist in your environment. Remember, VLANs are defined on each individual switch. It's possible to have different VLANs configured on different switches. To ensure you get a good handle on your VLANs, perform the exercises in this chapter on the central or core switch in your environment. If you've set up your own lab according to the online appendix, use Switch1.

6.2.1   *The VLAN database*

VLANs are defined on the switch and stored in what's called the local *VLAN database*. This database is stored in flash memory in the vlan.dat file and is distinct from the startup configuration.

You can view a pared-down version of the VLAN database using the `show vlan brief` command.

> **Try it now**
>
> Log into your switch and get into enable mode.
>
> Issue this command to view all VLANs:
>
> `show vlan brief`

You'll see a list of all VLANs configured on the switch:

```
Switch1#show vlan brief

VLAN Name                 Status    Ports
---- -------------------- --------- ------------------------------
1    default              active    Fa0/1, Fa0/2, Fa0/3, Fa0/4
                                    Fa0/5, Fa0/6, Fa0/7, Fa0/8
                                    Fa0/9, Fa0/10, Fa0/11, Fa0/12
                                    Fa0/13, Fa0/14, Fa0/15, Fa0/16
                                    Fa0/17, Fa0/18, Fa0/19, Fa0/20
                                    Fa0/21, Fa0/22, Fa0/23, Fa0/24
                                    Gi0/1, Gi0/2
1002 fddi-default         act/unsup
1003 token-ring-default   act/unsup
1004 fddinet-default      act/unsup
1005 trnet-default        act/unsup
```

The output you see may look the same, or it may look very, very different. Either way, what's important is being able to interpret what you're looking at.

VLAN

In the leftmost VLAN column are the VLAN IDs. The switch keeps track of VLANs using numeric VLAN identifiers. You can create new VLANs with identifiers 2 through 1001 inclusive, but you don't have to assign VLANs IDs sequentially. VLAN ID numbers by themselves have no significance, with the exception of VLAN 1. This is called the default Ethernet VLAN, and it exists on all Cisco switches. You can't delete or rename it. I'll cover VLAN 1 in a moment.

NAME

The next column, the Name column, is the name of the VLAN. You can optionally assign an alphanumeric name to a VLAN, but you don't have to. If you don't assign a name, the switch will create one for you based on the VLAN ID.

STATUS

The third column, the Status column, should be active for all VLANs that you're using. Notice that VLANs 1002–1005 are listed as act/unsup, which means active and unsupported. These VLANs are non-Ethernet default VLANs that exist on every Catalyst switch, and you don't need to worry about them. Just know that you can't use, modify, or delete them.

PORTS

The Ports column is the most important. It tells you which ports belong to which VLANs. In my output, every port is a member of the default VLAN 1.

Above and beyond

Because the VLAN database is stored in a separate file, you can blow away the startup configuration completely, and any configured VLANs will still be there. If you want to delete the entire VLAN database, you have to delete vlan.dat using the enable command `delete flash:vlan.dat`.

6.2.2   *The default VLAN*

By default, every switch port is a member of the default VLAN 1. When you take a brand-new Cisco switch out of the box, or if you blow away the VLAN database, every switch port automatically gets assigned to VLAN 1. This means that everything attached to the switch is in the same broadcast domain. Logically, it's the same thing as not using VLANs at all!

Sticking with VLAN 1 and having one big broadcast domain is a common practice, especially in small organizations that don't have a need or desire to separate broadcast domains by department or function. Today, your organization may not require any VLAN except the default VLAN 1. But there's always the possibility that growth or an acquisition could change that, so you need to know how to create new VLANs to accommodate that eventuality.

6.2.3   *How many VLANs should you create?*

The short answer is as many as you need and no more.

There's no hard-and-fast rule about how many devices can or should be in a single broadcast domain. If your organization plans to add more heads, you should start thinking about breaking out separate devices into VLANs when you have around 150 machines. When you get north of 200, you should definitely start making plans to create a new VLAN.

6.2.4   *Planning a new VLAN*

Divide the VLANs in a way that aligns with business units, but make sure each VLAN is large enough to justify its own existence. For example, if the Payroll department has 50 computers, and the Implementation department has only 10 computers, it makes sense to lump them together into a single VLAN instead of two. There's nothing wrong with having only 10 computers in a VLAN, but from an administrative standpoint, it's more efficient to minimize the total number of VLANs.

Security and availability are also important considerations. You probably don't want the locked-down Human Resources computers to be in the same VLAN as the less-secure Training computers. If one of the Training computers gets a nasty virus and starts flooding the network with a broadcast storm, you want to ensure the HR computers can still access the network without issue.

Don't fret if you aren't sure how or if you should create new VLANs. The point is that as a network administrator, you'll have to do it eventually—and likely sooner rather than later. Even if you have no need at the moment to create new VLANs, it's important that you follow along with the exercises to get a feel for the configuration so that you'll be ready when the time comes.

6.3   *Creating VLANs*

You can create, name, and delete VLANs in *VLAN configuration mode*. Even though the VLAN database isn't stored in the running or startup configuration, you still must get into global configuration mode to make changes to it. Suppose you've decided to create two new VLANs: VLAN 600 for Human Resources and VLAN 700 for Executives. Let's start with the former.

> **Try it now**
>
> Get into global configuration mode by typing `configure terminal`. Then create VLAN 600 using this command:
>
> ```
> vlan 600
> ```
>
> At this point, you should see the VLAN configuration mode prompt:
>
> ```
> Switch1(config-vlan)#
> ```
>
> Type `exit` to leave VLAN configuration mode and save your changes.
>
> Now do a `show vlan brief` to verify.

You should see the new VLAN:

```
Switch1#show vlan brief

VLAN Name                 Status    Ports
---- -------------------- --------- ----------------------------
1    default              active    Fa0/1, Fa0/2, Fa0/3, Fa0/4
                                    Fa0/5, Fa0/6, Fa0/7, Fa0/8
                                    Fa0/9, Fa0/10, Fa0/11, Fa0/12
                                    Fa0/13, Fa0/14, Fa0/15, Fa0/16
                                    Fa0/17, Fa0/18, Fa0/19, Fa0/20
                                    Fa0/21, Fa0/22, Fa0/23, Fa0/24
                                    Gi0/1, Gi0/2
600  VLAN0600             active
```

Notice that the name of the VLAN is VLAN0600. This is the name the switch automatically assigned to the VLAN because you didn't explicitly specify one. Again, a custom name isn't necessary, but it is helpful. Let's add one.

> **Try it now**
>
> Go back into VLAN configuration mode and assign VLAN 600 the name HR:
>
> ```
> vlan 600
> name HR
> ```
>
> Type `exit` to exit VLAN configuration mode.
>
> Verify with a `show vlan brief`.

```
Switch1#show vlan brief

VLAN Name                 Status     Ports
---- -------------------- ---------  -------------------------------
1    default              active     Fa0/1, Fa0/2, Fa0/3, Fa0/4
                                     Fa0/5, Fa0/6, Fa0/7, Fa0/8
                                     Fa0/9, Fa0/10, Fa0/11, Fa0/12
                                     Fa0/13, Fa0/14, Fa0/15, Fa0/16
                                     Fa0/17, Fa0/18, Fa0/19, Fa0/20
                                     Fa0/21, Fa0/22, Fa0/23, Fa0/24
                                     Gi0/1, Gi0/2
600  HR                   active
```

**VLAN you
just created**

Now the VLAN database output reflects the name of the new HR VLAN. Next up is the Executives VLAN.

Try it now

Create VLAN 700 and name it `Executives` using the following commands:

```
vlan 700
name Executives
exit
```

Verify again with a `show vlan brief`:

```
Switch1#show vlan brief

VLAN Name                 Status     Ports
---- -------------------- ---------  -------------------------------
1    default              active     Fa0/1, Fa0/2, Fa0/3, Fa0/4
                                     Fa0/5, Fa0/6, Fa0/7, Fa0/8
                                     Fa0/9, Fa0/10, Fa0/11, Fa0/12
                                     Fa0/13, Fa0/14, Fa0/15, Fa0/16
                                     Fa0/17, Fa0/18, Fa0/19, Fa0/20
                                     Fa0/21, Fa0/22, Fa0/23, Fa0/24
                                     Gi0/1, Gi0/2
600  HR                   active
700  Executives           active
```

**Notice there are
no member ports.**

Perfect! Believe it or not, that's all there is to creating VLANs. But creating VLANs is only one piece of the puzzle. Right now, all of the ports on the switch are members of the default VLAN 1. VLANs 600 and 700 don't have any port members, so there's no way for any end-user devices to access these new VLANs.

6.4   *Assigning VLANs*

To keep it simple, you're going to assign FastEthernet0/20 to VLAN 600 and FastEthernet0/21 to VLAN 700. As always, if you're working in a live environment, feel free to choose different ports so you don't interrupt anybody's work.

6.4.1   *Checking port configuration*

Before you change any VLAN membership assignment, it's always a good idea to check the current port configuration in case you need to revert if something goes wrong. As a practical matter, even if you're careful, you'll eventually slip up and reconfigure the wrong switch port, so being able to set it back to its original configuration quickly is important.

> **Try it now**
> Check FastEthernet0/20's running configuration:
>
> ```
> show run interface fa0/20
> ```

You should see the configuration only for the specified port:

```
Switch1#show run interface fa0/20
Building configuration...

Current configuration : 68 bytes
!
interface FastEthernet0/20          | Port is set to be a member
 switchport mode access          ◄──┘ of a single VLAN
 shutdown
End
```

That first line in the interface configuration—switchport mode access—might seem a bit strange. When a port is a member of a VLAN, Cisco calls it a *static access port* because the device connected to it always accesses that VLAN. But what VLAN is it accessing? The earlier show vlan brief indicates it's a member of VLAN 1, but there's nothing about VLAN 1 in the interface configuration. I mentioned in the last chapter that the switch removes certain configuration commands if they're redundant or unnecessary. Because VLAN 1 is the default VLAN, it doesn't explicitly show up in the interface configuration because the switch assumes it.

6.4.2   *Setting the access VLAN*

When you assign a VLAN to a port, you are, in Cisco parlance, setting the access VLAN on that port. Any device connected to that port becomes a member of that VLAN by virtue of being connected to the port. The command to set the access VLAN is switchport access vlan followed by the VLAN ID.

> **Try it now**
> Assign FastEthernet0/20 to VLAN 600 using the following commands:
>
> ```
> interface fa0/20
> switchport access vlan 600
> ```
>
> Verify with another show run interface fa0/20.

You should see a reference to VLAN 600:

```
Switch1#show run interface fa0/20
Building configuration...

Current configuration : 96 bytes
!
interface FastEthernet0/20
 switchport access vlan 600
 switchport mode access
 shutdown
End
```

> Port is in
> **VLAN 600**

> Port is a static
> **access port**

This is much clearer! There's no question that this port is a member of VLAN 600. The only part that may not be immediately clear to the uninitiated is *what* VLAN 600 is. Obviously, you know that it's the HR VLAN because you just configured it. But if you forgot, or if this were a different VLAN you didn't configure, you'd want to check the VLAN database again to find out.

> **Try it now**
> Determine what VLAN 600 is, and verify that FastEthernet0/20 is a member of it:
> ```
> show vlan brief
> ```

Now see if you can spot the difference in the output:

```
Switch1#show vlan brief

VLAN Name                   Status    Ports
---- -------------------- --------- -------------------------------
1    default              active    Fa0/1, Fa0/2, Fa0/3, Fa0/4
                                    Fa0/5, Fa0/6, Fa0/7, Fa0/8
                                    Fa0/9, Fa0/10, Fa0/11, Fa0/12
                                    Fa0/13, Fa0/14, Fa0/15, Fa0/16
                                    Fa0/17, Fa0/18, Fa0/19, Fa0/21
                                    Fa0/22, Fa0/23, Fa0/24, Gi0/1
                                    Gi0/2
600  HR                   active    Fa0/20
700  Executives           active
```

> **Notice the lone
> member of VLAN 600.**

Being a Cisco network administrator means paying close attention to details that others might miss. FastEthernet0/20 is the only member of VLAN 600. That `Fa0/20` almost blends in with the ports in VLAN 1, doesn't it? To make things a bit clearer, you can use a slightly different command.

> **Try it now**
> Filter the `show vlan brief` output to display only the columns and information pertinent to VLAN 600:
> ```
> show vlan brief | i VLAN|600
> ```

You should see something like this:

```
VLAN Name                   Status      Ports
600  HR                     active      Fa0/20
```

Much better! VLAN 600 is the HR VLAN, and it has one member, FastEthernet0/20. In a live environment, you'll likely have more VLANs and more ports, making the output even more muddled. Using the built-in parsing functions to filter your output can make things a lot more readable and even save you from making some mistakes.

6.4.3 Setting the access mode

So far, you've assigned the HR VLAN 600 to FastEthernet0/20, but there are no member ports in VLAN 700, the Executives VLAN. Next, you're going to make FastEthernet0/21 an access port in VLAN 700. But before you do, you need to check the existing configuration for that port.

Try it now

Determine the VLAN configuration on FastEthernet0/21:

```
show run interface fa0/21
```

You should see the interface configuration section of the running configuration:

```
Switch1#show run int fa0/21
Building configuration...

Current configuration : 44 bytes
!
interface FastEthernet0/21
 shutdown
end
```

This output looks a little different. The `switchport mode access` command is missing. In order to add this port to VLAN 700, you need both this command and the `switchport access vlan 700`.

Try it now

Make FastEthernet0/21 a static access port for VLAN 700:

```
interface fa0/21
switchport mode access
switchport access vlan 700
```

Then verify with a `show run interface fa0/21`.

Your output should include the two commands:

```
Switch1#show run interface fa0/21
Building configuration...

Current configuration : 96 bytes
!
interface FastEthernet0/21
 switchport access vlan 700
 switchport mode access
 shutdown
end
```

It's important to understand that these two commands serve two different purposes. The `switchport mode access` command forces the port to always be a static access port in the VLAN specified by `switchport access VLAN 700`. It's possible for a port to be a member of multiple VLANs, and you'll learn about that starting in chapter 10. The only reason I'm mentioning it now is so that you understand why both commands are necessary.

6.5   *Voice VLANs*

Many organizations use their existing computer network infrastructure to provide Voice over IP (VoIP) telephony. If you're familiar with how IP phones connect to the network, you know that the phone connects to a switch port, and a computer connects to the phone. In other words, the phone sits between the switch and the computer. This raises an interesting dilemma when it comes to VLANs.

Suppose you connect an IP phone to FastEthernet0/20, which is a member of the HR VLAN 600. Then you connect a computer to the phone. Both the computer and the phone are in VLAN 600, the HR VLAN. Here's the problem: voice traffic is especially sensitive to delays. Any heavy traffic in the HR VLAN could potentially make voice calls choppy and garbled. For example, if an HR employee starts a large download on their computer while interviewing a prospective employee on an IP phone, the download could crowd out voice traffic.

Cisco allows you to avoid this problem by dedicating a separate VLAN to IP phones. This is called a *voice VLAN*. A voice VLAN isn't a special type of VLAN. Rather, it's a term Cisco uses to describe the VLAN that an IP phone uses. If your organization uses IP phones, you should already have a voice VLAN configured. Chances are it's named something like VOICE.

If you already have a voice VLAN, you don't need to create another one. But if you don't, go ahead and create VOICE VLAN 20 for practice.

Try it now

Use the following commands to create VLAN 20 and name it `VOICE`:

```
vlan 20
name VOICE
exit
```

(continued)

Verify the new VLAN exists in the VLAN database:

```
sh vlan brief | i VLAN|20
```

Don't worry whether you have any ports in the voice VLAN. All that matters at this point is that it exists:

```
Switch1#sh vlan brief | i VLAN|20
VLAN Name                    Status     Ports
20   VOICE                   active
600  HR                      active     Fa0/20
```

Simply creating the VLAN and naming it VOICE isn't enough. You need a way to keep the phone's voice traffic in the voice VLAN while keeping traffic from the computer in the HR VLAN. The solution is to configure FastEthernet0/20 to use VLAN 20 as its voice VLAN. You do this using the `switchport voice vlan 20` command. This command causes the switch to send special instructions to the IP phone telling it to use VLAN 20 as the voice VLAN.

Try it now

Configure voice VLAN 20 on FastEthernet0/20:

```
interface fa0/20
switchport voice vlan 20
```

Verify with a `sh vlan brief | i VLAN|20`.

Your output should show both the HR and voice VLANs:

```
Switch1#sh vlan brief | i VLAN|20
VLAN Name                    Status     Ports
20   VOICE                   active     Fa0/20
600  HR                      active     Fa0/20
```

Notice that the same port is a member of both VLANs. The `switchport voice vlan 20` command turns FastEthernet0/20 into what Cisco calls a *multi-VLAN access port* that can access both the voice and HR VLANs simultaneously. This doesn't mean that both VLANs are in the same broadcast domain—quite the opposite. When the IP phone sends voice traffic, it appends a special *tag* to each voice packet indicating that it's for VLAN 20. The switch uses this tag to ensure that voice traffic from the IP phone goes into VLAN 20, while all other traffic from the computer goes into VLAN 600.

6.6 *Using your new VLANs*

At the beginning of this chapter, I presented VLANs as a way to easily create separate broadcast domains without having to incur the expense of buying additional switches.

But as you'll recall from chapter 2, separating devices into different broadcast domains creates another problem: a device in one broadcast domain can't communicate with a device in the other using its media access control (MAC) address.

If you want devices to communicate across broadcast domains, you have to give them IP addresses in different subnets, and you also have to provide a gateway to route packets between the broadcast domains. In the next chapter, you're going to learn how to create new IP subnets, associate them with the two new VLANs you created, and establish communication between them.

6.7   Commands in this chapter

Creating and assigning VLANs requires you to use three different configuration modes. Table 6.1 can help you remember which commands work in which configuration modes.

Table 6.1   Commands used in this chapter

Command	Configuration mode	Description
vlan 700	Global	Enters VLAN configuration mode for VLAN 700
name Executives	VLAN	Assigns the human-friendly name Executives to the specified VLAN
exits	VLAN	Saves the VLAN database and exits to global configuration mode
switchport access vlan 700	Interface	Makes the port a member of VLAN 700
switchport mode access	Interface	Makes the port a static access port in the specified VLAN
switchport voice vlan 20	Interface	Assigns VLAN 20 as the voice VLAN
show vlan brief	N/A	Displays the VLAN database

6.8   Hands-on lab

Perform all of the exercises in this chapter if you haven't done so already. If you have, go ahead and save the running configuration using the `write memory` command.

Before tomorrow, I recommend that you have two test computers plugged into FastEthernet0/20 and 0/21, or whatever ports you used for the exercises. If you don't have a couple of computers to spare, don't worry. You'll still be able to perform the exercises.

Breaking the VLAN barrier by using switched virtual interfaces

Although splitting devices into separate virtual LANs (VLANs) prevents excessive flooding and provides a bit of security, it creates another problem: devices in separate VLANs can't communicate with each other—at least not without a little help.

At the end of the last chapter, I recommended connecting two test computers to the two VLAN access ports you configured. If you weren't able to do that, don't worry. You can still follow along with most of the exercises, and I'll provide screenshots to fill in the gaps, using the computers shown in figure 7.1 as an example.

As you can see, HR-PC1 is connected to FastEthernet0/20, which is an access port in VLAN 600, and Executive-PC1 is connected to FastEthernet0/21, which is in VLAN 700. As it stands, these two devices can't communicate with each other. In

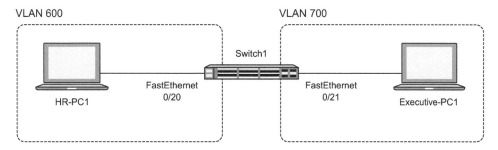

Figure 7.1   Two computers in separate VLANs

fact, they can't communicate with any devices outside their respective VLANs. Creating new VLANs and setting up access ports was the first step, but you need to do more before you can actually start *using* these new VLANs.

In this chapter, I'm going to teach you how to get these two computers talking to each other using a feature called *switched virtual interfaces (SVIs)*.

7.1   Understanding the VLAN–subnet connection

You can't just willy-nilly assign IP addresses to computers at random. In addition to uniquely addressing each device in a VLAN, an IP address needs to somehow indicate *which* VLAN the device is in.

Before you can decide on specific IP addresses, you need to decide which IP *subnets* to use for each VLAN. Remember that a subnet is just a range of IP addresses that usually all reside in the same broadcast domain. The specific IP addresses you choose for each device will come from the range of available IP addresses in the subnet.

Table 7.1 lists the subnets you'll be using for each VLAN. You can choose a different pair of subnets, but if you're practicing in an organizational environment, be sure the subnets you choose don't conflict with those already in your network. Most organizations maintain a list of subnets they're using internally.

Table 7.1   Subnets and corresponding VLANs

VLAN	Subnet address	Subnet mask	Usable IP address range
600	172.31.60.0	255.255.255.0	172.31.60.1–172.31.60.254
700	172.31.70.0	255.255.255.0	172.31.70.1–172.31.70.254

You may notice that I snuck a new term into the second column heading: *subnet address*. The subnet address along with the subnet mask actually determines the specific *range* of IP addresses that reside in the subnet. For example, look at the subnet address and subnet mask for VLAN 700, written out in table 7.2.

Table 7.2   Subnet address and subnet mask

	First octet	Second octet	Third octet	Fourth octet
Subnet address	172	31	70	0
Subnet mask	255	255	255	0

It helps to think of the subnet mask as a sort of secret code that tells you how to read the subnet address. The number 255 means "This octet has to stay the same." The number 0 means "This can be any number between 1 and 254!" Alternatively, you can think of the 0 as being a variable like *x*.

Using this information, let's pick an IP address for Executive-PC1's address (you'll manually configure Executive-PC1 with this IP address in a moment). The first three octets have to stay the same, so the IP address must begin with 172.31.70.*x*. The last octet, however, can be any number between 1 and 254. Choosing 1 for the last octet yields an IP address of 172.31.70.1.

Above and beyond

In case you can't use the subnets I suggested, you can select from the following subnet ranges, which are reserved for private networks:

```
10.0.0.0-10.255.255.0
172.16.0.0-172.31.255.0
192.168.0.0-192.168.255.0
```

When calculating individual IP addresses, remember to use the subnet mask 255.255.255.0.

I'll go ahead and assign this IP address to Executive-PC1, as shown in figure 7.2.

Make sure the Default Gateway field is blank. You'll fill in that field a little later.

Next, you need to come up with an IP address for HR-PC1 in VLAN 600. That's the 172.31.60.0 subnet. I'll pick 172.31.60.1 and assign that to the machine, as shown in figure 7.3. Notice that the Default Gateway field is blank here as well.

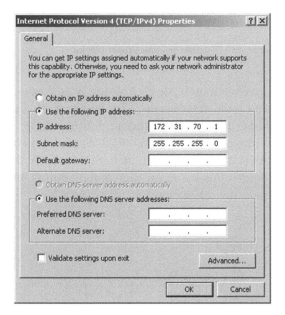

Figure 7.2   IP address and subnet mask configured for Executive-PC1

Figure 7.3   IP address and subnet mask for HR-PC1

Try it now

If you have two test computers plugged into VLANs 600 and 700, go ahead and con-figure them as follows:

```
VLAN 600, 172.31.60.1, 255.255.255.0
VLAN 700, 172.31.70.1, 255.255.255.0
```

Even if you don't have test computers to work with, keep reading. You can continue to follow along with the examples. The most important thing is that you practice the IOS commands.

Looking at figure 7.4, you should see the relationship between the VLANs and the sub-nets start to become clearer. You've arbitrarily chosen two IP subnets and associated them with the VLANs you created in the last chapter. But at this point, the computers still can't communicate with each other.

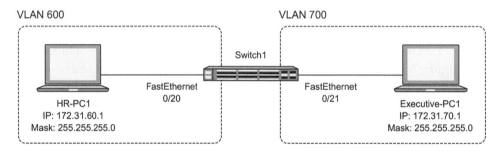

Figure 7.4 Computers in separate VLANs configured with IP addresses and subnet masks

It's important that you understand why these computers, despite having IP addresses, can't talk to each other. Using HR-PC1 as an example, let's revisit what happens when a computer tries to send an IP packet to another computer in a different subnet.

HR-PC1 has the IP address 172.31.60.1 with a subnet mask of 255.255.255.0. When it tries to send an IP packet to Executive-PC1 at 172.31.70.1, it notices that its IP address resides in a different subnet. It knows this based on the combination of IP address and subnet mask. Table 7.3 illustrates the calculation.

Table 7.3 Subnet address and subnet mask

HR-PC1	172	31	60	1
Subnet mask	255	255	255	0
Executive-PC1	172	31	70	1

Based on this, HR-PC1 knows that Executive-PC1 is in a different subnet. All HR-PC1 needs to do is create an IP packet addressed to 172.31.70.1, stick it inside an Ethernet frame, and send it along. But to whom should it address the Ethernet frame? It can't address it to Executive-PC1's media access control (MAC) address because even if HR-PC1 knew it (which it doesn't), the Ethernet frame would get stopped at the VLAN 600 boundary. Remember, Ethernet frames don't traverse broadcast domain boundaries.

Figure 7.5 represents VLANs 600 and 700 as separate boxes or containers inside Switch1. Remember, these VLANs represent isolated broadcast domains. Connecting them together directly would create a single broadcast domain, which would defeat the whole purpose of having VLANs.

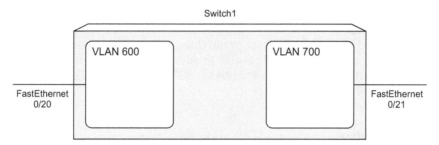

Figure 7.5 **Close-up view of VLANs inside Switch1. Notice that VLANs 600 and 700 aren't connected in any way.**

There's an invisible barrier between these VLANs, and the only way to cross it is to have a default gateway—a router—that's connected to both VLAN 600 and VLAN 700.

7.2   *Switches or routers?*

In chapter 2 I went into great detail explaining what switches and routers do. But I stopped short of making dogmatic statements like "Routers only route IP packets!" and "Switches only forward Ethernet frames!" I deliberately avoided those types of statements because they're not always true. There's quite a bit of overlap between the functionalities that switches and routers provide.

You've been performing the labs on what network folks call a layer-3 switch. A layer-3 switch provides both switching and routing functionality in the same device. You can think of a layer-3 switch as having a tiny virtual router living inside it. You're going to configure this virtual router to join together VLANs 600 and 700, as shown in figure 7.6.

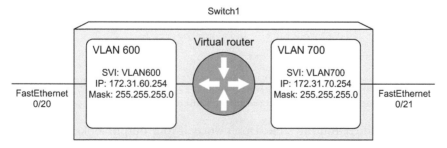

Figure 7.6 **Close-up view of VLANs, virtual router, and SVIs inside Switch1**

You'll perform three steps to get this working. I'll briefly summarize each of them here, and then I'll walk you through the details. First, you'll need to enable the IP routing functionality on the switch. This, in effect, turns on the virtual router. It's not on by default. Second, you'll create two switched virtual interfaces (SVIs) to provide a connection from the virtual router to each VLAN. Finally, you'll assign IP addresses to each of the SVIs. These IP addresses will become the default gateway IP addresses that HR-PC1 and Executive-PC1 will use. That may seem like a lot, and don't worry if you aren't totally clear yet on what you'll be doing. I'll go into more detail as you get to each step.

Above and beyond

The term *layer 3* refers to the layer of the Open Systems Interconnect (OSI) model, which roughly describes the purpose of IP addresses and subnets. It's often contrasted against *layer 2*, which is the layer that corresponds to MAC addresses and Ethernet frames.

7.2.1   Enabling IP routing

The first step is to enable IP routing on your switch using the `ip routing` global configuration command. In a live environment, there's a good chance it's already enabled, but it doesn't hurt to run the command again.

Try it now

Get into global configuration mode and enable IP routing:

```
ip routing
```

Verify with `show ip route`.

If IP routing is enabled, you should see some pretty verbose output:

```
Switch1#show ip route
Codes: L - local, C - connected, S - static, R - RIP, M - mobile, B - BGP
       D - EIGRP, EX - EIGRP external, O - OSPF, IA - OSPF inter area
       N1 - OSPF NSSA external type 1, N2 - OSPF NSSA external type 2
       E1 - OSPF external type 1, E2 - OSPF external type 2
       i - IS-IS, su - IS-IS summary, L1 - IS-IS level-1, L2 - IS-IS level-2
       ia - IS-IS inter area, * - candidate default, U - per-user static route
       o - ODR, P - periodic downloaded static route, H - NHRP, l - LISP
       + - replicated route, % - next hop override

Gateway of last resort is not set

       192.168.1.0/24 is variably subnetted, 2 subnets, 2 masks
C       192.168.1.0/24 is directly connected, Vlan1
L       192.168.1.101/32 is directly connected, Vlan1
```

This is called the IP routing table. Don't worry if your output looks significantly different from mine. In fact, you should expect it to look different. The specifics aren't important. What is important is that you get, at a minimum, the list of codes at the top and at least one IP subnet listed at the bottom. If you do, IP routing is enabled.

7.3 What are switched virtual interfaces?

A physical router has at least two physical interfaces. In the case of the virtual router inside your switch, you have to create and configure a *virtual* interface for each VLAN. These virtual interfaces are called switched virtual interfaces—SVIs for short.

The SVI serves two purposes. The first purpose is to provide a link between the individual VLANs and the virtual router. Because the router and VLANs are virtual rather than physical, you can't just connect them with physical Ethernet cables. You have to connect them using Cisco Internetwork Operating System (IOS) commands.

The second purpose is to provide a default gateway IP address for devices in each VLAN. Although you did learn about the significance of the default gateway in chapter 2, I'll go over it again in more detail in a moment. Notice that each SVI has an address in each VLAN, as shown in table 7.4.

Table 7.4 SVI IP addresses and subnet masks

VLAN	IP address	Subnet mask
600	172.31.60.254	255.255.255.0
700	172.31.70.254	255.255.255.0

This information should look familiar. These IP addresses came from the same subnets that you created for VLANs 600 and 700 earlier. The specific IP addresses I selected for the SVIs are arbitrary. For example, I could have chosen 172.31.60.177 for VLAN 600's SVI. But I chose 172.31.60.254 because 254 is the highest value allowed for the last octet, which makes it easier to remember. Alternatively, you could have chosen 172.31.60.1 instead.

Above and beyond

Although 255 is a valid value for an IP address octet, it's reserved for the broadcast IP address. The IP broadcast address is the IP corollary to the broadcast MAC address (FFFF.FFFF.FFFF). If you were to try to send an IP packet to the address 172.31.60.255, your computer would stuff that packet into an Ethernet frame addressed to FFFF.FFFF.FFFF. It would never leave the broadcast domain! This is why you don't want to use it to address individual devices.

7.3.1 Creating and configuring SVIs

Now that you know what an SVI is and have a general idea of its purpose, it's time to create one for each VLAN. After you create them, I'm going to show you how to use them.

IOS treats an SVI as just another interface, like FastEthernet0/20. But there's one exception: SVIs don't exist by default. Simply creating a VLAN as you did in the last chapter doesn't create an SVI. Neither does enabling IP routing. You have to explicitly create your SVIs individually.

> **Try it now**
> Start by creating an SVI for VLAN 600. In global configuration mode, type
>
> ```
> interface vlan 600
> ```

Immediately after issuing the command, you should get at least one message:

```
Switch1(config)#interface vlan 600
Switch1(config-if)#
*Mar  1 00:10:33.306: %LINK-3-UPDOWN: Interface Vlan600, changed state to up
*Mar  1 00:10:33.314: %LINEPROTO-5-UPDOWN: Line protocol on Interface
    Vlan600, changed state to up
```

Notice that once you issue the command, IOS puts you into interface configuration mode. The specific messages it gives you after that may differ depending on a couple of factors. If you don't have a device connected to FastEthernet0/20 (your access port for VLAN 600), or if the port is shut down, then the Vlan600 interface won't come up. If you get any messages saying that the Vlan600 interface is down, don't worry. Before the chapter is over, I'll tell you how to fix this. What's important now is that the Vlan600 interface exists, even if it's down.

Once you get the Vlan600 interface created, you need to assign an IP address to it. This is critically important: the IP address you assign *must* be in the same subnet that you created for VLAN 600. In this case, I'm going to use 172.31.60.254.

While still in interface configuration mode, I'll type `ip address ?`:

```
Switch1(config-if)#ip address ?
  A.B.C.D  IP address
  dhcp     IP Address negotiated via DHCP
  pool     IP Address autoconfigured from a local DHCP pool
```

There are three ways you can assign an IP address to the SVI, but in almost all cases, you want to assign a *static* IP address. To do that, I'll type the address 172.31.60.254, followed by another question mark (?):

```
Switch1(config-if)#ip address 172.31.60.254 ?
  A.B.C.D  IP subnet mask
```

Next, IOS asks for the subnet mask. This will be 255.255.255.0:

```
Switch1(config-if)#ip address 172.31.60.254 255.255.255.0
```

Try it now

While still in interface configuration mode for the Vlan600 SVI, assign the IP address 172.31.60.254 with the subnet mask 255.255.255.0:

```
ip address 172.31.60.254 255.255.255.0
```

Verify using the command `show ip interface brief | i Vlan600|Status`.

Here's what you should see:

```
Interface     IP-Address      OK?   Method    Status      Protocol
Vlan600       172.31.60.254   YES   manual    up          up
```

If you see this, then you've successfully configured the SVI for VLAN 600. Again, don't worry if the Status or Protocol column shows down. You're not finished yet!

Now it's time to create and configure the SVI for VLAN 700.

Try it now

Create and configure an SVI for VLAN 700 using the IP address 172.31.70.254 and the subnet mask 255.255.255.0:

```
interface vlan 700
ip address 172.31.70.254 255.255.255.0
```

Verify with `show ip interface brief | i 00|Status`.

You should get the following output:

```
Interface     IP-Address      OK?   Method    Status    Protocol
Vlan600       172.31.60.254   YES   manual    up        up
Vlan700       172.31.70.254   YES   manual    up        up
```

Excellent! As long as you see the SVI names and IP addresses, you've successfully created and configured two new SVIs for VLANs 600 and 700. Now on to the big question: what do you *do* with these SVIs?

7.4 *Default gateways*

I mentioned earlier that the IP addresses you assigned to the SVIs would become the default gateway IP addresses that HR-PC1 and Executive-PC1 will use. Recall that when I configured the IP addresses and subnet masks for these machines, I left the Default Gateway fields blank. Now it's time to fill them in.

Above and beyond

If you know in advance what IP address you'll use for an SVI, you may pre-populate the default gateway address before creating the SVI. Pointing a machine to a nonexistent default gateway won't cause any problems, but that machine won't be able to reach other subnets until you configure the SVI.

Figure 7.7 illustrates the current network topology along with the default gateway IPs for each VLAN/subnet. Notice that the default gateway IP address corresponds to the subnet of the VLAN it resides in.

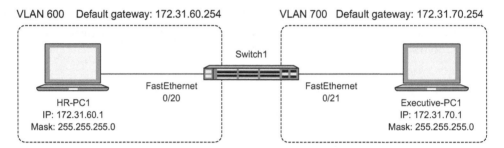

VLAN 600   Default gateway: 172.31.60.254   VLAN 700   Default gateway: 172.31.70.254

Switch1

FastEthernet   FastEthernet
0/20   0/21

HR-PC1   Executive-PC1
IP: 172.31.60.1   IP: 172.31.70.1
Mask: 255.255.255.0   Mask: 255.255.255.0

Figure 7.7   Default gateway IP addresses for each subnet

I'll start by configuring HR-PC1, as shown in figure 7.8.

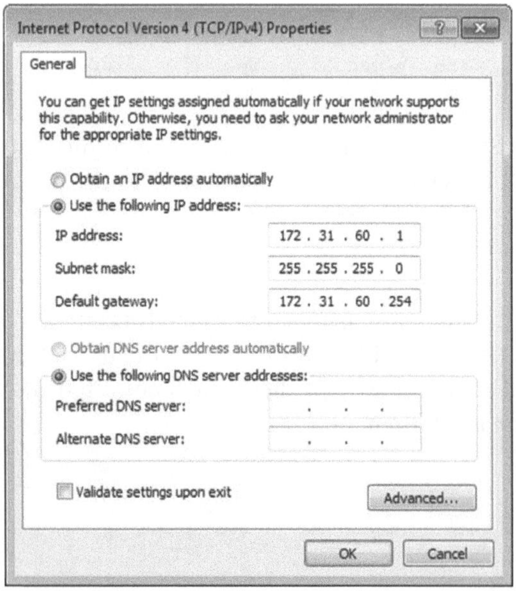

Figure 7.8   HR-PC1 configured with IP address, subnet mask, and default gateway

Remember, the default gateway IP address must be in the same subnet as the computer's IP address. That's not an issue here, but when dealing with a live environment, it's something you always want to check for.

Next, I'll configure Executive-PC1 with its default gateway, as shown in figure 7.9.

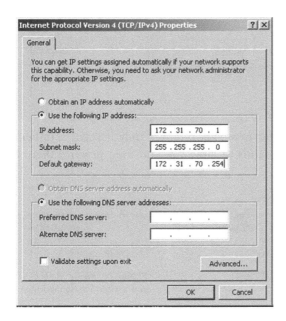

Figure 7.9   Executive-PC1 configured with IP address, subnet mask, and default gateway

Try it now

Configure a default gateway IP address on each of your test computers.

7.4.1   *Testing inter-VLAN connectivity*

Now it's time to test whether HR-PC1 in VLAN 600 can actually communicate with Executive-PC1 in VLAN 700. One of the most common ways to do this is to use the ping command.

From Executive-PC1, I'll ping HR-PC1's IP address, 172.31.60.1. Figure 7.10 shows the promising results.

Figure 7.10   Successful ping from Executive-PC1 (172.31.70.1) to HR-PC1 (172.31.60.1)

```
Administrator: C:\Windows\system32\cmd.exe

C:\>ping 172.31.60.1

Pinging 172.31.60.1 with 32 bytes of data:
Reply from 172.31.60.1: bytes=32 time=1ms TTL=127
Reply from 172.31.60.1: bytes=32 time<1ms TTL=127
Reply from 172.31.60.1: bytes=32 time<1ms TTL=127
Reply from 172.31.60.1: bytes=32 time<1ms TTL=127

Ping statistics for 172.31.60.1:
    Packets: Sent = 4, Received = 4, Lost = 0 (0% loss),
Approximate round trip times in milli-seconds:
    Minimum = 0ms, Maximum = 1ms, Average = 0ms

C:\>
```

The Reply from messages indicate that HR-PC1 received and replied to my test ping.

Try it now

Use the ping command to test connectivity between your test computers. Assuming you're using the same IP address scheme as I am, use the following commands:

```
ping 172.31.60.1
ping 172.31.70.1
```

If successful, you should get a Reply from message.

7.5 Commands in this chapter

Enabling IP routing and creating new SVIs requires only a small number of commands. Take a look at the commands in table 7.5, and then practice them by doing the hands-on lab.

Table 7.5 Commands used in this chapter

Command	Configuration mode	Description
ip routing	Global	Enables IP routing
interface vlan 600	Global	Creates an SVI for VLAN 600 and enters interface configuration mode
ip address 172.31.70.254 255.255.255.0	Interface	Configures an IP address and subnet mask on the selected interface
show ip route	N/A	Displays the IP routing table

7.6 Hands-on lab

Now would be a good time to practice what you've learned in this chapter and the last. Perform the following tasks:

1 Create a new VLAN on your switch.
2 Configure a switch port to be an access port in that new VLAN.
3 Create an SVI in the new VLAN.
4 Configure the SVI with an IP address and subnet mask.
5 Remember to save your configuration!

IP address assignment by using Dynamic Host Configuration Protocol

In the last chapter, you got your two virtual LANs (VLANs) talking to each other by coming up with two IP subnets and configuring two switched virtual interfaces (SVIs), one for each VLAN. Configuring an SVI for a VLAN is something you typically have to do only once per VLAN because each subnet needs only one default gateway to reach other subnets.

But when it comes to devices *within* a VLAN—computers, printers, security systems, and so on—manually assigning IP addresses one by one as you did in the last chapter is too tedious and prone to error. You need a way to automatically assign IP addresses from a subnet to devices in any given VLAN.

Dynamic Host Configuration Protocol (DHCP) is a service that takes a range of IP addresses from a subnet and automatically assigns them to devices in a VLAN. It can also automatically assign other network parameters, such as the default gateway and *Domain Name System (DNS)* servers. Many organizations also use DHCP to automatically tell Cisco IP phones which Call Manager server to connect to. Regardless of the application, the goal of DHCP is to save you from ever having to touch the network configuration on a networked device.

In this chapter, you'll learn how to configure a Cisco switch to automatically assign IP addresses using DHCP. If your organization already has a DHCP server, you'll learn how to configure your switch to play nicely with it.

8.1 To switch or not to switch?

DHCP is not a Cisco-proprietary protocol. In fact, most server operating systems, including the Windows Server family and Linux, provide DHCP services out of the box. Even consumer-grade routers and access points provide DHCP (this is how you get an IP address when you connect your smartphone to your home Wi-Fi). For the purposes of this book, I'll refer to these devices as non-Cisco DHCP servers.

Cisco switches and routers can also provide DHCP services. They don't always do this by default, so it's something you have to configure. Fortunately, configuring a Cisco switch to automatically assign IP addresses requires typing only a handful of intuitive IOS commands. It's quick, straightforward, cheap, and painless.

Yet the majority of networks I've seen use non-Cisco DHCP servers. Your organization may already have a non-Cisco DHCP server configured to provide IP addresses. If this is the case, you'll still want to read this chapter because even a non-Cisco DHCP server requires some specialized configuration on your Cisco switches.

8.2   Configuring a Cisco DHCP server

Suppose your organization has decided to open up a new branch office that—initially, anyway—won't have enough people to justify having servers on premises. Instead, users at the branch office will connect to a data center to access network resources such as file and database servers.

> ### Above and beyond
> You have a few options when it comes to connecting geographically separated sites. Private T1/E1 lines, MPLS virtual private networks (VPNs), and secure VPNs that traverse the internet are three of the most popular methods. When it comes to DHCP, the specific type connecting the sites usually doesn't matter.

Take a look at figure 8.1. Let's assume that Switch1 and the two computers we've been working with—Executive-PC1 and HR-PC1—are in this new, hypothetical branch office. Recall from the last chapter that you configured each of these computers with static IP addresses.

Your task is to configure DHCP on Switch1 to provide IP addresses to each of the machines in this branch office. Because the switch is in the same office as the machines, it will work even if the connectivity to the data center fails.

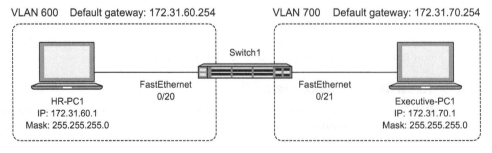

Figure 8.1   HR-PC1 and Executive-PC1 with hardcoded IP addresses

8.2.1 Scopes

Before you can get down to configuring DHCP, you need to know more than from which IP subnet DHCP should assign addresses.

The goal of DHCP is to automate the assignment of not just IP addresses but *all* network configuration parameters that you'd otherwise have to configure manually. To refresh your memory on what some of these items are, take another look at the network settings for Executive-PC1 in figure 8.2.

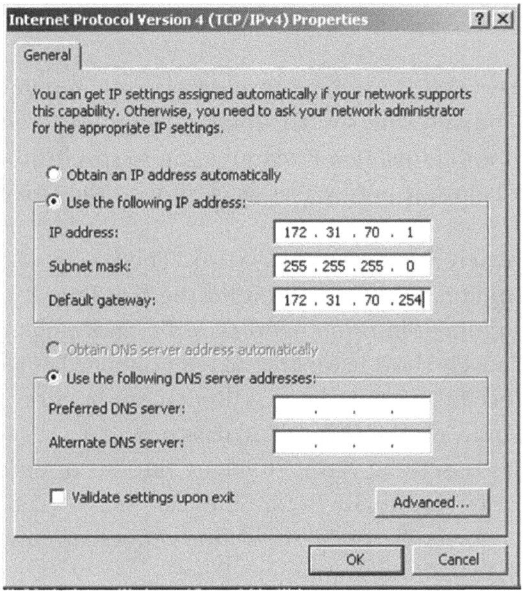

Figure 8.2   Executive-PC1's network settings

You've already filled in several fields, including IP Address, Subnet Mask, and Default Gateway. There are also two blank fields: Preferred DNS Server and Alternate DNS Server.

DHCP can automatically populate each of these fields—and then some. Recall that the IP subnet and subnet mask together give you a range of IP addresses in that subnet. In DHCP parlance, this range is called a *scope*. When configuring DHCP, at the bare minimum you have to define the scope because it's the *pool* from which the switch pulls and assigns IP addresses.

8.2.2 Options

The other fields—Default Gateway and DNS Servers—are *DHCP options*. They're called options because DHCP doesn't require them. But that doesn't mean they're not important. Modern organizations almost universally use IP gateways and DNS for accessing internal resources and the internet.

Another lesser-known DHCP option is the *domain name*. Modern operating systems let you specify a domain name to help with DNS name resolution. For example, suppose I have a server named fileserver.benpiper.com. On my desktop computer, I'd like to be able to reach that server by just typing "fileserver" and leaving off "benpiper.com." I can do this by configuring my computer's domain name as benpiper.com. When I try to access "fileserver," my computer will automatically append "benpiper.com" to yield the fully qualified domain name fileserver.benpiper.com. DHCP lets you automatically assign the domain name to computers on your network to enable this kind of network shortcut.

8.2.3   Lease time

It doesn't make much sense to have DHCP assign an IP address to a computer and let that computer use it forever. Eventually, the subnet would run out of IP addresses. This is called *DHCP exhaustion*. To avoid this, DHCP requires you to specify how long a computer can use an IP address before it must check back in with the DHCP server. This is called the *lease time*.

The lease time can range anywhere from minutes to years. The length of the lease time depends on how often computers move in and out of the building. If users are bringing in their laptops, plugging them into the network in the morning, and then taking them home at night, a relatively short lease time like 8 hours makes sense. On the other hand, if you have an office full of desktops that don't move but once or twice a year, you can set a longer lease time, on the order of 30 days or so.

It's important to note that the lease time is the *minimum* amount of time a computer can use an IP address. It's not a maximum. Before the lease expires (about halfway through), the computer will contact the DHCP server and request a *renewal*. If the DHCP server doesn't object, it will extend the computer's lease.

8.2.4   Subnets and VLANs

You configure DHCP on a per-VLAN basis. Remember that it's a good idea to keep one VLAN associated with only one subnet. Because all DHCP does is assign IP addresses from a subnet, sticking with this approach will make your life a lot easier. Table 8.1 lays out the DHCP scopes, options, and lease times you'll configure for each of the VLANs.

Table 8.1   DHCP scopes, options, and lease times for each VLAN

VLAN	Subnet	Mask	Default gateway	DNS1	DNS2	Lease time
600	172.31.60.0	255.255.255.0	172.31.60.254	192.168.100.10	192.168.100.11	7 days
700	172.31.70.0	255.255.255.0	172.31.70.254	192.168.100.10	192.168.100.11	3 days, 12 hours

Incidentally, you may recognize the default gateway addresses. They're the switched virtual interfaces (SVIs) that you configured in chapter 7. Because we've been looking at Executive-PC1 on VLAN 700, you'll start by configuring DHCP for VLAN 700.

8.3 Configuring a DHCP pool

The combination of a DHCP scope, options, and lease time forms what Cisco calls a DHCP *pool.* You'll configure your core DHCP settings in DHCP pool configuration mode.

Try it now

On Switch1, get into global configuration mode and create a new DHCP pool called Executives:

```
ip dhcp pool Executives
```

Notice that the prompt changes to reflect that you're in DHCP configuration mode:

```
Switch1(dhcp-config)#
```

Next, you need to specify the scope—the IP subnet and netmask. For VLAN 700, the subnet is 172.31.70.0 and the subnet mask is 255.255.255.0:

```
Switch1(dhcp-config)#network 172.31.70.0 255.255.255.0
```

IOS will assign IP addresses from the range specified by this subnet and mask combination—172.31.70.1 through 172.31.70.254, inclusive. IOS will hand out IP addresses beginning at the low end of the range and work its way up.

Above and beyond

Some DHCP implementations, like those of many non-Cisco DHCP servers, don't ask for a subnet and mask. Instead, they just ask for a range of consecutive IP addresses. But behind the scenes, they use this information to arrive at a subnet and mask. Cisco's DHCP implementation skips the extra step and makes you input the subnet and mask directly.

Try it now

Now it's time to specify the options. Start by configuring the default gateway for VLAN 700, which is 172.31.70.254:

```
Switch1(dhcp-config)#default-router 172.31.70.254
```

Cisco has a habit of calling the same thing by multiple names. For example, in DHCP configuration mode IOS requires the command default-router, whereas in other places it takes the default-gateway command instead. Always take advantage of the inline help to discover which command you're supposed to use and when.

Try it now

Specify the two DNS servers, 192.168.100.10 and 192.168.100.11, with one command:

```
Switch1(dhcp-config)#dns-server 192.168.100.10 192.168.100.11
```

If you have more than two DNS servers that you need to specify, you can append those to the command as well. IOS lets you specify up to eight unique DNS servers.

Next, specify the domain name. I'm going to use benpiper.com, but you can use whatever is appropriate for your environment:

```
Switch1(dhcp-config)#domain-name benpiper.com
```

Next, specify the lease time of 3 days, 12 hours, 0 minutes:

```
Switch1(dhcp-config)#lease 3 12 0
```

Type exit and press Enter to exit DHCP configuration mode:

```
Switch1(dhcp-config)# exit
```

Finally, verify your configuration with show run | section dhcp.

Here's what you should see:

```
Switch1#show run | section dhcp
ip dhcp pool Executives
 network 172.31.70.0 255.255.255.0
 dns-server 192.168.100.10 192.168.100.11
 default-router 172.31.70.254
 domain-name benpiper.com
 lease 3 12
```

Notice that all of the subcommands after ip dhcp pool Executives are indented, indicating that they apply only to the Executives DHCP pool.

8.4   *Excluding addresses from assignment*

Take a look at the network command in the output. Earlier I said that IOS will assign IP addresses sequentially starting at 172.31.70.1 and move through the subnet until it has assigned the last available address, 172.31.70.254. This presents an interesting problem.

Remember that Switch1 is already using 172.31.70.254 for its VLAN 700 SVI. As you might expect, IOS is smart enough not to assign its own IP address. But what if other devices are using statically assigned IP addresses? Perhaps there are file servers, firewalls, wireless access points, or printers in the same subnet that you *want* to be statically assigned. Or maybe you don't have any such devices currently, but you want to exclude a range—a subset—of IP addresses from DHCP assignment so that you can use them in the future.

You can prevent IOS from assigning IP addresses using the `ip dhcp excluded-address` global configuration command. The specific addresses you exclude, if any, are entirely up to you. In this example, I'll exclude the ranges in table 8.2.

Table 8.2 IP addresses that DHCP will not assign

Address ranges excluded from DHCP assignment
172.31.70.1–49
172.31.70.251–254

Try it now

Get into global configuration mode and exclude the ranges in table 8.2 from DHCP assignment:

```
ip dhcp excluded-address 172.31.70.1 172.31.70.49
ip dhcp excluded-address 172.31.70.251 172.31.70.254
```

Execute `show run | section dhcp` to verify.

You should see the following:

```
Switch1#sh run | s dhcp
ip dhcp excluded-address 172.31.70.1 172.31.70.49
ip dhcp excluded-address 172.31.70.251 172.31.70.254
ip dhcp pool Executives
 network 172.31.70.0 255.255.255.0
 dns-server 192.168.100.10 192.168.100.11
 default-router 172.31.70.254
 domain-name benpiper.com
 lease 3 12
```

When assigning addresses to devices in VLAN 700, Switch1 will choose only IP addresses between 172.31.70.50 and 172.31.70.250, inclusive.

Notice that you don't issue the `ip dhcp excluded-address` commands in DHCP configuration mode. The reason is that DHCP exclusions are independent of any DHCP pools. In fact, you can configure exclusions before any DHCP pools even exist! When IOS parses the running configuration, it places the exclusion before any of the DHCP pool definitions.

Try it now

Even though you haven't yet configured DHCP for VLAN 600, go ahead and configure exclusions for it as well. Exclude the IP addresses 172.31.60.1–49 and 172.31.60.251–254:

```
ip dhcp excluded-address 172.31.60.1 172.31.60.49
ip dhcp excluded-address 172.31.60.251 172.31.60.254
```

The next step is to get Executive-PC1 to stop using its statically assigned address and request a DHCP-assigned address instead.

8.5   Configuring devices to request DHCP addresses

Nowadays, most networked devices come configured out of the box to automatically request an IP address from DHCP. But in this case Executive-PC1 is configured with a static IP address. In order to get it to pick up an address from DHCP, you'll need to tell the machine "Obtain an IP address automatically," as reflected in figure 8.3.

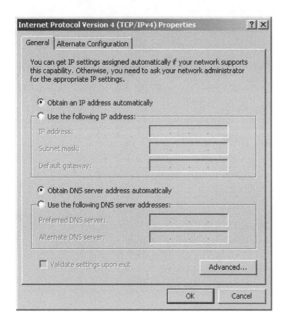

Figure 8.3   Configuring Executive-PC1 to use DHCP

The radio button Obtain an IP Address Automatically tells the computer that it should obtain its IP address, subnet mask, and default gateway from whatever DHCP server happens to be serving the VLAN that it's on.

The other radio button, Obtain DNS Server Address Automatically, tells the machine to set its DNS servers to whatever the DHCP server provides. In some cases, like when testing or troubleshooting, it may be necessary to manually set DNS servers. Under normal circumstances, however, you'll stick with the DNS servers configured in DHCP.

After you click OK to accept the new settings, Executive-PC1 attempts to locate the DHCP server to request an address. Although the nerdy details of how a device requests and receives an address are well beyond the scope of this book, there are a couple of technical terms you should know.

The first thing Executive-PC1 does is send a *DHCP Discover* message contained inside an Ethernet frame addressed to the broadcast MAC address. Switch1 sees this frame, checks to see if it has any IP addresses available in the Executives pool, and then sends a *DHCP Offer* message to Executive-PC1. The offer contains the IP address, subnet mask, default gateway, DNS servers, and domain name—all the parameters you specified when you configured the Executives pool on Switch1.

> **Above and beyond**
> Recall that Ethernet frames addressed to the broadcast MAC address stay within the VLAN. This means that the DHCP server and client machines must be in the same VLAN in order for the machines to request IP addresses.

Once Executive-PC1 accepts the offer, it automatically applies the network settings. The entire process typically takes a few seconds. Figure 8.4 illustrates the output of an `ipconfig /all` on Executive-PC1 after it has received and accepted a DHCP offer.

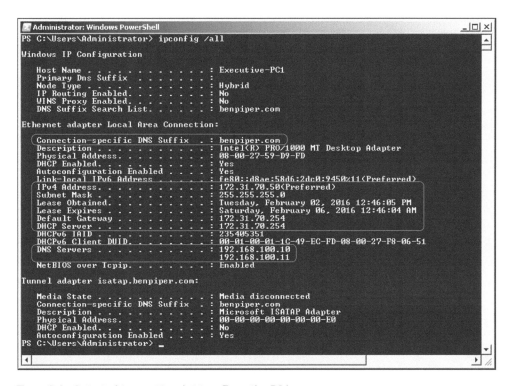

Figure 8.4 Output of `ipconfig /all` on **Executive-PC1**

Every bit of information inside the rectangles comes from DHCP! Imagine how long it would take you to manually configure these same network settings on hundreds of computers.

8.6   *Associating DHCP Pools with VLANs*

So far, you've configured a DHCP pool for VLAN 700. From now on, any device that connects to VLAN 700 and requests an IP address from DHCP will receive one from Switch1.

But what about VLAN 600? Right now, HR-PC1 is configured with a static IP address in the 172.31.60.0 subnet, as shown in figure 8.5. Even if you were to reconfigure it to request a DHCP-assigned address, Switch1 would completely ignore its request. The reason is that you haven't configured a DHCP pool for VLAN 600.

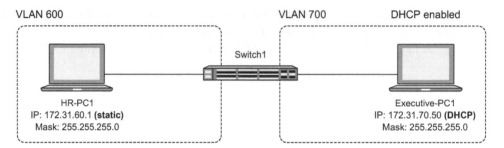

Figure 8.5   DHCP enabled only for VLAN 700

At this point, I want to address something that may be lurking in the back of your mind. Here's the DHCP pool configuration for VLAN 700:

```
Switch1#sh run | section pool Executives
ip dhcp pool Executives
 network 172.31.70.0 255.255.255.0
 dns-server 192.168.100.10 192.168.100.11
 default-router 172.31.70.254
 domain-name benpiper.com
 lease 3 12
```

Notice that there's nothing in here about VLAN 700. No command in this output even suggests that Switch1 should provide addresses to devices only in VLAN 700. Yet under no circumstances will Switch1 ever try to assign any IP addresses in the 172.31.70.0 subnet to devices in VLAN 600—or any other VLAN for that matter.

The reason for this behavior is shown in the following output:

```
Switch1#show ip interface brief vlan 700
Interface      IP-Address         OK? Method Status    Protocol
Vlan700        172.31.70.254      YES manual up        up
```

Switch1 has an SVI in VLAN 700, and that SVI is in the 172.31.70.0 subnet. Switch1 therefore assumes that this subnet belongs solely to VLAN 700. When it looks at its DHCP configuration for the Executives pool, it recognizes that the IP subnet you specified with the network command corresponds to the subnet that the VLAN 700 SVI is in.

The implication of this is that when you go to configure a new DHCP pool and specify the 172.31.60.0 subnet, Switch1 will realize that it should assign IP addresses in this subnet only to devices in VLAN 600. The bottom line is that this will make your life as a Cisco administrator a lot easier!

8.7 Creating a second DHCP pool

Now it's time to configure another DHCP pool for the HR VLAN 600. Remember that you already configured the IP exclusions. Table 8.3 lays out everything you need to build a second pool for the HR VLAN.

Table 8.3   DHCP scope, options, and lease time for VLAN 600

VLAN	Subnet	Mask	Default gateway	DNS1	DNS2	Lease time
600	172.31.60.0	255.255.255.0	172.31.60.254	192.168.100.10	192.168.100.11	7 days

Try it now

Create a new DHCP pool called HR. Use table 8.3 as a guide:

```
ip dhcp pool HR
 network 172.31.60.0 255.255.255.0
 dns-server 192.168.100.10 192.168.100.11
 default-router 172.31.60.254
 domain-name benpiper.com
 lease 7
```

As always, verify with `show run | section pool HR`.

HR-PC1 still has a static IP address, so the next step is to set it to request an address from DHCP. Figure 8.6 illustrates the two radio buttons that should be selected: Obtain an IP Address Automatically and Obtain DNS Server Address Automatically.

Figure 8.6   Configuring HR-PC1 to use DHCP

```
Administrator: Windows PowerShell

PS C:\Users\Administrator> ipconfig /all

Windows IP Configuration

   Host Name . . . . . . . . . . . . : HR-PC1
   Primary Dns Suffix  . . . . . . . :
   Node Type . . . . . . . . . . . . : Hybrid
   IP Routing Enabled. . . . . . . . : No
   WINS Proxy Enabled. . . . . . . . : No
   DNS Suffix Search List. . . . . . : benpiper.com

Ethernet adapter Local Area Connection:

   Connection-specific DNS Suffix  . : benpiper.com
   Description . . . . . . . . . . . : Intel(R) PRO/1000 MT Desktop Adapter
   Physical Address. . . . . . . . . : 08-00-27-F8-06-51
   DHCP Enabled. . . . . . . . . . . : Yes
   Autoconfiguration Enabled . . . . : Yes
   Link-local IPv6 Address . . . . . : fe80::d130:ec7c:b25d:2f8a%11(Preferred)
   IPv4 Address. . . . . . . . . . . : 172.31.60.50(Preferred)
   Subnet Mask . . . . . . . . . . . : 255.255.255.0
   Lease Obtained. . . . . . . . . . : Tuesday, February 02, 2016 12:48:07 PM
   Lease Expires . . . . . . . . . . : Tuesday, February 09, 2016 12:48:07 PM
   Default Gateway . . . . . . . . . : 172.31.60.254
   DHCP Server . . . . . . . . . . . : 172.31.60.254
   DHCPv6 IAID . . . . . . . . . . . : 235405351
   DHCPv6 Client DUID. . . . . . . . : 00-01-00-01-1C-49-EC-FD-08-00-27-F8-06-51
   DNS Servers . . . . . . . . . . . : 192.168.100.10
                                       192.168.100.11
   NetBIOS over Tcpip. . . . . . . . : Enabled

Tunnel adapter isatap.benpiper.com:

   Media State . . . . . . . . . . . : Media disconnected
   Connection-specific DNS Suffix  . :
   Description . . . . . . . . . . . : Microsoft ISATAP Adapter
   Physical Address. . . . . . . . . : 00-00-00-00-00-00-00-E0
   DHCP Enabled. . . . . . . . . . . : No
   Autoconfiguration Enabled . . . . : Yes
PS C:\Users\Administrator> _
```

Figure 8.7   Output of `ipconfig /all` **on HR-PC1**

Figure 8.7 reveals the results of `ipconfig /all` on HR-PC1.

8.8   *Viewing DHCP leases*

In a real network, there could be hundreds of machines, and if you need to view IP information for each one of them, going to each machine and running `ipconfig` is not feasible. Fortunately, there's an easy way to view this information from IOS.

You can view active DHCP leases directly from the IOS command line using the `show ip dhcp binding` command. (Not surprisingly, Cisco also refers to DHCP leases as *bindings*.)

Try it now

View the current DHCP leases using the `show ip dhcp binding` command.

The resulting output shows two leases:

```
Switch1#show ip dhcp binding
Bindings from all pools not associated with VRF:
IP address          Client-ID/            Lease expiration        Type
                    Hardware address/
                    User name
172.31.60.50        0108.0027.f806.51     Feb 09 2016 12:47 PM    Automatic
172.31.70.50        0108.0027.59d9.fd     Feb 06 2016 12:45 AM    Automatic
```

Take a look at the first lease for 172.31.60.50. This is for HR-PC1. Notice that the lease expiration date matches up closely with the Lease Expires time in the `ipconfig /all` output in figure 8.7. It's off by about a minute because the clocks on HR-PC1 and Switch1 aren't synchronized.

Above and beyond

In an organizational environment, it's not uncommon to have the clocks of individual devices be off by several seconds or even a minute or two. This isn't a concern because a device configured to use DHCP will attempt to renew its lease well before it expires.

8.9 *Using non-Cisco DHCP servers*

At the beginning of this chapter I acknowledged that there may be cases where you just don't want to use a Cisco switch as your DHCP server. You may already have an existing non-Cisco DHCP server somewhere on your network, or you may choose to build one.

How to configure a Windows or Linux DHCP server is beyond the scope of this book. But if you decide to use one, you need to make some configuration changes on your Cisco switch to accommodate this setup.

Figure 8.8 shows a hypothetical non-Cisco DHCP server in VLAN 900. For the rest of this chapter, assume that Switch1 isn't providing DHCP services at all. Also assume that HR-PC1 and Executive-PC1 don't have DHCP-assigned IP addresses.

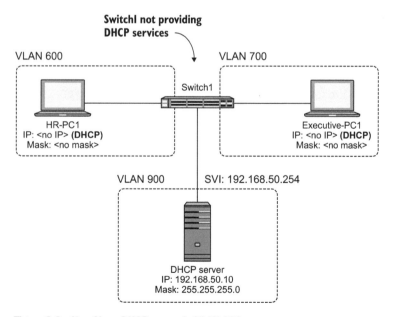

Figure 8.8 Non-Cisco DHCP server in VLAN 900

Switch1 has an SVI in this VLAN with the IP address 192.168.50.254 and a subnet mask of 255.255.255.0. The DHCP server has a hardcoded IP address of 192.168.50.10. Assume that this DHCP server is already configured with the appropriate DHCP scopes and options for VLANs 600 and 700, which correspond to the 172.31.60.0 and 172.31.70.0 subnets, respectively.

Earlier I said that when a device tries to obtain an IP address, it sends a DHCP Discover message—contained in an Ethernet frame—to the Ethernet broadcast address. Suppose that HR-PC1 sends a DHCP Discover message to VLAN 600. This message gets flooded throughout the VLAN but does not reach the DHCP server because that server resides in VLAN 900.

This poses what seems like an insurmountable problem. Remember that by default, a switch won't forward an Ethernet frame outside the VLAN whence it originated. But in order for the DHCP server to assign an address to HR-PC1, it *must* receive the DHCP Discover message, which is inside an Ethernet frame. In order for this to work, some rules have to be broken.

8.9.1   *Asking the switch for help using the ip helper-address command*

The solution is to configure Switch1 to forward the DHCP Discover message from VLAN 600 to VLAN 900. You might be thinking that doing this would turn VLANs 600 and 900 into a single broadcast domain, defeating the purpose of VLANs altogether. But there's a catch. Switch1 doesn't need to forward *all* Ethernet frames between VLANs 600 and 900. Instead, it needs to forward *only* those frames containing DHCP messages!

The `ip helper-address` interface command causes the switch to forward *only* select Ethernet frames to a given IP address. In this case, you want Switch1 to forward all DHCP messages from VLAN 600 to the DHCP server at the IP address 192.168.50.10.

Try it now

Configure Switch1 to forward all DHCP messages from VLAN 600 to 192.168.50.10:

```
interface vlan600
ip helper-address 192.168.50.10
```

Verify with `show run interface vlan 600`.

You should see the `ip helper-address` command in the running configuration as follows:

```
interface Vlan600
 ip address 172.31.60.254 255.255.255.0
 ip helper-address 192.168.50.10
end
```

Keep in mind that this configuration will cause Switch1 to forward DHCP broadcasts *only from* VLAN 600. If you want to forward DHCP broadcasts from VLAN 700 as well, you'll have to issue the same command under the interface configuration for the VLAN 700 SVI.

Try it now

Configure an `ip helper-address` under the VLAN 700 SVI as follows:

```
interface vlan700
ip helper-address 192.168.50.10
```

8.10 Commands in this chapter

If you can remember how to get into DHCP pool configuration mode, you can rely on the IOS inline help to guide you to the rest of the commands. Feel free to use table 8.4 as a checklist to ensure you don't forget anything.

Table 8.4 Commands used in this chapter

Command	Configuration mode	Description
`ip dhcp pool MoL`	Global	Creates a DHCP pool named MoL
`network 172.29.1.0 255.255.255.0`	DHCP pool	Sets the scope from which the DHCP pool will assign addresses
`default-router 172.29.1.254`	DHCP pool	Sets the default gateway the IOS DHCP server will assign to clients
`dns-server 192.168.10.100 192.168.10.101`	DHCP pool	Sets the DNS servers the IOS DHCP server will assign to clients
`domain-name benpiper.com`	DHCP pool	Sets the DNS domain name the IOS DHCP server will assign to clients
`lease 7 4 15`	DHCP pool	Sets the IP lease time to 7 days, 4 hours, 15 minutes
`ip dhcp excluded-address 172.29.1.1 172.29.1.19`	Global	Excludes 172.29.1.1–19 from being assigned to clients
`ip helper-address 192.168.5.5`	Interface	Forwards received DHCP broadcasts to a non-Cisco DHCP server at 192.168.5.5
`show ip dhcp binding`	N/A	Displays current DHCP bindings

8.11   *Hands-on lab*

In this lab, you'll practice creating a new DHCP pool from scratch. Perform the following steps:

1 Create a DHCP pool named MoL.
2 Choose a subnet and configure the pool to assign IP addresses from the subnet.
3 From the subnet, select an IP for the default gateway. Configure the pool to tell DHCP clients about this gateway.
4 Configure a lease time of 14 days, 6 hours.
5 As always, save your configuration!

Securing the network by using IP access control lists

In the last chapter, you configured IP routing and switched virtual interfaces (SVIs) to allow hosts on one subnet to talk to hosts on another. By default, IOS doesn't restrict this sort of inter-VLAN communication. Any device on one subnet can reach any device on another, provided you've set up routing correctly.

If these were the 1990s, you could probably leave it at that. But security is a big deal nowadays, and many organizations require tight control over how traffic flows between devices. If you want to be taken seriously as a Cisco network administrator, you have to know how to configure your switches and routers to restrict IP traffic according to those requirements.

The most common way to do this is by using IP *access control lists (ACLs)*. An ACL is a set of rules that defines whether a given IP address can talk to another IP address. At first blush, the idea of writing rules like this may sound monumentally tedious. In a network of 5,000 devices, you can't write ACL rules for every device—nor should you. The good news is that ACLs are extremely flexible and powerful, and you can cover a large number of use cases with a small number of rules.

When it comes to restricting traffic, you'll most often encounter three basic scenarios:

- Blocking a single IP address from reaching another IP address
- Blocking a single IP address from reaching another subnet
- Blocking a subnet from reaching another subnet

In this chapter, I'm going to show you how to configure ACLs to cover each of these scenarios. To get you started off on the right foot, here's a high-level overview of the steps you'll be performing:

1 Creating an ACL
2 Adding rules to it
3 Applying the ACL to an interface

9.1   Blocking IP-to-IP traffic

Take a look at figure 9.1. As it stands, any device with an IP address in VLAN 600 can talk to any device in VLAN 700 and vice versa.

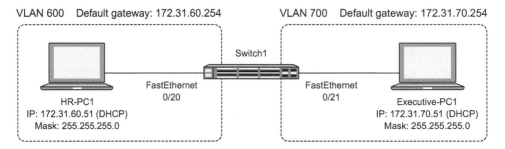

Figure 9.1   HR-PC1 and Executive-PC1 with DHCP-assigned IP addresses

Suppose you need to prevent HR-PC1 from reaching Executive-PC1, but you don't want to restrict traffic from HR-PC1 in any other way. It's vitally important that you, as a network administrator, can take a requirement like this and translate it into IOS-speak by rephrasing the requirement in terms of source and destination IP addresses.

In this case, HR-PC1 with its IP address of 172.31.60.51 shouldn't be able to reach Executive-PC1 at 172.31.70.51. In networking parlance, HR-PC1 is the *source* and Executive-PC1 is the *destination*, as shown in table 9.1.

Table 9.1   Prototype rule to deny traffic from HR-PC1 to Executive-PC1

Action	Source	Destination
Deny	172.31.60.51 (HR-PC1)	172.31.70.51 (Executive-PC1)

Notice that I snuck in another term: *action.* The action is what you want the switch to do with traffic that matches the source and destination addresses. In this case, if 172.31.60.51 sends any traffic to 172.31.70.51, the switch should *deny*, or block, it.

Once you have this information, you're ready to create your access list, which you'll apply to an interface later in the chapter.

9.1.1 Creating an access list

To block IP-to-IP traffic, you create what's called an *extended IP access list*. The only reason I mention this ridiculously long name is to help you remember the equally long command you must use to create it, which I'll share in a moment. You also have to assign it either a name or a number. There's no technical reason to use one over the other, but my personal preference is to stick with numbers.

Try it now

Get into global configuration mode. Then create ACL 100 using this command:

```
ip access-list extended 100
```

You should see the extended named access control list (NACL) configuration prompt:

```
Switch1(config-ext-nacl)#
```

As I said, an ACL is just a list of rules. You've created the list, ACL 100, but you haven't created any rules. Using the information from table 9.1, you need to create a new rule inside the ACL.

Try it now

Make sure you're still at the `(config-ext-nacl)#` prompt, and issue the following command to deny traffic from 172.31.60.51 to 172.31.70.51:

```
Switch1(config-ext-nacl)#deny ip host 172.31.60.51 host 172.31.70.51
```

By the way, Cisco calls this rule an *access control entry (ACE)*, but I prefer the term *rule* because it's more descriptive.

The format of an ACL rule is pretty simple, as you can see in figure 9.2. The action comes first—in this case, `deny`. Next, the `IP` indicates you want this rule to apply only to IP traffic. The next two parameters—`host 172.31.60.51`—indicate that the rule applies to traffic from the single *source* IP address, 172.31.60.51. Last, the `host 172.31.70.51` indicates the rule applies if 172.31.70.51 is the *destination* IP address.

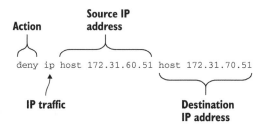

Figure 9.2 Breakdown of a simple ACL rule

Even though the terms *source* and *destination* don't appear explicitly in the command, IOS infers them based on the order.

Keep in mind that when you create a rule, IOS doesn't check whether the IP addresses you specify are valid. Always double-check your IP addresses when creating an access list.

Try it now

Exit ACL configuration mode:

```
Switch1(config-ext-nacl)#exit
```

Verify the ACL and that the new rule exists:

```
Switch1#show access-lists 100
```

You should see the following:

```
Switch1#sh access-lists 100
Extended IP access list 100                          # IOS added
    10 deny ip host 172.31.60.51 host 172.31.70.51  ← sequence
    ➥ number 10 to the beginning
```

It's important to note that by itself, an ACL doesn't do anything. It is, as the name suggests, just a list of rules. At this point, Switch1 is not blocking any traffic because you haven't explicitly told Switch1 to use ACL 100. Later on in the chapter, I'll show you how to configure Switch1 to use this new ACL.

Notice that there's a 10 preceding the rule you just created. When you create a rule, IOS assigns a *sequence number* in increments of 10. The first rule is 10, the second is 20, and so on. It's called a sequence number because when IOS looks at an ACL to determine what to do with a given packet, it evaluates each rule in order, starting with the lowest sequence number. To understand how this works, let's look at two examples.

The first example may strike you as painfully obvious, but it illustrates an important point. If IOS sees a packet with the source IP address 172.31.60.51 and the destination IP address 172.31.70.51, it first looks at rule 10. Because the source and destination IP addresses match what the rule specifies, IOS performs the action required by the rule, in this case, deny. IOS drops the packet, and it's done.

Now let's take a contrasting example. Suppose IOS sees a packet with the source IP address 172.31.60.51 and the destination IP address 192.168.100.1. IOS first looks at the rule with the lowest sequence number, which is 10. The source IP address—172.31.60.51—matches what's in the rule. But the destination IP address—192.168.100.1—does not. Because the packet doesn't match the rule exactly, IOS doesn't take the deny action specified in rule 10. But then what happens to the packet?

You might assume that IOS allows the packet through, and that's a reasonable assumption. After all, the point of ACLs is to block packets, and the only rule you specified in the ACL—rule 10—does not prohibit the packet in question. But there's another rule—a hidden rule—that does prohibit the packet.

THE IMPLICIT DENY RULE

Every ACL, as soon as you create it, contains a secret, hidden rule called the *implicit deny rule*. The rule looks like this:

```
deny ip any any
```

You can blame Cisco for being counterintuitive on a lot of things, but this command does exactly what it says. It denies traffic from any IP address to any IP address. In other words, the implicit deny rule blocks all IP traffic.

IOS ensures that the implicit deny rule exists at the bottom of every ACL. No matter how many rules you explicitly define in an ACL, the implicit deny rule is always waiting at the bottom of the list. The rule is hidden, so you can't see it, but it's there! Table 9.2 illustrates how IOS views ACL 100.

Table 9.2   ACL 100 with the implicit deny rule

Sequence	Action	Source	Destination
10	Deny	172.31.60.51 (HR-PC1)	172.31.70.51 (Executive-PC1)
Last (hidden)	Deny	Any	Any

Sequence 10 corresponds to the rule you just configured. But the rule immediately following it—the last in the sequence—is the implicit deny rule that IOS inserts automatically.

Your goal is to prevent HR-PC1 from reaching Executive-PC1, and ACL 100 accomplishes that, but it goes way too far. The implicit deny rule causes the ACL to deny all IP traffic, including traffic that you want to permit.

The obvious solution would be to get rid of the implicit deny rule—except you can't do that. Instead, you have to circumvent it by creating another rule to *permit* all traffic.

Try it now

Get back into ACL configuration mode for ACL 100:

```
Switch1(config)#ip access-list extended 100
```

Create another rule to explicitly permit all IP traffic:

```
Switch1(config-ext-nacl)# permit ip any any
```

IOS will automatically insert this rule at the bottom of the access list.

Exit ACL configuration mode:

```
Switch1(config-ext-nacl)#exit
```

Verify the new rule exists:

```
Switch1#sh access-lists 100
```

You should see the new rule in sequence 20:

```
Switch1#sh access-l 100
Extended IP access list 100
    10 deny ip host 172.31.60.51 host 172.31.70.51
    20 permit ip any any
```

> **Explicitly permitting all IP traffic overcomes the implicit deny rule.**

Going back to the earlier example, if IOS sees a packet with the source IP address 172.31.60.51 and the destination IP address 192.168.100.1, it first compares the packet against the rule in sequence 10. The packet doesn't match the rule, so IOS continues down the list. The rule in sequence 20—`permit ip any any`—matches the packet, so IOS takes the configured action: `permit`.

This effectively circumvents the implicit deny rule because once IOS takes some action on a packet—`permit` or `deny`—it stops processing subsequent rules.

Now's a good time to point out that in highly restrictive, Fort Knox–style environments, you may want an ACL to block all IP traffic by default. If that's the case, you should not place the `permit ip any any` statement in your ACL. Instead, you should explicitly permit *only* the traffic you want allowed and then let the implicit deny do its thing for all other traffic. Alternatively, you could configure an explicit deny—`deny ip any any`—as the last rule in the ACL.

In this case, the ACL is exactly the way you want it. It denies traffic from HR-PC1 to Executive-PC1 and allows everything else. But as I mentioned earlier, an ACL does nothing by itself. To configure Switch1 to use the ACL and actually start blocking traffic, you must apply the ACL to an interface.

9.2   Applying an ACL to an interface

As a general rule, you should apply an ACL on the interface closest to the source of the traffic you want to block. In this case, ACL 100 blocks traffic from HR-PC1 from reaching Executive-PC1, so the best place to apply the ACL is the port that HR-PC1 is connected to, FastEthernet0/20. To understand the logic behind this, look at figure 9.3.

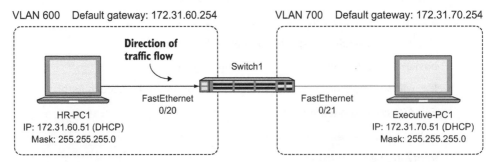

Figure 9.3   Determining which interface to apply ACL 100 to. FastEthernet0/20 is the closest interface to the source of traffic.

Traffic coming from HR-PC1 flows into FastEthernet0/20. In networking parlance, traffic *sourced* from HR-PC1 *ingresses* FastEthernet0/20. If you want Switch1 to block any traffic from HR-PC1, the best place to do it is at the interface where that traffic comes in. Hence, you would apply the ACL to the FastEthernet0/20 interface.

Try it now

Apply ACL 100 to FastEthernet0/20 using the following commands.

Get into interface configuration mode for FastEthernet0/20:

```
Switch1(config)#interface fastEthernet 0/20
```

Apply ACL 100 to the interface:

```
Switch1(config-if)#ip access-group 100 in
```

The `ip access-group 100 in` command throws off a lot of newcomers. Even though it says nothing about "access list," it does in fact refer to ACL 100. As I've pointed out before (and probably will again), Cisco likes to use multiple terms for the same thing.

The significance of the `in` keyword at the end of the command is a bit less obvious. It means that IOS should apply the ACL rules only to *inbound* traffic—that is, traffic coming into FastEthernet0/20. It shouldn't touch traffic exiting, or *egressing*, FastEthernet0/20.

Try it now

Verify that ACL 100 is applied to FastEthernet0/20:

```
Switch1#show ip interface fastEthernet 0/20
```

You should see the following:

```
Switch1#sh ip interface fastEthernet 0/20
FastEthernet0/20 is up, line protocol is up
  Inbound access list is 100
```

In case you didn't believe me that the `access-group` command really refers to an access list, the last line in the output should erase any doubts. At this point, IOS checks all IP traffic ingressing FastEthernet0/20 against ACL 100.

It's a good idea to always verify your configurations in multiple ways, if possible. So far, you've verified that the ACL exists, has the proper rules in place, and is applied to the correct interface. But the best way to verify that all of these pieces are working together is to attempt to ping Executive-PC1 from HR-PC1. If you've done everything correctly, the ping should fail.

> **Try it now**
>
> Use the `ping` command to verify that HR-PC1 (172.31.60.51) can't reach Executive-PC1 (172.31.70.51). Assuming your test machines have the same IP addresses as mine, issue the following command on HR-PC1:
>
> `ping 172.31.70.51`

The following output is from HR-PC1:

```
C:\>ping 172.31.70.51
Pinging 172.31.70.51 with 32 bytes of data:
Request timed out.
```

Remember that the goal is to prevent HR-PC1 from reaching Executive-PC1 without restricting traffic from HR-PC1 in any other way. The consistent ping failure indicates that the ACL is blocking traffic from HR-PC1 to Executive-PC1. But to confirm that Switch1 allows all other traffic from HR-PC1, let's try to ping a different IP address to confirm that all other traffic is allowed.

> **Try it now**
>
> On HR-PC1, ping the VLAN 700 SVI (172.31.70.254):
>
> `ping 172.31.70.254`

You should see the following:

```
C:\>ping 172.31.70.254

Pinging 172.31.70.254 with 32 bytes of data:
Reply from 172.31.70.254: bytes=32 time=4ms TTL=255
```

Success! Switch1 blocks HR-PC1 from reaching Executive-PC1 without interfering with any other IP traffic sourced from HR-PC1.

9.3   *Blocking IP-to-subnet traffic*

As it stands, the ACL you applied inbound to FastEthernet0/20—ACL 100—blocks only traffic from HR-PC1 to Executive-PC1. Now suppose that you want to block traffic from HR-PC1 to all devices in the Executives VLAN. The simplest, safest way to accomplish this is to create a new ACL with the rules listed in table 9.3 and apply it to FastEthernet0/20.

Table 9.3   **ACL rules to block IP traffic to an entire subnet**

Sequence	Action	Source	Destination
10	Deny	172.31.60.51 (HR-PC1)	172.31.70.0/255.255.255.0 (Executives VLAN 700)
20	Permit	Any	Any

The Executives VLAN corresponds to the 172.31.70.0 subnet. Notice that for sequence 10, the destination contains both the subnet (172.31.70.0) and a subnet mask (255.255.255.0). Recall that the subnet mask is the code that tells you the IP addresses that are part of the VLAN. When specifying an entire subnet as the destination in an ACL, you must tell IOS the subnet mask. But there's a catch: you can't use the subnet mask in an ACL.

Try it now

Because ACL 100 is already in use, you don't want to modify or delete it. Instead, create a brand-new ACL:

```
Switch1(config)#ip access-list extended 101
```

Add a rule to block access to the Executives VLAN from HR-PC1:

```
Switch1(config)#deny ip host 172.31.60.51 172.31.70.0 0.0.0.255
```

I know that last parameter looks a little weird, and I'll explain it in a moment. But first, you must overcome the implicit deny rule:

```
Switch1(config)#permit ip any any
```

Verify the new ACL with `show access-lists 101`.

You should see the following:

```
Switch1#sh access-lists 101
Extended IP access list 101
    10 deny ip host 172.31.60.51 172.31.70.0 0.0.0.255
    20 permit ip any any
```

9.3.1 *Wildcard masks*

The destination portion of the command looks noticeably different than the one you configured earlier. The last two parameters, `172.31.70.0 0.0.0.255`, indicate the destination subnet. But 0.0.0.255 isn't a valid subnet mask. In fact, it's called a *wildcard mask*, and it's the inverse of a subnet mask. Table 9.4 illustrates what I mean.

Table 9.4   Subnet mask to wildcard mask conversion

Subnet mask	Wildcard mask
255.0.0.0	0.255.255.255
255.255.0.0	0.0.255.255
255.255.255.0	0.0.0.255
255.255.255.255	0.0.0.0

I'm not going to get into the nerdy details of why Cisco ACLs use wildcard masks instead of subnet masks. It involves a lot of binary math, which you'll pick up should you decide

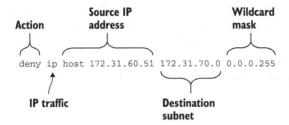

Figure 9.4   Breakdown of an ACL rule to deny IP traffic to an entire subnet

to pursue Cisco certifications. What you need to know is that when configuring an ACL rule, instead of specifying the subnet mask, you must specify the corresponding wildcard mask. Bookmark the previous page so you can come back to this table as needed.

It's important that you understand what the command in figure 9.4 does. Notice that immediately preceding the destination subnet and wildcard mask there's no host. That's because the destination is not a host but a subnet.

9.3.2   Replacing an ACL

Now that you've configured ACL 101, it's time to replace ACL 100 with it. To refresh your memory, you need to apply ACL 101 to FastEthernet0/20.

Try it now

Use the following commands to apply ACL 101 to FastEthernet0/20:

```
Switch1(config)#int fa0/20
Switch1(config-if)#ip access-group 101 in
```

If you configured everything correctly, HR-PC1 shouldn't be able to reach any device in the 172.31.70.0 subnet. Let's test it out.

Try it now

Try to ping Executive-PC1 again from HR-PC1:

```
ping 172.31.70.51
```

You should get nothing but failures, as shown:

```
C:\>ping 172.31.70.51

Pinging 172.31.70.51 with 32 bytes of data:
Request timed out.
```

Now for the real test! You shouldn't be able to ping any IP address in the 172.31.70.0 subnet, including the VLAN 700 SVI (172.31.70.254).

> **Try to ping the VLAN 700 SVI:**
> ping 172.31.70.254

This ping should fail as well:

```
C:\>ping 172.31.70.254

Pinging 172.31.70.254 with 32 bytes of data:
Request timed out.
```

Excellent! The ACL works exactly the way you configured it. But there's a potential problem. You applied ACL 101 to FastEthernet0/20, which is connected to HR-PC1. Suppose someone (not you, of course) moves HR-PC1 to a different port, say FastEthernet0/19. Let's look at the configuration of that port to figure out what might happen:

```
Switch1#sh run int fa0/19

interface FastEthernet0/19
 switchport access vlan 600
 switchport mode access
end
```

Notice two things. First, this port is a member of VLAN 600, the HR VLAN, so HR-PC1 still has network connectivity. But there's no ACL applied to this interface, so HR-PC1 can still reach the Executives VLAN! A show ip interface fa0/19 confirms this:

```
Switch1#show ip interface fa0/19
FastEthernet0/19 is up, line protocol is up
  Inbound  access list is not set
```

> **Try it now**
> Move HR-PC1 to another port in VLAN 600; then try to ping Executive-PC1 again:
>
> ping 172.31.70.51

You can see that HR-PC1 has unrestricted access now:

```
C:\> ping 172.31.70.51

Pinging 172.31.70.51 with 32 bytes of data:
Reply from 172.31.70.51: bytes=32 time=1ms TTL=127
```

Applying the ACL at the port level works fine as long as the device you're blocking traffic from doesn't move to a different port. But if the device does move, the ACL becomes moot. You could apply the ACL to every port in the VLAN, but that would be cumbersome. Fortunately, you have a better option.

9.3.3 *Applying an access control list to a switched virtual interface*

Rather than applying ACL 101 to every port in VLAN 600, you can apply it to the VLAN 600 switched virtual interface.

You need to block HR-PC1 from getting to the Executives subnet regardless of which port it's plugged into. You can do this by applying the access list directly to the VLAN 600 SVI.

> **Try it now**
> Enter interface configuration mode for the VLAN 600 SVI:
>
> ```
> Switch1(config)#int vlan600
> Switch1(config-if)#ip access-group 101 in
> ```
>
> Verify your configuration:
>
> ```
> show ip interface vlan 600 | i 600|101
> ```

You should see the following output:

```
Switch1#show ip interface vlan 600 | i 600|101
Vlan600 is up, line protocol is up
  Inbound  access list is 101
```

Because you applied ACL 101 to the VLAN 600 SVI, IOS applies ACL 101 to all traffic hitting the VLAN 600 SVI, regardless of which physical port the traffic came from. That means even though HR-PC1 is connected to a port that doesn't have an ACL applied, any traffic from HR-PC1 destined to the Executives VLAN will still get blocked.

> **Try it now**
> On HR-PC1, ping Executive-PC1:
>
> ```
> ping 172.31.70.51
> ```

You should see a ping failure:

```
C:\>ping 172.31.70.51

Pinging 172.31.70.51 with 32 bytes of data:
Reply from 172.31.60.254: Destination net unreachable.
```

Another ping to the VLAN 700 SVI should yield the same result:

> **Try it now**
> On HR-PC1, ping the VLAN 700 SVI:
>
> ```
> ping 172.31.70.254
> ```

You should see the following:

```
C:\>ping 172.31.70.254

Pinging 172.31.70.254 with 32 bytes of data:
Reply from 172.31.60.254: Destination net unreachable.
```

At this point, you have a pretty robust ACL configuration. Regardless of which physical port HR-PC1 is connected to, it can't reach any device in the Executives VLAN. But there's still another problem. Because HR-PC1 receives its IP address via DHCP, its IP address could change, rendering the ACL once again useless. To overcome this, you need to make your ACL fully DHCP-proof.

9.4 *Blocking subnet-to-subnet traffic*

When configuring ACLs, it's easy to get lost in all the details. But as a network administrator, you should always keep in mind the ultimate goal you're trying to accomplish. At the beginning of the chapter, I laid out a simple requirement: prevent HR-PC1 from reaching Executive-PC1. I later modified that requirement to prohibit HR-PC1 from reaching any device in the Executives VLAN. You might be sensing a pattern here, and can probably guess what's coming next!

Given that devices in the HR and Executives VLANs get their IP addresses from DHCP, it's clear that configuring ACLs to block traffic to or from individual IP addresses isn't going to cut it. This leaves you with only one option: prevent all IP traffic from VLAN 600 from reaching VLAN 700. It's time to create another ACL!

Try it now

Create ACL 102 to block all traffic from the 172.31.60.0 subnet to the 172.31.70.0 subnet:

```
Switch1(config)#ip access-list extended 102
Switch1(config-ext-nacl)#deny ip 172.31.60.0 0.0.0.255 172.31.70.0
0.0.0.255
Switch1(config-ext-nacl)#permit ip any any
```

Apply the ACL to the VLAN 600 SVI:

```
Switch1(config)#int vlan 600
Switch1(config-if)#ip access-group 102 in
```

Now no devices in the 172.31.60.0 subnet should be able to reach devices in the 172.31.70.0 subnet. Let's test it by pinging a few IP addresses:

Try it now

From HR-PC1, ping Executive-PC1 and the VLAN 700 SVI:

```
ping 172.31.70.51
ping 172.31.70.254
```

Both pings should fail:

```
C:\>ping 172.31.70.51

Pinging 172.31.70.51 with 32 bytes of data:
Reply from 172.31.60.254: Destination net unreachable.

C:\>ping 172.31.70.254

Pinging 172.31.70.254 with 32 bytes of data:
Reply from 172.31.60.254: Destination net unreachable.
```

This looks good, but it's inconclusive because these are exactly the same results you saw before. The real test is to change HR-PC1's IP address and ping again.

> **Try it now**
>
> Change HR-PC1's IP address to a static one outside the configured DHCP range.
>
> Set the default gateway to 172.31.60.254.

In the last chapter, you configured the DHCP range for VLAN 600 to be 172.31.60.50–172.31.60.250. Figure 9.5 illustrates how to statically configure HR-PC1 with the IP address 172.31.60.49, which is outside the DHCP scope. Remember to set the default gateway!

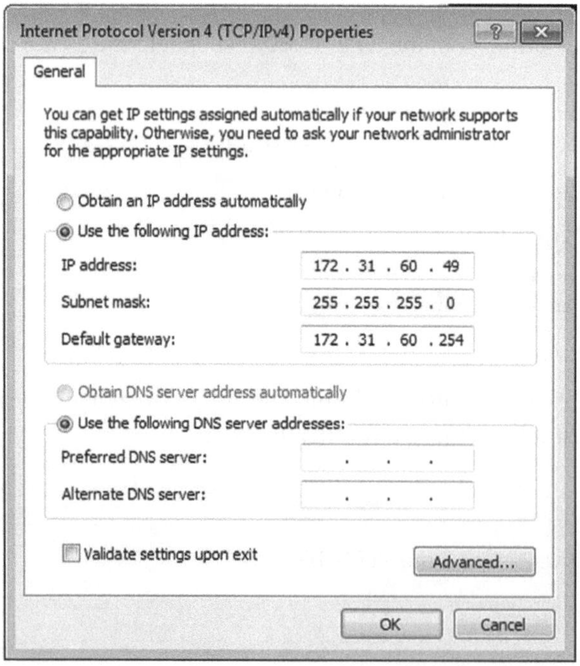

Figure 9.5   Configuring HR-PC1 with a static IP address and default gateway

Try it now
From HR-PC1, ping 172.31.70.51 and 172.31.70.254 again.

You should get the same results as you did before changing the IP address:

```
C:\>ping 172.31.70.51

Pinging 172.31.70.51 with 32 bytes of data:
Reply from 172.31.60.254: Destination net unreachable.
C:\>ping 172.31.70.254

Pinging 172.31.70.254 with 32 bytes of data:
Reply from 172.31.60.254: Destination net unreachable.
```

As it stands, Switch1 prevents every device in the 172.31.60.0 subnet from accessing any device in the 172.31.70.0 subnet. But you might be thinking, "What if I don't want to do that? What if I just want to restrict a few IP addresses here and there?" Suppose that you want HR-PC1 to be able to access only 172.31.70.254 but nothing else in that subnet. You can accomplish this using ACLs but with one minor change.

Try it now
Create a new ACL 103:

```
Switch1(config)#ip access-list extended 103
```

Permit any device in the HR VLAN to access only 172.31.70.254, the VLAN 700 SVI:

```
Switch1(config-ext-nacl)#permit ip 172.31.60.0 0.0.0.255 host
172.31.70.254
```

Prohibit all other devices in the HR VLAN from accessing any device in the 172.31.70.0 subnet:

```
deny ip 172.31.60.0 0.0.0.255 172.31.70.0 0.0.0.255
```

Overcome the implicit deny rule:

```
permit ip any any
```

Verify the new ACL with `show access-list 103`.

You should see the following:

```
Switch1#show access-lists 103
Extended IP access list 103
    10 permit ip 172.31.60.0 0.0.0.255 host 172.31.70.254
    20 deny ip 172.31.60.0 0.0.0.255 172.31.70.0 0.0.0.255
    30 permit ip any any
```

Now all you have to do is apply this new ACL to the VLAN 600 SVI.

> ### Try it now
> Apply ACL 103 to the VLAN 600 SVI:
>
> ```
> Switch1(config)#int vlan 600
> Switch1(config-if)#ip access-group 103 in
> ```
>
> Verify that HR-PC1 can ping 172.31.70.254 but nothing else in the Executives subnet:
>
> ```
> ping 172.31.70.254
> ping 172.31.70.51
> ```

HR-PC1 can ping the VLAN 700 SVI without any problem:

```
C:\>ping 172.31.70.254

Pinging 172.31.70.254 with 32 bytes of data:
Reply from 172.31.70.254: bytes=32 time=2ms TTL=255
```

But it can't ping Executive-PC1:

```
C:\>ping 172.31.70.51

Pinging 172.31.70.51 with 32 bytes of data:
Reply from 172.31.60.254: Destination net unreachable.
```

9.5   *Commands in this chapter*

The order of operations in an ACL is not something you want to mess up, because it can mean the difference between a working ACL and one that doesn't do anything. Refer to table 9.5 as you complete the hands-on lab. To make things easier, I've listed the commands in the order in which you would execute them.

Table 9.5   Commands used in this chapter

Command	Configuration mode	Description
ip access-list extended 150	Global	Creates ACL 150 and enters IP extended access list configuration mode
deny ip host 1.2.3.4 host 5.6.7.8	IP extended access list	Denies IP traffic from 1.2.3.4 to 5.6.7.8
permit ip 172.31.10.0 0.0.0.255 host 7.7.7.7	IP extended access list	Permits any IP traffic from the 172.31.10.0/255.255.255.0 subnet to 7.7.7.7
permit ip any any	IP extended access list	Permits all IP traffic
ip access-group 150 in	Interface	Applies ACL 150 to the selected interface

9.6 *Hands-on lab*

In this chapter, you used ACLs to control IP traffic from VLAN 600 to VLAN 700. For the lab, you're going to configure an ACL to restrict traffic in the opposite direction, from VLAN 700 to VLAN 600.

Perform the following tasks:

1 Configure an ACL to prevent Executive-PC1 (172.31.70.51) from accessing *any* device in the 172.31.60.0/255.255.255.0 subnet.

2 Apply this ACL to the appropriate interface.

3 Configure another ACL to prevent all devices in the 172.31.70.0/255.255.255.0 subnet from accessing any device in the 172.31.60.0/255.255.255.0 subnet.

4 Replace the ACL you created in step 1 with the ACL you created in step 3.

Connecting switches using trunk links

10

The switch I've been working with in this book has only 24 ports. Yours may have 24 or 48, but regardless of the exact number, in an organization of any size, you can imagine that one switch isn't going to cut it. As you add more devices to a network, eventually you're going to run out of switch ports. When that happens, you'll have to add another switch.

In this chapter, you're going to connect your second switch, Switch2, to Switch1. You'll then move Executive-PC1 from Switch1 to Switch2. Before starting this chapter, be sure you've configured Switch2 using the lab setup instructions found under the Source Code link at https://www.manning.com/books/learn-cisco-network-administration-in-a-month-of-lunches. If you haven't, you won't be able to complete the labs in this chapter.

Adding another switch isn't as simple as connecting the new switch to an existing switch and powering it on. It's *almost* that simple, but you have to perform a few key steps to get everything working. Here's a quick overview of those steps:

1 Physically connect the new switch.
2 Configure the switch ports to form a VLAN trunk.
3 Configure VLANs on the new switch.

That second step references a new term, *VLAN trunk*. I'll explain trunks in detail later on, but for now, understand that a VLAN trunk link is a special type of logical connection that carries traffic for multiple VLANs. Unlike an access port, which carries traffic for only one VLAN, a trunk port carries traffic for multiple VLANs

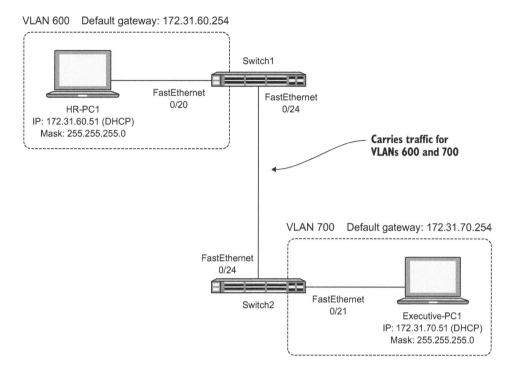

VLAN 600   Default gateway: 172.31.60.254

Switch1

FastEthernet
0/20

HR-PC1
IP: 172.31.60.51 (DHCP)
Mask: 255.255.255.0

FastEthernet
0/24

**Carries traffic for
VLANs 600 and 700**

VLAN 700   Default gateway: 172.31.70.254

FastEthernet
0/24

Switch2

FastEthernet
0/21

Executive-PC1
IP: 172.31.70.51 (DHCP)
Mask: 255.255.255.0

Figure 10.1   Connecting Switch2 to Switch1 via a VLAN trunk and moving Executive-PC1 to Switch2

simultaneously. Chances are you already have VLAN trunks operating in your organization's environment.

Look at figure 10.1 to get a clear picture of what you'll build out in this chapter. Notice the addition of Switch2 and the migration of Executive-PC1 from Switch1 to Switch2. Also, notice that the trunk link between the switches carries traffic for VLANs 600 and 700.

10.1 *Connecting the new switch*

Once again, if you haven't already configured Switch2 according to the lab setup instructions, stop reading and do that now. It's important to note that there's more than one way to physically connect Cisco switches. Some models support Cisco Stack-Wise, a proprietary Cisco technology that allows you to connect switches using thick (and expensive) StackWise cables. But only certain models support StackWise, and the Catalyst 3560s I've recommended for the lab do not. That's why in this chapter you'll connect your switches using a plain-old Ethernet cable. Even if your switches do support StackWise, you can still follow along with this chapter.

Try it now

Log into Switch1.

Take an Ethernet cable and connect FastEthernet0/24 on Switch1 to FastEthernet0/24 on Switch2.

You should see the link come up on Switch1, like so:

```
*Mar  1 05:23:11.869: %LINK-3-UPDOWN: Interface FastEthernet0/24, changed
    state to up
*Mar  1 05:23:12.875: %LINEPROTO-5-UPDOWN: Line protocol on Interface
    FastEthernet0/24, changed state to up
```

If you don't see this, make sure your cable is good and that Switch2 is configured according to the lab setup instructions. If you do see the link come up, you're ready to move on to the next step.

Above and beyond

Using a regular, straight-through Ethernet cable will work fine to connect most Cisco switches that you're likely to find out in the wild. But if you're using older gear that doesn't include the auto-cross or auto-MDIX feature (for example, Catalyst 3550), there's a chance a straight-through cable won't work. If that's the case, you may have to find a crossover cable to connect your switches.

10.2   *Understanding VLAN trunk links*

A moment ago, I said that a VLAN trunk link is a special connection that carries traffic for multiple VLANs. You may hear it referred to as a *VLAN trunk*, a *trunk link*, or just a *trunk*. All of these terms mean the same thing. The idea behind a trunk link is that you can use a *single* physical connection between switches to carry traffic for multiple VLANs without having to worry about traffic moving *between* VLANs. Figure 10.2 illustrates the VLAN trunk that you'll be configuring in this chapter.

You might be wondering why there appear to be two connections between Switch1 and Switch2 even though there's just one physical connection. These two lines represent two separate *logical* connections, one for each VLAN. Even though the switches use one physical link, they internally separate traffic for each VLAN as it traverses the link. Later on in this chapter, I'll delve a bit into the technical details of how they do this.

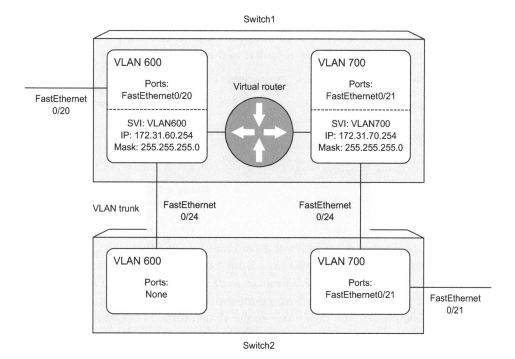

Figure 10.2   Close-up view of a trunk between Switch1 and Switch2

10.2.1 Configuring a trunk link

Back in the day, Cisco made the process of creating a trunk link very easy. In older model switches, all you had to do was connect them together and they'd magically form a trunk through a process called *negotiation*. In newer models, however, this is no longer the case, and you have to perform a bit of manual configuration to get your trunk.

DYNAMIC TRUNKING PROTOCOL

The *Dynamic Trunking Protocol (DTP)* is a Cisco-proprietary feature that automatically configures a port as either a VLAN access port or a trunk port. DTP is an optional feature, and you can configure a trunk without it, but it's enabled by default and most Cisco networks you'll encounter use it. Before you can use DTP to configure a trunk, you need to see how DTP is configured on your switch.

Try it now

Issue the following command to see how DTP is configured on FastEthernet0/24:

```
Switch1#show interfaces fa0/24 switchport
```

Because I don't know what particular model or IOS version you're using, it's important that you do this for yourself and don't assume that my configuration is the same as yours. You should see output similar to this:

```
Switch1#show interfaces fa0/24 switchport
Name: Fa0/24
Switchport: Enabled
Administrative Mode: dynamic auto
Operational Mode: static access
Administrative Trunking Encapsulation: negotiate
Operational Trunking Encapsulation: native
Negotiation of Trunking: On
Access Mode VLAN: 1 (default)
[extraneous output truncated]
```

DTP is configured to form either an access port or a trunk based on what the other side requests.

By default, DTP makes the port a VLAN access port.

Also by default, DTP places the port in VLAN I.

The `Administrative Mode` is `dynamic auto` (the word *dynamic* refers to DTP). This setting means that the switch will sit and wait for the other side (in this case, Switch2) to tell it whether to make this port a trunk port or a VLAN access port.

The `Operational Mode` is `static access`. Remember that in chapter 5 you used the `switchport mode access` command to configure a port to access a specific VLAN. Technically, you don't have to use that command because, as you can see, DTP defaults to making the port a static VLAN access port in VLAN 1, as indicated by the `Access Mode VLAN` setting.

Above and beyond

It's still a good idea to use the `switchport mode access` command when configuring an access port. Doing so eliminates DTP as a potential point of failure, avoids accidental trunk links, and makes the configuration easier to read.

As it stands, FastEthernet0/24 on Switch1 is configured as a VLAN access port in VLAN 1. That means this port is not a trunk link and hence can't carry traffic for VLAN 600 or 700. It's time to fix that.

10.2.2 *Configuring DTP to automatically negotiate a trunk*

I just said that the `dynamic auto` setting configured on Switch1's FastEthernet0/24 causes DTP to sit around and wait for the other side—Switch2—to tell it whether to form a trunk. Because the switches have yet to form a trunk, you can conclude that Switch2 is likely also configured with the `dynamic auto` setting. In other words, both switches are waiting for the other to make the first move.

Getting DTP to negotiate a VLAN trunk requires changing the `dynamic auto` setting on Switch1 to `dynamic desirable`. This setting causes Switch1 to reach out to Switch2 and say, "Hey, I desire to form a trunk!"

Try it now

Issue the following commands to configure FastEthernet0/24 on Switch1 to negotiate a trunk with Switch2:

```
Switch1(config)#interface fa0/24
Switch1(config-if)#switchport mode dynamic desirable
```

You should see the interface go down and come back up, like so:

```
%LINEPROTO-5-UPDOWN: Line protocol on Interface FastEthernet0/24,
    changed state to down
%LINEPROTO-5-UPDOWN: Line protocol on Interface FastEthernet0/24,
    changed state to up
```

By the way, this is sometimes called flapping or *bouncing*. You probably won't get any other output, so you need to manually verify that a trunk has formed.

Try it now

Verify that Switch1 and Switch2 have formed a trunk:

```
Switch1#show interfaces fa0/24 switchport
```

You should see output similar to the following:

```
Name: Fa0/24
Switchport: Enabled
Administrative Mode: dynamic desirable          ← DTP is configured to try
Operational Mode: trunk                         ←   to negotiate a trunk.
Administrative Trunking Encapsulation: negotiate
Operational Trunking Encapsulation: isl           VLAN trunk is present
Negotiation of Trunking: On                       between Switch1 and Switch2.
Access Mode VLAN: 1 (default)
[extraneous output truncated]
```

Notice that the Administrative Mode of dynamic desirable now reflects the configuration change you just made. The Operational Mode of trunk indicates this port is now a trunk port. Although this is a good verification command, it's missing some important details about the trunk.

As I said, a VLAN trunk can carry traffic for multiple VLANs. But it doesn't *have* to. In this case, because you're going to be moving Executive-PC1 to Switch2, you need to ensure that traffic for the Executives VLAN 700 actually traverses the trunk link.

Try it now

Issue a show interfaces trunk command on Switch1 to view the details of the new trunk.

You should see the following:

```
Switch1#show interfaces trunk

Port         Mode              Encapsulation  Status        Native vlan
Fa0/24       desirable         n-isl          trunking      1

Port         Vlans allowed on trunk
Fa0/24       1-4094

Port         Vlans allowed and active in management domain
Fa0/24       1,20,600,700

Port         Vlans in spanning tree forwarding state and not pruned
Fa0/24       1,20,600,700
```

VLANs traversing the trunk

The first two lines indicate that FastEthernet0/24 is a trunk port formed by DTP (as indicated by the `desirable` mode).

Look at the line below `Vlans allowed and active in management domain`. This indicates that Switch1 is *sending* traffic for VLANs 1, 20, 600, and 700 across this trunk. When you have a trunk, IOS will, by default, send all configured VLANs across that trunk. Again, this does not mean that these VLANs are all in the same broadcast domain. It just means that for the purpose of getting across to Switch2, they're all sharing the same physical port.

Even though you're only going to be moving Executive-PC1 to Switch2, there's no harm in allowing all VLANs to traverse the trunk. What's important is that VLAN 700 traffic makes it from Switch1 to Switch2.

10.3   *Configuring Switch2*

Before you move Executive-PC1 to Switch2, you have to configure Switch2. But before you can do that, you have to log into it. You've already configured Switch2's VLAN1 SVI with the IP address 192.168.1.102. Remember that VLAN 1 exists on all Cisco switches by default, and you can't delete it or turn it off. Hence, VLAN 1 will always traverse all trunk ports. This makes it perfect for testing out your new trunk.

> **Try it now**
> Test the trunk link to Switch2 by pinging its VLAN1 SVI:
>
> ```
> Switch1#ping 192.168.1.102
> ```

If you've configured the trunk correctly, you should get a response:

```
Switch1#ping 192.168.1.102
Type escape sequence to abort.
Sending 5, 100-byte ICMP Echos to 192.168.1.102, timeout is 2 seconds:
!!!!!
```

If your pings are successful, you're ready to configure Switch2. You'll do this by Telnetting to it from Switch1. IOS has a built-in Telnet client, which often comes in handy, especially when configuring a new switch!

Try it now
Telnet to Switch2 from Switch1:

```
Switch1#telnet 192.168.1.102
```

Log in using the following credentials:

```
Username: admin
Password: cisco
```

Here's what you should see:

```
Switch1#telnet 192.168.1.102
Trying 192.168.1.102 ... Open

User Access Verification

Username: admin
Password:
Switch2#
```

Notice that the prompt indicates you're on Switch2. If you don't believe me, you can see for yourself with `show ip interface vlan 1 | i up|Internet`:

```
Switch2#show ip interface vlan 1 | i up|Internet
Vlan1 is up, line protocol is up
  Internet address is 192.168.1.102/24
```

The fact that you're connected to this SVI indicates that VLAN 1 traffic is successfully traversing the trunk. As it stands, you have a trunk link between Switch1 and Switch2, and VLAN 1 traffic is flowing freely across that trunk. The next step is to move Executive-PC1 from Switch1 to Switch2.

10.3.1 Configuring VLANs on the new switch

Before you physically move Executive-PC1 to Switch2, you need to make sure that VLAN 700 exists there.

Try it now
On Switch2, issue `show vlan brief` to verify that VLAN 700 exists.

You should see the following:

```
Switch2#show vlan brief

VLAN Name                             Status    Ports
---- -------------------------------- --------- -------------------------------
1    default                          active    Fa0/1, Fa0/2, Fa0/3, Fa0/4
                                                Fa0/5, Fa0/6, Fa0/7, Fa0/8
                                                Fa0/9, Fa0/10, Fa0/11, Fa0/12
                                                Fa0/13, Fa0/14, Fa0/15, Fa0/16
                                                Fa0/17, Fa0/18, Fa0/19, Fa0/20
                                                Fa0/21, Fa0/22, Fa0/23, Gi0/1
                                                Gi0/2
1002 fddi-default                     act/unsup
1003 token-ring-default               act/unsup
1004 fddinet-default                  act/unsup
1005 trnet-default                    act/unsup
```

VLAN 700 doesn't exist! In fact, none of the VLANs on Switch1—20, 600, or 700—exist on Switch2. Initially, this may not seem like a big deal. But if you look at the VLAN trunk from the perspective of Switch2, you should spot a big problem.

> **Try it now**
> On Switch2, do a show interfaces trunk.

You should see this:

```
Switch2#show interfaces trunk

Port        Mode             Encapsulation  Status        Native vlan
Fa0/24      auto             n-isl          trunking      1

Port        Vlans allowed on trunk
Fa0/24      1-4094

Port        Vlans allowed and active in management domain
Fa0/24      1

Port        Vlans in spanning tree forwarding state and not pruned
Fa0/24      1
```

Only VLAN1 is allowed and active, but none of the other VLANs are anywhere to be found. This means that Switch2 can receive traffic only for VLAN 1.

Remember that by default, Cisco switches come with only VLAN 1 enabled. Because Switch2 is a brand-new switch that you're adding to the network, the VLANs you configured on Switch1—VLANs 20, 600, and 700—don't exist on it yet. In order for Switch2 to send and receive traffic for these VLANs across the trunk, you must configure them manually.

Try it now

On Switch2, configure VLANs 20, 600, and 700:

```
Switch2(config)#vlan 20,600,700
Switch2(config-vlan)#exit
```

Issue another `show interfaces trunk` to verify.

A subsequent `show interfaces trunk` reveals that the newly configured VLANs are now active:

```
Switch2#sh interfaces trunk

Port          Mode             Encapsulation  Status        Native vlan
Fa0/24        auto             n-isl          trunking      1

Port          Vlans allowed on trunk
Fa0/24        1-4094

Port          Vlans allowed and active in management domain
Fa0/24        1,20,600,700

Port          Vlans in spanning tree forwarding state and not pruned
Fa0/24        1
```

The lesson here is that if a VLAN doesn't exist on the switch, the switch won't be able to send or receive traffic for that VLAN. Whenever you add a new switch to an environment, make sure you configure the necessary VLANs on it!

10.4　*Moving devices to the new switch*

At this point, you're ready to move Executive-PC1 to Switch2. This might be the simplest part of the whole process!

Try it now

Unplug Executive-PC1 from Switch1 and connect it to FastEthernet0/21 on Switch2. Configure the port as an access port for VLAN 700 using the following commands:

```
Switch2(config)#interface fa0/21
Switch2(config-if)#switchport access vlan 700
```

Verify the configuration with `show interfaces fa0/21 switchport | i Mode`.

You should see the following output:

```
Switch2# show interfaces fa0/21 switchport | i Mode
Administrative Mode: dynamic auto
Operational Mode: static access
Access Mode VLAN: 700 (VLAN0700)
```

To refresh your memory, Executive-PC1 belongs in the Executives VLAN 700, so you must manually configure the port as an access port for VLAN 700. But notice that you're not using the `switchport mode access` command this time. Recall that earlier in the chapter I said that if DTP can't negotiate a VLAN trunk on a port, it will make that port into a VLAN access port. That's what happened here. All you had to do was configure the access VLAN to be 700 with the `switchport access vlan 700` command, and DTP took care of the rest.

At this point, you're finished with your Switch2 configuration. The next step is to hop on Executive-PC1 and verify that it can communicate just as it did before the move. Remember that Executive-PC1 is configured to automatically get an IP address via DHCP. Whenever you move a PC from one port to another, it's a good idea to either reboot it or do an `ipconfig /release` and `ipconfig /renew` to ensure that it's able to pick up an IP address when connected to the new port.

Try it now

On Executive-PC1, issue an `ipconfig /release` and `ipconfig /renew` to ensure that it picks up an IP address in the 172.31.70.0 subnet.

Confirm IP connectivity by pinging the IP address of Switch1's VLAN700 SVI:

```
ping 172.31.70.254
```

You should see successful pings all around:

```
PS C:\>ping 172.31.70.254

Pinging 172.31.70.254 with 32 bytes of data:
Reply from 172.31.70.254: bytes=32 time<1ms TTL=255
Reply from 172.31.70.254: bytes=32 time=1ms TTL=255
Reply from 172.31.70.254: bytes=32 time<1ms TTL=255
Reply from 172.31.70.254: bytes=32 time=1ms TTL=255

Ping statistics for 172.31.70.254:
    Packets: Sent = 4, Received = 4, Lost = 0 (0% loss),
Approximate round trip times in milli-seconds:
    Minimum = 0ms, Maximum = 1ms, Average = 0ms
```

10.5 *Changing the trunk encapsulation*

As traffic for multiple VLANs moves across the trunk, both switches need a way to identify which Ethernet frames belong to which VLAN. They accomplish this by using a trunk encapsulation protocol called Inter-Switch Link (ISL), which marks, or tags, each Ethernet frame with a VLAN identifier as it traverses the trunk.

Try it now

You can verify that your switches are using ISL as the encapsulation type by looking for `isl` in certain output. Issue the following commands and review the output:

```
show interfaces trunk | i Encap|isl
show interfaces fa0/24 switchport | i isl
```

Note that both commands reveal ISL as the trunk encapsulation protocol:

```
Switch1#show interfaces trunk | i isl|Encap
Port        Mode            Encapsulation  Status       Native vlan
Fa0/24      auto            n-isl          trunking     1

Switch1#show interfaces fa0/24 switchport | i isl
Operational Trunking Encapsulation: isl
```

ISL works fine between Cisco switches, and in this case there's no reason to change it. But ISL is a Cisco-proprietary protocol, and it doesn't work with non-Cisco switches. If you need to form a trunk between a Cisco switch and a non-Cisco switch, there's another encapsulation type you'll have to use called 802.1Q.

Virtualization products like VMware ESXi, Microsoft Hyper-V, Citrix XenServer, and Linux KVM also use 802.1Q trunks. Although those are beyond the scope of this book, knowing how to configure 802.1Q encapsulation on your Cisco switches is a must. It's also really easy!

Try it now

If you're still on Switch2, type `exit` at the `Switch2#` prompt to get back to Switch1's command line.

Get into interface configuration mode for FastEthernet0/24 and issue the following command:

```
switchport trunk encapsulation dot1q
```

The command referencing `dot1q` instead of `802.1q` may seem a little odd, but that's the way Cisco did it. Remember, if you forget that little detail, you can always rely on the inline help.

Verify with a `show interfaces trunk`.

You should see `802.1q` listed as the trunk encapsulation type:

```
Switch1#show interfaces trunk | i Encap|trunking
Port        Mode            Encapsulation  Status       Native vlan
Fa0/24      auto            802.1q         trunking     1
```

Functionally, you won't see any difference between the performance of an 802.1Q trunk and an ISL trunk. Both achieve the same goal, but under the hood they're different technologies.

Manually setting the trunk encapsulation type has an interesting side effect: it lets you stop using DTP. Instead of depending on DTP to negotiate a trunk, you can now configure the port to *always* behave like a trunk port by setting it as an unconditional trunk port.

Try it now

On Switch1, get into interface configuration mode for FastEthernet0/24 and issue the following command to make it an unconditional trunk port:

```
switchport mode trunk
```

You should get no output, so go ahead and issue a `show run int fa0/24` to view the running configuration.

You should see some interesting output:

```
Switch1#show run | section FastEthernet0/24
interface FastEthernet0/24
 switchport trunk encapsulation dot1q
 switchport mode trunk
 switchport port-security maximum 3
 switchport port-security aging time 10
 switchport port-security violation restrict
```

The `dynamic desirable` command is completely gone! DTP is completely out of the picture, and so is ISL. This means that if you wanted to, you could connect a non-Cisco switch or virtualization host to this port and seamlessly create an 802.1Q trunk. Most likely, though, in a typical office environment, the majority of trunk links you'll encounter will be between Cisco switches.

Notice that there's some Port Security configuration from an earlier chapter. In the hands-on lab, you're going to experiment with this and see whether Port Security affects your new trunk link.

10.6   *Commands in this chapter*

Refer to the commands in table 10.1 as you complete the hands-on lab.

Table 10.1   Commands used in this chapter

Command	Configuration mode	Description
`show interfaces fa0/24 switchport`	N/A	Displays verbose information about the operational state of the port, including whether it's in trunk or access mode

Table 10.1 Commands used in this chapter

Command	Configuration mode	Description
`switchport mode dynamic desirable`	Interface	Sets the port to attempt to negotiate a trunk with the device on the other end
`show interfaces trunk`	N/A	Displays information about all active VLAN trunks
`telnet 192.168.1.102`	N/A	Launches the IOS Telnet client and connects to 192.168.1.102
`switchport trunk encapsulation dot1q`	Interface	Sets the trunk encapsulation type to 802.1Q (as opposed to ISL)
`switchport mode trunk`	Interface	Sets the port as a static trunk port, effectively disabling DTP

10.7 *Hands-on lab*

For this lab, you'll get a feel for how various settings can impact your trunk link. As a Cisco network administrator, you need to understand how technologies you configured in previous chapters can impact what you're doing right now. You already saw how not having the VLANs configured on Switch2 prevented those VLANs from traversing your newly created trunk. Follow these steps and answer the questions:

1 On Switch2, configure FastEthernet0/24 in `dynamic desirable` mode. Verify that the trunk is still up.

2 Reconfigure the port again as an unconditional trunk port. Is the trunk still up?

3 Attempt to enable Port Security on the port by issuing the `switchport port-security` command. What happens?

4 On Executive-PC1, attempt to ping HR-PC1's IP address, 172.31.60.51. Does it work? If not, why not?

5 Save your running configurations on both Switch1 and Switch2.

Automatically configuring VLANs using the VLAN Trunking Protocol

Now that you've set up a trunk between your switches, it's time to introduce you to another cool feature of IOS that can save you a bit of time when configuring VLANs on your new switches.

In the last chapter, when you were configuring Switch2 you had to manually create VLANs 600 and 700 on it. This wasn't a big deal because you had to do this on only one switch, but what if you had to add 10 new switches and each switch needed 100 VLANs? Although manually adding VLANs isn't a difficult process, it doesn't scale well.

To solve this, Cisco has given us a cool feature called the VLAN Trunking Protocol (VTP). VTP saves you from having to manually create VLANs on each switch in your topology. Instead, you create your VLANs on only one switch, and VTP automatically creates and names those same VLANs on all your other switches, provided they're connected via trunk links and you've configured VTP properly.

Figure 11.1 illustrates what you'll be building out in this chapter. VTP uses a client/server configuration. The VTP server is the switch where you'll configure all your VLANs—Switch1 in this case. The VTP process running on Switch1 will send out VTP advertisements across the trunk connected to Switch2. A VTP advertisement is a message that contains a list of VLANs configured on Switch1. Switch2 will receive the advertisements and automatically create the VLANs that exist on Switch1.

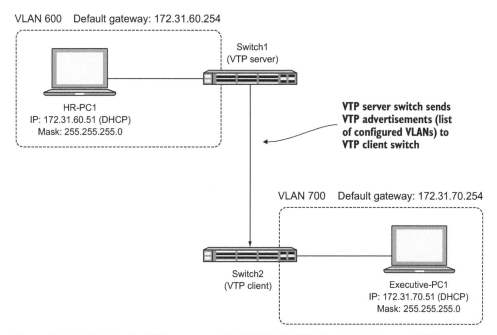

VLAN 600   Default gateway: 172.31.60.254

Switch1
(VTP server)

HR-PC1
IP: 172.31.60.51 (DHCP)
Mask: 255.255.255.0

**VTP server switch sends
VTP advertisements (list
of configured VLANs) to
VTP client switch**

VLAN 700   Default gateway: 172.31.70.254

Switch2
(VTP client)

Executive-PC1
IP: 172.31.70.51 (DHCP)
Mask: 255.255.255.0

**Figure 11.1   Switch1 is the VTP server, and Switch2 is the VTP client. Switch1 sends VTP
advertisements containing information about the VLANs configured on it.**

11.1   *Two words of warning*

Before beginning, I need to give you two big warnings about VTP. First, VTP, if misconfigured, has the ability to bring down a network in seconds. Because it can create and
delete VLANs automatically, there's the potential for it to delete very, very important
VLANs in a production environment. I noted earlier in the book that I would warn you
if anything I'm going to teach you could negatively impact a live network. This is your
warning. *Do not configure VTP on a live network without following whatever process your organization has for making potentially catastrophic changes!*

Second, because of VTP's potential to do very nasty things (like deleting VLANs),
many organizations don't allow it. Personally, I choose not to implement it in most
environments I manage. But many organizations do use it, and more important, as a
Cisco network administrator, you need to understand how to configure it so that you
can fix it when it breaks!

Here are the basic steps you'll be performing to get VTP up and running:

1   Configure Switch1 as a VTP server.
2   Configure Switch2 as a VTP client.

   3 Create VLANs 900-999 on Switch1.

   4 Configure VTP pruning.

I told you it was simple! Let's get started.

11.2   *Configuring Switch1 as a VTP server*

Before making a configuration change, it's always good to get an idea of the current configuration. That way, if something breaks badly, you have at least some idea of what changed.

> **Try it now**
>
> On Switch1, do a `show vtp status` to view the current VTP configuration.

You should see something like this:

```
Switch1#show vtp status
VTP Version capable             : 1 to 3
VTP version running             : 1
VTP Domain Name                 : cisco
VTP Pruning Mode                : Disabled
VTP Traps Generation            : Disabled
Device ID                       : 0023.ab40.8e00
Configuration last modified by 0.0.0.0 at 0-0-00 00:00:00

Feature VLAN:
--------------
VTP Operating Mode              : Transparent
Maximum VLANs supported locally : 1005
Number of existing VLANs        : 8
Configuration Revision          : 0
MD5 digest                      : 0xF9 0xD6 0xB0 0x82 0x71 0x06 0x3B 0x92
                                  0x04 0xC3 0xCB 0xC8 0xFD 0x37 0x91 0xC7
```

Don't worry if your output doesn't look exactly like mine. You're going to be changing it anyway. I want to draw your attention to the specific configuration parameters you'll be modifying on Switch1.

    `VTP Domain Name` is a string that each VTP participant uses to determine whether it should heed or ignore the information in a VTP advertisement. Think of it as a last name or surname. If your last name is Smith, and you hear someone yelling for Mr. or Mrs. Smith, you're probably going to pay attention. If your last name isn't Smith, you'll just ignore it.

    The `VTP Operating Mode` is `Transparent`, which means that VTP will ignore VTP advertisements, but it will pass them along to other connected switches. Transparent mode effectively disables VTP on a switch, regardless of what the `VTP Domain Name` is.

    In this case, you want Switch1 to act as a VTP server so that it will send out VTP advertisements to connected switches.

> **Try it now**
> On Switch1, issue the following command to make it a VTP server for the cisco VTP domain:
>
> ```
> Switch1(config)#vtp mode server
> ```

You should see a single line of output:

```
Setting device to VTP Server mode for VLANS.
```

The next step is to set a VTP password. The purpose of the VTP password is to prevent someone from accidentally bringing down a network through a VTP misconfiguration.

> **Try it now**
> Set a VTP password of "MoL" on Switch1:
>
> ```
> Switch1(config)#vtp password MoL
> ```

You should get this confirmation:

```
Setting device VTP password to MoL
```

And that's it for configuring Switch1 as a VTP server!

11.3 *Configuring Switch2 as a VTP client*

Again, it's a good idea to check the existing configuration before making changes. Go ahead and check the VTP configuration of Switch2.

> **Try it now**
> On Switch2, do a show vtp status.

You should see the following output:

```
Switch2#sh vtp status
VTP Version capable             : 1 to 3        Switch2 automatically
VTP version running             : 1             populated the domain name
VTP Domain Name                 : cisco    ←    that it received from Switch1.
VTP Pruning Mode                : Disabled
VTP Traps Generation            : Disabled
Device ID                       : 0024.5088.6d80
Configuration last modified by 192.168.1.102 at 3-1-93 00:58:04
Local updater ID is 192.168.1.102 on interface Vl1 (lowest numbered VLAN
        interface found)
```

```
Feature VLAN:
--------------
VTP Operating Mode                 : Server
Maximum VLANs supported locally    : 1005          The VTP passwords on Switch1
Number of existing VLANs           : 8               and Switch2 don't match.
Configuration Revision             : 0
MD5 digest                         : 0xB2 0x50 0x7A 0x9B 0x04 0x97 0xBD 0x83
                                     0x5A 0xFD 0xC4 0x15 0xFB 0xF5 0x4C 0x6F
*** MD5 digest checksum mismatch on trunk: Fa0/24 ***    ◄
```

Notice two things here. The `VTP Domain Name` is `cisco`. I didn't configure that, and neither did you. It happened automatically. By default, VTP starts out with a null domain name. When you configured Switch1 as a VTP server, it sent out a VTP advertisement that included the VTP domain name. Switch2 received this advertisement and automatically set its own VTP domain name to match.

The next thing to notice is that there's an error indicating `MD5 digest checksum mismatch`. Although not obvious, this indicates that the VTP password you configured on Switch1 doesn't match the nonexistent password on Switch2. This message will go away once you complete the configuration.

Try it now

Configure Switch2 as a VTP client using the following command:

```
Switch2(config)#vtp mode client
```

You should see this message:

```
Setting device to VTP Client mode for VLANS.
```

Next, set the VTP password to "MoL":

```
Switch2(config)#vtp password MoL
```

You should see this confirmation message:

```
Setting device VTP password to MoL
```

11.4 Creating new VLANs on Switch1

At this point, you're ready to test your new VTP setup. You'll do this by creating some new VLANs on Switch1 and then verifying that they propagated to Switch2.

Try it now

On Switch1, create VLANs 900-999:

```
Switch1(config)#vlan 900-999
Switch1(config-vlan)#exit
```

Go back over to Switch2, and check the VTP status again:

```
Switch2(config)#do sh vtp status
```

You should see the following output:

```
VTP Version capable         : 1 to 3
VTP version running         : 1
VTP Domain Name             : cisco
VTP Pruning Mode            : Disabled
VTP Traps Generation        : Disabled
Device ID                   : 0024.5088.6d80
Configuration last modified by 192.168.1.101 at 3-1-93 01:39:02        ←─┐
                                                            **The IP address of**
Feature VLAN:                                               **Switch1's VLAN I SVI**
--------------
VTP Operating Mode              : Client
Maximum VLANs supported locally : 1005      **The number of**
Number of existing VLANs        : 108    ←─┘ **VLANs on Switch2**
Configuration Revision          : 1
MD5 digest                      : 0x6B 0xCB 0x64 0xBE 0x29 0x9D 0xBF 0xB9
                                  0x8C 0x04 0xC0 0xE9 0x3E 0x7F 0x51 0x52
```

Notice the line that says `Configuration last modified by 192.168.1.101.`
That's the IP address of Switch1's VLAN 1 SVI. If you ever forget which switch is the VTP
server, do a `show vtp status` and look at that line in the output.

Also notice that the number of existing VLANs has increased from 8 to 108, thanks
to the addition of VLANs 900–999. You just created 100 new VLANs on Switch1 and
Switch2 by making a single configuration change only on Switch1! To really appreciate this, take a look at the VLANs on Switch2.

Try it now
On Switch2, do a `show vlan`.

I won't put the full output here, but you should have several screens of output listing
each of the new VLANs:

```
Switch2#sh vlan

VLAN Name                         Status    Ports
---- ------------------------- --------- -----------------------------
1    default                     active    Fa0/1, Fa0/2, Fa0/3, Fa0/4
                                           Fa0/5, Fa0/6, Fa0/7, Fa0/8
                                           Fa0/9, Fa0/10, Fa0/11, Fa0/12
                                           Fa0/13, Fa0/14, Fa0/15, Fa0/16
                                           Fa0/17, Fa0/18, Fa0/19, Fa0/20
                                           Fa0/22, Fa0/23, Gi0/1, Gi0/2
```

```
20    VOICE                      active
600   HR                         active
700   Executives                 active    Fa0/21
900   VLAN0900                   active
901   VLAN0901                   active
902   VLAN0902                   active
903   VLAN0903                   active
904   VLAN0904                   active
905   VLAN0905                   active
906   VLAN0906                   active
907   VLAN0907                   active
908   VLAN0908                   active
909   VLAN0909                   active
910   VLAN0910                   active
--More--
```

As cool as it is to be able to create hundreds of VLANs on multiple switches in seconds, there is a tradeoff. If you want to create, delete, or rename a VLAN on a VTP client—in this case, Switch2—you must do so on the server—Switch1. If you attempt to change a VLAN on Switch2, VTP will stop you.

Try it now
On Switch2, attempt to get into VLAN configuration mode:

```
Switch2(config)#vlan 900
```

You won't get far. As soon as you try to enter VLAN configuration mode, VTP kicks you out with the following message:

```
VTP VLAN configuration not allowed when device is in CLIENT mode.
```

This can be a bit of a bummer, especially when you're in a hurry to create a new VLAN. The solution is to go to the VTP server—Switch1—and make your change there.

Try it now
On Switch1, assign a name of your choice to VLAN 900:

```
Switch1(config)#vlan 900
Switch1(config-vlan)#name Marketing
Switch1(config-vlan)#exit
```

You should get no errors this time.

> Go to Switch2 and verify that the information propagated:
>
> ```
> Switch2#show vlan brief | i Name|900
> ```

You should see VLAN 900 along with its corresponding new name:

```
VLAN Name                        Status    Ports
900  Marketing                   active
```

11.5   *Enabling VTP pruning*

The term *VLAN Trunking Protocol* is a little misleading in that it seems to suggest a role in creating a VLAN trunk. But as you already know from the last chapter, you can create a VLAN trunk without using VTP at all. So where does the *VLAN Trunking* part of VTP come from?

When you use VTP to automatically create VLANs on multiple switches, the traffic from each of those VLANs automatically transits your existing trunks. In this case, VTP doesn't (and can't) create a VLAN trunk between Switch1 and Switch2. But because those switches are already trunked, the act of creating a VLAN on both switches—VLAN 900, for example—results in VLAN 900 traffic traversing that trunk. To see what I mean, look at the VLANs that are active on the trunk.

> **Try it now**
> On Switch1, issue a show interfaces trunk.

You should see the following output:

```
Switch1#sh interfaces trunk

Port        Mode              Encapsulation  Status      Native vlan
Fa0/24      on                802.1q         trunking    1

Port        Vlans allowed on trunk
Fa0/24      1-4094

Port        Vlans allowed and active in management domain
Fa0/24      1,20,600,700,900-999

Port        Vlans in spanning tree forwarding state and not pruned
Fa0/24      1,20,600,700,900-999
```

All VLANs that exist on Switch1 are traversing the trunk to Switch2.

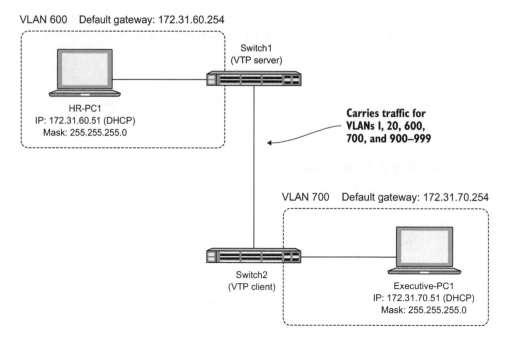

Figure 11.2   All VLANs are traversing the trunk between Switch1 and Switch2.

Look at the list of VLANs under Vlans in spanning tree forwarding state and not pruned. Every single one of the VLANs you just created—900 through 999—as well as the existing VLANs are traversing the trunk, as shown in figure 11.2.

As you know, each VLAN is a separate broadcast domain. If this was a live network and each of these VLANs had traffic, every broadcast in every VLAN would be going across this trunk! That could consume most if not all of the bandwidth of this 100 Mbps trunk link.

The solution is to use a feature called *VTP pruning* to prevent traffic from unused VLANs from traversing the trunk. What constitutes an unused VLAN isn't as cut-and-dry as it sounds.

Take another look at figure 11.2. Notice that there are no devices in VLANs 900–999. Putting it more technically, there are no switched virtual interfaces (SVIs) or access ports that are members of those VLANs. Hence, those VLANs are unused. You can verify this by looking at the VLAN database on Switch1 and Switch2.

Try it now
On Switch1 and Switch2, issue a show vlan brief | i Fa.

On Switch1, you should see port membership only in VLANs 1, 20, 600, and 700:

```
Switch1#show vlan brief | i Fa
1    default                  active     Fa0/1, Fa0/2, Fa0/3, Fa0/4
                                         Fa0/5, Fa0/6, Fa0/7, Fa0/8
                                         Fa0/9, Fa0/10, Fa0/11, Fa0/12
                                         Fa0/13, Fa0/14, Fa0/15, Fa0/16
                                         Fa0/17, Fa0/18, Fa0/22, Fa0/23
20   VOICE                    active     Fa0/19, Fa0/20
600  HR                       active     Fa0/19, Fa0/20
700  Executives               active     Fa0/21
```

On Switch2, you should see membership only in VLANs 1 and 700:

```
Switch2#sh vlan brief | i Fa
1    default                  active     Fa0/1, Fa0/2, Fa0/3, Fa0/4
                                         Fa0/5, Fa0/6, Fa0/7, Fa0/8
                                         Fa0/9, Fa0/10, Fa0/11, Fa0/12
                                         Fa0/13, Fa0/14, Fa0/15, Fa0/16
                                         Fa0/17, Fa0/18, Fa0/19, Fa0/20
                                         Fa0/22, Fa0/23, Gi0/1, Gi0/2
700  Executives               active     Fa0/21
```

By process of elimination, VLANs 900–999 are unused on Switch1 and Switch2. The VTP pruning feature can automatically determine which VLANs are unused and prune them from the trunk, but first you have to explicitly enable it.

Try it now

Enable VTP pruning on Switch1 by issuing the following command in global configuration mode:

```
vtp pruning
```

You should see a message indicating pruning is on:

```
Switch1(config)#vtp pruning
Pruning switched on
```

By the way, you must issue this command on the VTP server. It won't work on any VTP clients. To confirm that VTP pruning is working as you expect, it's always a good idea to look at the trunk.

Try it now

On Switch1, issue a `show interfaces trunk`.

You should see the following output:

```
Switch1#show interfaces trunk

Port       Mode          Encapsulation  Status      Native vlan
Fa0/24     on            802.1q         trunking    1
```

```
Port          Vlans allowed on trunk
Fa0/24        1-4094
                                                         Only VLANs 1 and
Port          Vlans allowed and active in management domain    700 are traversing
Fa0/24        1,20,600,700,900-999                              the trunk.

Port          Vlans in spanning tree forwarding state and not pruned
Fa0/24        1,700
```

Look at the Vlans in spanning tree forwarding state and not pruned section again. The VTP pruning feature removed or pruned all VLANs except VLANs 1 and 700. The removal of VLANs 900–999 should come as no surprise, but why did VTP prune VLAN 600? To understand why, take a look at figure 11.3.

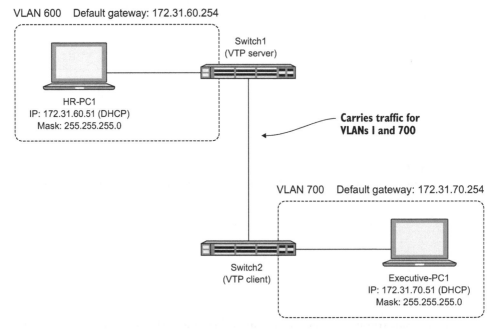

Figure 11.3   VLANs 1 and 700 allowed on the trunk port from Switch1 to Switch2

The only device that's a member of VLAN 600 is HR-PC1 on Switch1. But on Switch2, there are no devices in VLAN 600. Hence, VLAN 600 is unused on Switch2, so the VTP process on Switch1 pruned it from the trunk.

Above and beyond

VTP will never prune VLAN 1 from a trunk. I call VLAN 1 the immutable VLAN because you can't delete or disable it. That's a good thing, because VTP itself uses VLAN 1 for sending and receiving VTP advertisements.

That raises this question: how does Switch1 know which VLANs to prune? Switch2 tells it.

> **Try it now**
> On Switch2, issue a `show interfaces pruning`.

Here's what you should see:

```
Switch2#show interfaces pruning

Port                Vlans pruned for lack of request by neighbor
Fa0/24              900-999

Port                Vlan traffic requested of neighbor
Fa0/24              1,700
```

Switch2 has requested that Switch1 send traffic for these VLANs.

The Vlan traffic requested of `neighbor` lists the VLANs that Switch2 wants to receive from Switch1: VLANs 1 and 700. In other words, these are the VLANs that Switch2 doesn't want Switch1 to prune from the trunk. Not coincidentally, these are the only VLANs Switch1 allows on the trunk.

One thing to keep in mind is that the pruned VLANs aren't symmetrical; that is, the VLANs Switch1 prunes aren't necessarily the same as the VLANs Switch2 prunes. In the hands-on lab, you're going to get into Switch2 and see exactly what I mean.

11.6   *Commands in this chapter*

Refer to table 11.1 as you complete the hands-on lab.

Table 11.1   Commands used in this chapter

Command	Configuration mode	Description
`show vtp status`	N/A	Displays information about the current VTP configuration
`vtp mode server`	Global	Configures the switch as a VTP server
`vtp password MoL`	Global	Sets the VTP password to "MoL"
`vtp mode client`	Global	Configures the switch as a VTP client
`vlan 900-999`	Global	Creates VLANs 900 through 999 inclusive
`show interfaces trunk`	N/A	Displays information on trunk links, including which VLANs are traversing which trunks
`vtp pruning`	Global	Enables VTP pruning
`show interfaces pruning`	N/A	Displays which VLANs VTP has pruned

11.7   *Hands-on lab*

For this lab, you're going to see how changes you make to VTP affect the client—Switch2. You're also going to see how changes you make on Switch2 affect VTP pruning:

1 Delete VLANs 901–999 on Switch1 using the command `no vlan 901-999`. What happens to those VLANs on Switch2?

2 On Switch2, create an SVI for VLAN 900. Does Switch1 still prune VLAN 900 from the trunk?

3 Switch1 is pruning VLANs 20 and 600 on the trunk facing Switch2. Which VLANs is Switch2 pruning on the trunk?

4 Which VLANs is Switch2 not pruning?

5 Save your configurations!

Protecting against bridging loops by using the Spanning Tree Protocol

In the last chapter, you connected two switches—Switch1 and Switch2—via a single Ethernet connection. Imagine for a moment that both of these switches are in a live network and have dozens of end users connected to them. If the link between the switches goes down, devices on Switch1 won't be able to communicate with devices on Switch2 and vice versa.

The solution is to add a redundant connection between FastEthernet0/23 on Switch1 and Switch2, as shown in figure 12.1. If the original link fails for whatever reason, the switches can communicate across the redundant link.

At first glance, this looks like a wonderful configuration. It appears that by adding an additional connection, you're adding not only redundancy but additional bandwidth as well. But this configuration isn't as wonderful as it looks.

When you add a redundant connection, by default you can't have traffic traversing both links simultaneously. To understand why, consider the following scenario.

Suppose that Executive-PC1 generates a broadcast Ethernet frame and sends it out onto the network. Recall from chapter 2 that Switch2 will forward such a broadcast out every port, including both ports connected to Switch1—FastEthernet0/23 and FastEthernet0/24. Figure 12.2 illustrates what this would look like.

Switch1 would receive the same frame on both ports. Seeing that both identical frames are broadcast frames, it would forward them out of all its ports, including the ports connected to Switch2. In short, the frames would bounce back and forth between Switch1 and Switch2 indefinitely. This is called a *bridging loop*.

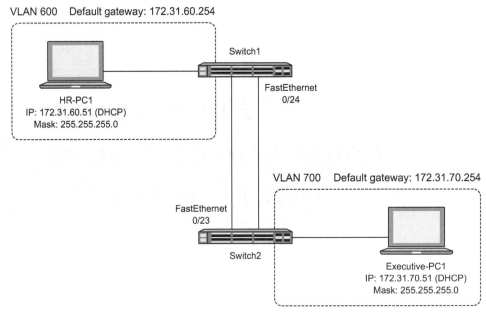

Figure 12.1   Switch1 and Switch2 with redundant links. Note that the interface numbers are the same on each end of the link.

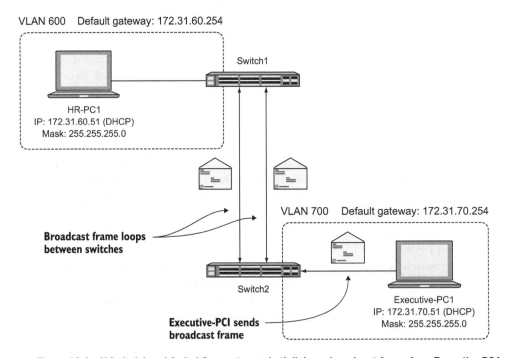

Figure 12.2   If Switch1 and Switch2 were to use both links, a broadcast frame from Executive-PC1 would cause a bridging loop.

Without getting into the nerdy details, a bridging loop results in the original broadcast frame getting multiplied and sent across the inter-switch links over and over again, until all the bandwidth on both links is consumed or each switch's CPU is overloaded. The ending is always the same: devices connected to both switches lose network connectivity. Ironically, that's the very problem the redundant connection was supposed to prevent!

12.1　How Spanning Tree works

To solve the problem of bridging loops, a network engineer named Radia Perlman invented something called the *Spanning Tree Protocol*. Most network folks just call it *Spanning Tree* or, even more mercifully, *STP*. Spanning Tree resolves the problem of bridging loops, and on Cisco switches it's enabled by default. But before you can get a hands-on feel for how it works, you need to create another trunk between your switches.

Try it now

Connect an Ethernet cable between ports FastEthernet0/23 on Switch1 and Switch2.

On Switch1, configure FastEthernet0/23 to be a VLAN trunk port:

```
Interface fa0/23
switchport trunk encapsulation dot1q
switchport mode trunk
```

As always, verify your configuration with a show `interfaces trunk`.

Don't worry about creating a bridging loop. Remember, Spanning Tree is enabled by default and will prevent this. To see how it does this, look at figure 12.3.

Notice that Spanning Tree blocks FastEthernet0/24 on Switch2. By default, Spanning Tree blocks the higher-numbered ports in favor of the lower-numbered ports. It's important to understand that *blocked* doesn't mean shut down, disabled, or disconnected. It just means that the Spanning Tree process on Switch2 blocks Ethernet frames from ingressing or egressing FastEthernet0/24. As always, you can verify this at the command line.

Try it now

On Switch2, issue a show `spanning-tree vlan 700`.

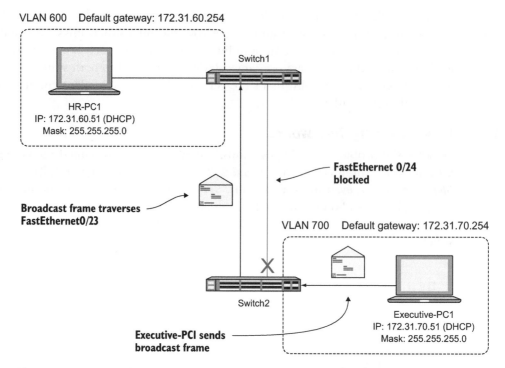

VLAN 600   Default gateway: 172.31.60.254

Switch1

HR-PC1
IP: 172.31.60.51 (DHCP)
Mask: 255.255.255.0

FastEthernet 0/24
blocked

Broadcast frame traverses
FastEthernet0/23

VLAN 700   Default gateway: 172.31.70.254

Switch2

Executive-PC1
IP: 172.31.70.51 (DHCP)
Mask: 255.255.255.0

Executive-PCI sends
broadcast frame

Figure 12.3   Spanning Tree preventing a bridging loop by blocking FastEthernet0/24 on Switch2

You should get some cryptic-looking output:

```
Switch2#show spanning-tree vlan 700

VLAN0700
  Spanning Tree enabled protocol ieee
  Root ID    Priority    33468
             Address     0023.ab40.8e00
             Cost        19
             Port        25  (FastEthernet0/23)
             Hello Time   2 sec  Max Age 20 sec  Forward Delay 15 sec

  Bridge ID  Priority    33468  (priority 32768 sys-id-ext 700)
             Address     0024.5088.6d80
             Hello Time   2 sec  Max Age 20 sec  Forward Delay 15 sec
             Aging Time  300 sec

Interface          Role Sts Cost      Prio.Nbr Type
------------------ ---- --- --------- -------- -----
Fa0/21             Desg FWD 19        128.23   P2p
Fa0/23             Root FWD 19        128.25   P2p
Fa0/24             Altn BLK 19        128.26   P2p
```

**Spanning Tree has
blocked this port to
prevent a bridging loop.**

Although not very obvious, the last line of the output indicates Spanning Tree has placed FastEthernet0/24 in a BLK status, which means *blocked*. In contrast, it leaves FastEthernet0/23 in a FWD state, meaning *forwarding*—as in *forwarding frames*. To use more generic terminology, you can think of FastEthernet0/24 as the *standby* or *backup* port and FastEthernet0/23 as the *active* port.

> **Above and beyond**
> Spanning Tree is an advanced topic that makes even experienced network administrators scratch their head. This book isn't going to cover how Spanning Tree determines which ports to block, only how to tweak it to suit your environment.

12.1.1 How Spanning Tree deals with link failures

The point of having two links is to avoid a network outage if one of them goes down. You have two links, but Spanning Tree allows traffic on only one of them: FastEthernet0/23. Now let's simulate a failure of that link to see how Spanning Tree responds.

> **Try it now**
> On Switch2, shut down the FastEthernet0/23 interface:
>
> ```
> interface fa0/23
> shutdown
> ```
>
> Issue another show spanning-tree vlan 700.

You should see the following:

```
Switch2#sh spanning-tree vlan 700

VLAN0700
  Spanning Tree enabled protocol ieee
  Root ID    Priority    33468
             Address     0023.ab40.8e00
             Cost        19
             Port        26 (FastEthernet0/24)
             Hello Time   2 sec  Max Age 20 sec  Forward Delay 15 sec

  Bridge ID  Priority    33468  (priority 32768 sys-id-ext 700)
             Address     0024.5088.6d80
             Hello Time   2 sec  Max Age 20 sec  Forward Delay 15 sec
             Aging Time  15   sec

Interface           Role Sts Cost       Prio.Nbr Type
------------------- ---- --- ---------  -------- -----
Fa0/21              Desg FWD 19         128.23   P2p
Fa0/24              Root FWD 19         128.26   P2p
```

Spanning Tree has placed FastEthernet0/24 into a forwarding state because FastEthernet0/23 is no longer available.

Notice that FastEthernet0/23, which you just shut down, is nowhere to be found. Instead, you see FastEthernet0/24 in a forwarding state, meaning that Switch2 is now using this link to send traffic to Switch1. By the way, if your output doesn't indicate a forwarding state for FastEthernet0/24, wait about 30 seconds and try again. I'll explain why in a moment.

As good as Spanning Tree is, it's not all roses. There's another downside that shows up whenever a port goes up or down.

> **Try it now**
>
> On Executive-PC1, start a continuous ping to Switch1's VLAN 700 SVI:
>
> ```
> Ping 172.31.70.254 -t
> ```
>
> On Switch2, bring FastEthernet0/23 back up:
>
> ```
> Interface fa0/23
> No shut
> ```
>
> Wait patiently for 30 seconds.

After about 30 seconds, you should see these few lines of output:

```
Switch2(config-if)#no shut
Switch2(config-if)#
*Mar  1 03:07:47.234: %LINK-3-UPDOWN: Interface FastEthernet0/23, changed
    state to up
*Mar  1 03:07:50.883: %LINEPROTO-5-UPDOWN: Line protocol on Interface
    FastEthernet0/23, changed state to up
*Mar  1 03:08:19.899: %LINEPROTO-5-UPDOWN: Line protocol on Interface
    Vlan900, changed state to up
*Mar  1 03:08:19.916: %LINEPROTO-5-UPDOWN: Line protocol on Interface Vlan1,
    changed state to up
```

Pay special attention to the timestamp. The interface came back up at 3:07:47, but the SVIs for VLANs 1 and 900 didn't come up until 30 seconds later. The reason for this is that Spanning Tree doesn't place the port back into a forwarding state right away. During these 30 seconds, no traffic can pass between Switch1 and Switch2.

Checking the continuous ping on Executive-PC1 makes this painfully evident:

```
PS C:\Users\Administrator> ping 172.31.70.254 -t

Pinging 172.31.70.254 with 32 bytes of data:
Reply from 172.31.70.254: bytes=32 time<1ms TTL=255
Reply from 172.31.70.254: bytes=32 time=1ms TTL=255
Request timed out.
Request timed out.
Request timed out.
Request timed out.
Request timed out.
Request timed out.
Reply from 172.31.70.254: bytes=32 time=2ms TTL=255
Reply from 172.31.70.254: bytes=32 time=1ms TTL=255
```

Although six ping time-outs isn't earth-shattering, it's something users would certainly notice. More importantly, Spanning Tree does its job, as indicated by the eventual success of the pings. You can further verify this by checking the Spanning Tree status again.

Try it now

Verify that FastEthernet0/23 is back in a forwarding state:

```
Show spanning-tree vlan 700
```

You should see this output:

```
Switch2#sh spanning-tree vlan 700

VLAN0700
  Spanning Tree enabled protocol ieee
  Root ID    Priority    33468
             Address     0023.ab40.8e00
             Cost        19
             Port        25 (FastEthernet0/23)
             Hello Time   2 sec  Max Age 20 sec  Forward Delay 15 sec

  Bridge ID  Priority    33468  (priority 32768 sys-id-ext 700)
             Address     0024.5088.6d80
             Hello Time   2 sec  Max Age 20 sec  Forward Delay 15 sec
             Aging Time  15  sec

Interface           Role Sts Cost      Prio.Nbr Type
------------------- ---- --- --------- -------- ----
Fa0/21              Desg FWD 19          128.23   P2p
Fa0/23              Root FWD 19          128.25   P2p
Fa0/24              Altn BLK 19          128.26   P2p
```

Now you can see everything's back to the way it was immediately after you originally set up the redundant connection.

Above and beyond

Again, I'm not going to get into the dirty details of how Spanning Tree works or why. Just know that, by default, Spanning Tree comes with this 30-second delay. The delay is twice the value of the *forward delay timer*, and it's possible to shorten this delay to as little as 8 seconds by adjusting the forward delay timer to 4 seconds using the command `spanning-tree vlan 1-4094 forward-time 4`.

You or the powers that be in your organization might find the 30-second delay unacceptable. In that case, you have another option.

12.2   Rapid Spanning Tree

As you might have guessed, *Rapid Spanning Tree Protocol (RSTP)* does the same thing as Spanning Tree; it just does it faster. The biggest downside is that you have to manually enable it on all the switches that you want to use it. As a general rule, I recommend using RSTP whenever possible. But if your organization won't allow it, or if you're just not comfortable doing it, there's absolutely no harm in sticking with regular old Spanning Tree.

> **Try it now**
>
> Enable Rapid Spanning Tree on Switch1 and Switch2 by issuing the following configuration mode command:
>
> ```
> spanning-tree mode rapid-pvst
> ```
>
> Verify with a show spanning-tree vlan 700.

You should see the following familiar-looking output:

```
Switch2#sh spanning-tree vlan 700
```

Notice that the output doesn't look very different:

```
VLAN0700
  Spanning Tree enabled protocol rstp                    ◁───┐ Rapid Spanning
  Root ID    Priority    33468                                │ Tree is enabled.
             Address     0023.ab40.8e00
             Cost        19
             Port        25 (FastEthernet0/23)
             Hello Time  2 sec  Max Age 20 sec  Forward Delay 15 sec

  Bridge ID  Priority    33468  (priority 32768 sys-id-ext 700)
             Address     0024.5088.6d80
             Hello Time  2 sec  Max Age 20 sec  Forward Delay 15 sec
             Aging Time  300 sec

Interface           Role Sts Cost      Prio.Nbr Type
------------------- ---- --- --------- -------- ----
Fa0/21              Desg FWD 19         128.23   P2p
Fa0/23              Root FWD 19         128.25   P2p
Fa0/24              Altn BLK 19         128.26   P2p
```

The biggest difference is a subtle one: Spanning Tree enabled protocol is rstp—Rapid Spanning Tree Protocol. To really appreciate the difference, you need to see how it behaves when the active link fails.

> **Try it now**
>
> Shut down interface FastEthernet0/23 on Switch2:
>
> ```
> Int fa0/23
> Shut
> ```
>
> Issue a show spanning-tree vlan 700.

Without any noticeable delay, you should see FastEthernet0/24 in the forwarding state:

```
Switch2#sh spanning-tree vlan 700

VLAN0700
  Spanning Tree enabled protocol rstp
  Root ID    Priority    33468
             Address     0023.ab40.8e00
             Cost        19
             Port        26 (FastEthernet0/24)
             Hello Time   2 sec  Max Age 20 sec  Forward Delay 15 sec

  Bridge ID  Priority    33468  (priority 32768 sys-id-ext 700)
             Address     0024.5088.6d80
             Hello Time   2 sec  Max Age 20 sec  Forward Delay 15 sec
             Aging Time  300 sec

Interface          Role Sts Cost      Prio.Nbr Type
------------------ ---- --- --------- -------- ----
Fa0/21             Desg BLK 19        128.23   P2p
Fa0/24             Root FWD 19        128.26   P2p
```

If you bring FastEthernet0/23 back up, you should see Rapid Spanning Tree respond just as quickly.

Try it now

Bring FastEthernet0/23 back up:

```
Int fa0/23
No shut
```

As fast as your fingers can type, do another `show spanning-tree vlan 700`.

You should see everything back to normal:

```
Switch2#show spanning-tree vlan 700

VLAN0700
  Spanning Tree enabled protocol rstp
  Root ID    Priority    33468
             Address     0023.ab40.8e00
             Cost        19
             Port        25 (FastEthernet0/23)
             Hello Time   2 sec  Max Age 20 sec  Forward Delay 15 sec

  Bridge ID  Priority    33468  (priority 32768 sys-id-ext 700)
             Address     0024.5088.6d80
             Hello Time   2 sec  Max Age 20 sec  Forward Delay 15 sec
             Aging Time  300 sec

Interface          Role Sts Cost      Prio.Nbr Type
------------------ ---- --- --------- -------- ----
Fa0/21             Desg BLK 19        128.23   P2p
Fa0/23             Root FWD 19        128.25   P2p
Fa0/24             Altn BLK 19        128.26   P2p
```

FastEthernet0/23 is once again in the forwarding state. Notice that Spanning Tree seems to prefer FastEthernet0/23 whenever it's available. By default, all Spanning Tree implementations, Rapid or otherwise, will select the lowest numbered port.

You might be thinking that this still isn't an optimal configuration. You have redundant connections, but it costs you a port on each switch. It would be nice to be able to use both connections simultaneously without encountering a bridging loop. In the next chapter, I'll show you how to achieve this.

12.3   PortFast

Because Spanning Tree attempts to prevent bridging loops, it operates on all ports, not just those connected to switches. This has some interesting implications for end-user devices like PCs and IP phones. In an organizational environment, this becomes quite obvious when a user reboots and can't get on the network for about 30 seconds. The act of rebooting a PC (and certainly turning it off and back on) causes the network interface card (NIC) to reset, which to the switch looks like someone unplugged the Ethernet cable and plugged it back in.

> **Try it now**
>
> On Executive-PC1, start a continuous ping to the VLAN 700 SVI:
>
> ```
> ping 172.31.70.254 -t
> ```
>
> On Switch2, bounce the FastEthernet0/21 interface connected to Executive-PC1:
>
> ```
> Int fa0/21
> Shut
> No shut
> ```

On Executive-PC1, you should see something like this:

```
PS C:\Users\Administrator> ping 172.31.70.254 -t

Pinging 172.31.70.254 with 32 bytes of data:
Reply from 172.31.70.254: bytes=32 time<1ms TTL=255
Request timed out.
Request timed out.
Request timed out.
Reply from 172.31.70.50: Destination host unreachable.
Reply from 172.31.70.50: Destination host unreachable.
Reply from 172.31.70.50: Destination host unreachable.
Request timed out.
Reply from 172.31.70.50: Destination host unreachable.
Request timed out.
Reply from 172.31.70.50: Destination host unreachable.
Reply from 172.31.70.254: bytes=32 time=2ms TTL=255
Reply from 172.31.70.254: bytes=32 time=1ms TTL=255
Reply from 172.31.70.254: bytes=32 time=1ms TTL=255
```

There's a single successful ping, followed by a series of failures, and then finally successful pings again. Spanning Tree doesn't know what's connected to that port, so it waits a long time (30 seconds) to make sure that forwarding traffic across that port won't cause a bridging loop.

As brilliant as Spanning Tree is, it's not human, and it's not smart enough to quickly figure out that the only thing connected to that port is a PC. Fortunately, you, being the smart network administrator you are, can tell Spanning Tree not to wait to place the port into a forwarding state.

Cisco switches have as part of their Spanning Tree implementations a feature called *PortFast*. It's an appropriate name, given that it causes Spanning Tree to enable the port—fast.

Try it now

Enable PortFast on FastEthernet0/21:

```
Int fa0/21
Spanning-tree portfast
```

You should get a scary-looking warning:

```
Switch2(config-if)#spanning-tree portfast
%Warning: portfast should only be enabled on ports connected to a single
 host. Connecting hubs, concentrators, switches, bridges, etc... to this
 interface when portfast is enabled, can cause temporary bridging loops.
 Use with CAUTION

%Portfast has been configured on FastEthernet0/21 but will only
 have effect when the interface is in a non-trunking mode.
```

Translated into non-geek, the warning means that you should never enable PortFast on an interface connected to a switch. If you do, it could cause a bridging loop because it effectively disables Spanning Tree on that port.

By the way, enabling PortFast on an interface has the same effect whether you're using STP or RSTP. Now that you've enabled PortFast, it's time to test it out.

Try it now

On Executive-PC1, restart a continuous ping to the VLAN 700 SVI:

```
ping 172.31.70.254 -t
```

On Switch2, bounce the FastEthernet0/21 interface connected to Executive-PC1:

```
Int fa0/21
Shut
No shut
```

You should see no more than one dropped ping:

```
PS C:\Users\Administrator> ping 172.31.70.254 -t

Pinging 172.31.70.254 with 32 bytes of data:
Reply from 172.31.70.254: bytes=32 time=1ms TTL=255
Reply from 172.31.70.254: bytes=32 time=1ms TTL=255
Reply from 172.31.70.254: bytes=32 time=1ms TTL=255
Request timed out.
Reply from 172.31.70.254: bytes=32 time=1ms TTL=255
Reply from 172.31.70.254: bytes=32 time=1ms TTL=255
Reply from 172.31.70.254: bytes=32 time<1ms TTL=255
```

Most users wouldn't even notice this split-second blip in network connectivity. Although you certainly don't have to enable PortFast on ports connected to end-user devices, it can potentially save you the occasional gripe from a user who has rebooted or kicked a network cable loose.

12.4   *Commands in this chapter*

Although you didn't learn a lot of new commands in this chapter, the few you did learn are powerful, so it's important to be clear on what each one does. Refer to table 12.1 for a refresher.

Table 12.1   Commands used in this chapter

Command	Configuration mode	Description
show spanning-tree vlan 700	N/A	Displays information about the current (R)STP configuration
spanning-tree mode rapid-pvst	Global	Enables Rapid Spanning Tree globally
spanning-tree portfast	Interface	Enables PortFast, causing (R)STP to place the port into a forwarding state immediately

Remember, regular Spanning Tree (STP) is enabled by default. It's stable and works fine, but in the event of a topology change (for example, a link between switches going down) it can take about 30 seconds for STP to catch up. Rapid Spanning Tree (RSTP) doesn't take as long, hence the name, which is why I recommend using it whenever possible.

12.5   *Hands-on lab*

1 Enable PortFast on the port connected to HR-PC1.
2 Physically disconnect the Ethernet cable connected to one of the FastEthernet0/23 ports (it doesn't matter which). Can Executive-PC1 ping 172.31.70.254?
3 Physically disconnect the cable connected to FastEthernet0/24. Can Executive-PC1 still ping 172.31.70.254?
4 Reconnect both cables and save your configurations!

Optimizing network performance by using port channels

Remember from the last chapter that you have two connections between Switch1 and Switch2, and that the Spanning Tree Protocol (STP) allows traffic to traverse only one of those links. This prevents bridging loops but has a downside: it consumes an additional port on each switch without letting you use the bandwidth of those ports.

A *port channel*—also known as an *EtherChannel*—lets you have the best of both worlds. It allows traffic to flow simultaneously across both links while still preventing bridging loops.

As you go through this chapter, you'll learn how to configure a port channel to achieve the configuration shown in figure 13.1.

Notice that the port channel consists of FastEthernet0/23 and 0/24 and is called Port-channel1. When you configure a port channel on a switch, the switch creates a logical or virtual interface to represent the port channel.

In keeping with Cisco tradition, a port channel may also be called an *EtherChannel*, a *bundle*, or a *port group*. I'll use the term *port channel* most of the time, but in the configuration commands and output, you'll see some of these other terms pop up.

As you spend more time learning how to administer Cisco networks, you'll begin to notice that there are often multiple ways to achieve the same result. Which particular method you use depends not so much on the result you want to achieve but on how long it will take and how scalable it will be. Port channel configuration is no different.

171

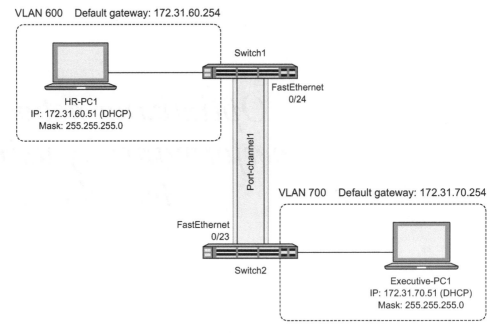

Figure 13.1   Port channel between Switch1 and Switch2

Think back to chapter 10 when you configured VLAN trunks between your switches. The Dynamic Trunking Protocol (DTP), which is enabled by default on Catalyst switches, made it possible for you to set up a trunk by configuring a switch on only one end of the link.

You can't get away with that with port channels. Unlike VLAN trunks, the only way to get a port channel up and going is to touch both switches.

13.1 *Static or dynamic?*

Before setting out to configure a port channel, you need to decide how you want to go about it. When it comes to configuring a port channel between Cisco switches, you have two basic options: static or dynamic.

13.1.1 *Static*

A static port channel is analogous to an unconditional VLAN trunk port. A switch configured with an unconditional trunk port has no regard for how the switch on the other end is configured. In the same way, a static port channel binds two or more physical ports into a single logical port channel interface regardless of what the switch on the other end is doing.

The big downside to this is that it creates a tremendous potential for bridging loops and dropping or "black-holing" traffic. I'll get into more detail on this later in the chapter, but when you configure a port channel, it hides the physical interfaces from Spanning Tree so that Spanning Tree can no longer place any of the individual interfaces into a blocked state.

The upside to creating a static port channel is that a quick glance at the running configuration makes it abundantly clear that there is a port channel, as well as which physical ports it comprises.

13.1.2 Dynamic

A dynamic port channel is somewhat analogous to negotiating a VLAN trunk using DTP. But there are two big differences.

The first difference is that there isn't just one protocol that can negotiate a port channel. There are two: the *Link Aggregation Control Protocol (LACP)* and Cisco's *Port Aggregation Protocol (PAgP)*. In this chapter, I cover only LACP because it's the most widely used.

The second difference is that unlike DTP, LACP and PAgP aren't enabled by default. You still have to touch both switches, and you have to specify which protocol you want to use.

The big advantage of using LACP or PAgP is that they perform sanity-checking to ensure that a port channel will work properly before actually creating it. This is similar to how DTP does its own checking before creating a VLAN trunk. By providing this sanity-checking, these dynamic protocols ensure your port channel won't black-hole traffic or create bridging loops.

The relatively small disadvantage of the dynamic protocols is that they entail a slight initial delay, which you'll witness in a moment when you configure a port channel using LACP.

13.2   Configuring a dynamic port channel using the Link Aggregation Control Protocol

Creating a port channel dynamically using the Link Aggregation Control Protocol is the most common method, so you'll start with that. Using LACP to dynamically form a port channel is so common that in the minds of many, the terms *LACP* and *port channel* are synonymous. By understanding the subtle distinction between a port channel and one of the protocols used to negotiate it—LACP—you'll be well ahead of the pack.

To reiterate, the Link Aggregation Control Protocol is just that—a protocol. You configure it on two switches, and it works to establish a port channel between those switches. Simply configuring LACP doesn't guarantee that you'll end up with a working port channel.

Try it now

On Switch1 and Switch2, issue the following commands:

```
interface range fa0/23-24
channel-group 1 mode active
```

(continued)

The active keyword indicates that you want to use LACP, as opposed to PAgP or a static port channel.

Among a slew of output, you should see this on both switches:

```
*Mar  2 04:26:38.669: %LINK-3-UPDOWN: Interface Port-channel1, changed state
    to up
*Mar  2 04:26:39.676: %LINEPROTO-5-UPDOWN: Line protocol on Interface Port-
    channel1, changed state to up
```

Notice that the Port-channel1 interface doesn't come up until you issue the commands on both switches. This is because all you did was configure LACP to try to negotiate a port channel. In order for LACP to do that, you must configure both Switch1 and Switch2 to speak to each other using LACP. Before either switch creates the Port-channel1 interface, both switches must explicitly agree with each other via LACP to form an EtherChannel before either of them actually does it.

Once the port channel comes up, you can verify which specific ports are parts of the EtherChannel.

Try it now

On Switch1 and Switch2, issue a show etherchannel summary.

You should see this:

```
Switch2#show etherchannel summary
Flags:  D - down         P - bundled in port-channel
        I - stand-alone  s - suspended
        H - Hot-standby (LACP only)
        R - Layer3       S - Layer2
        U - in use       f - failed to allocate aggregator

        M - not in use, minimum links not met
        u - unsuitable for bundling
        w - waiting to be aggregated
        d - default port


Number of channel-groups in use: 1
Number of aggregators:           1

Group  Port-channel  Protocol    Ports
------+-------------+-----------+--------------------
1      Po1(SU)       LACP        Fa0/23(P)   Fa0/24(P)
```

Notice that the protocol is LACP. Both physical ports, FastEthernet0/23 and 0/24, are part of the bundle.

Another reliable way to verify the presence of a port channel is to check Spanning Tree.

The output should differ slightly from what you saw earlier:

```
Switch2#sh spanning-tree vlan 700

VLAN0700
  Spanning tree enabled protocol rstp
  Root ID      Priority      33468
               Address       0023.ab40.8e00
               Cost          12
               Port          64 (Port-channel1)
               Hello Time    2 sec  Max Age 20 sec  Forward Delay 15 sec

  Bridge ID  Priority      33468  (priority 32768 sys-id-ext 700)
             Address       0024.5088.6d80
             Hello Time    2 sec  Max Age 20 sec  Forward Delay 15 sec
             Aging Time    300 sec

Interface           Role Sts Cost      Prio.Nbr Type
------------------- ---- --- --------- -------- ----
Fa0/21              Desg FWD 19        128.23   P2p Edge
Po1                 Root FWD 12        128.64   P2p
```

Notice that FastEthernet0/23 and 0/24 don't show up here. Only Po1—short for Port-channel1—appears. As I said earlier, the port channel hides the physical ports from Spanning Tree.

If this configuration seems ridiculously easy, it's because it is. LACP does the dirty work of making sure everything is in order before attempting to bring up a port channel. To really appreciate this, it helps to contrast it with a static configuration. But before you can do that, you need to get things back to square one by deleting the existing port channel.

This command might seem a bit strange because it deletes an interface. But remember that Port-channel1 is (or was) a virtual interface. It's an abstraction of two physical interfaces: FastEthernet0/23 and 0/24.

When you delete the port channel interface, IOS does something that you probably wouldn't expect. It shuts down those interfaces!

You should see the following:

```
Switch2#show run int fa0/23
interface FastEthernet0/23
 shutdown
end

Switch2#show run int fa0/24
interface FastEthernet0/24
 shutdown
end
```

It goes without saying that you're not going to have a port channel with both member interfaces shut down. To verify that the port channel is truly gone for good, you need to re-enable the physical interfaces.

You should no longer see the port channel:

```
Switch2#show etherchannel summary
Flags:  D - down         P - bundled in port-channel
        I - stand-alone  s - suspended
        H - Hot-standby (LACP only)
        R - Layer3       S - Layer2
        U - in use       f - failed to allocate aggregator

        M - not in use, minimum links not met
        u - unsuitable for bundling
        w - waiting to be aggregated
        d - default port
```

```
Number of channel-groups in use: 0
Number of aggregators:           0

Group  Port-channel  Protocol    Ports
------+------------+-----------+-----
```

Now that the port channel is completely gone, you're ready to reconfigure it statically.

13.3 *Creating a static port channel*

Configuring a static port channel is just as easy as using LACP, but it doesn't provide you the same sanity checks and protection that LACP does. Given that, you might question why anyone would even dream of creating a static port channel.

Generally, there are two main reasons. First, some organizations don't like the idea of using dynamic protocols. If possible, they avoid DTP, LACP, and anything else that has the ability to dynamically alter the network without direct human intervention. The second reason is that if you need to create a port channel between a Cisco switch and an older switch that doesn't support LACP or PAgP, then a static port channel is the only option.

If you want (or have) to go the static route, the *EtherChannel Misconfiguration Guard* feature provides some protection against bridging loops caused by a misconfigured port channel. It's enabled by default.

> **Try it now**
>
> On Switch1 and Switch2, ensure that EtherChannel Misconfiguration Guard is enabled:
>
> ```
> spanning-tree etherchannel guard misconfig
> ```
>
> Configure a static port channel:
>
> ```
> interface range fa0/23-24
> channel-group 1 mode on
> ```
>
> Verify with a show etherchannel summary.

You should get this familiar output:

```
Switch2#sh etherchannel summary
Flags:  D - down        P - bundled in port-channel
        I - stand-alone s - suspended
        H - Hot-standby (LACP only)
        R - Layer3       S - Layer2
        U - in use       f - failed to allocate aggregator

        M - not in use, minimum links not met
        u - unsuitable for bundling
        w - waiting to be aggregated
        d - default port
```

```
Number of channel-groups in use: 1
Number of aggregators:           1

Group  Port-channel  Protocol     Ports
------+-------------+-----------+--------------------
1      Po1(SU)          -         Fa0/23(P)   Fa0/24(P)
```

It's almost identical to what you saw before, but this time the `Protocol` column is empty because you're not using LACP or PAgP. The port channel, however, is still up and FastEthernet0/23 and 0/24 are members of it.

This might seem a bit too perfect. After my dire warning about possibly creating bridging loops, so far everything seems to be humming along smoothly. So let's make things interesting. Let's break something!

Try it now

On Switch1 only, delete the port channel:

```
No interface po1
```

Remember that when you delete a port channel interface, IOS shuts down the physical member interfaces: FastEthernet0/23 and 0/24. Bring them back up:

```
Int range fa0/23-24
No shut
```

On Switch1, you won't get any output indicating a problem. And on Switch1, nothing obvious will happen at first. But after about a minute, you may see this error indicating a bridging loop:

```
*Mar  1 00:50:03.809: %SW_MATM-4-MACFLAP_NOTIF: Host 2c27.d737.9ad1 in vlan
    700 is flapping between port Fa0/21 and port Po1
```

Almost another minute later, EtherChannel Misconfiguration Guard will kick in and shut down the port channel:

```
*Mar  1 00:50:31.265: %PM-4-ERR_DISABLE: channel-misconfig (STP) error
    detected on Po1, putting Po1 in err-disable state
```

The `channel-misconfig (STP) error detected` message indicates that the Ether-Channel Misconfiguration Guard feature detected a bridging loop and shut down the port channel interface.

To sharpen the distinction between creating a port channel statically versus using LACP, note that it took about two minutes for EtherChannel Misconfiguration Guard to shut down the port channel. In a live network, this could have resulted in two minutes of downtime or at least very poor network performance. LACP, on the other hand, would have detected the problem and shut down the port channel immediately.

To get the port channel back up, you need to re-create the port channel on Switch1 and get FastEthernet0/23 and 0/24 out of error-disabled state on Switch2.

> **Try it now**
>
> On Switch1, issue the following configuration commands to re-create the port channel:
>
> ```
> interface range fa0/23-24
> channel-group 1 mode on
> ```
>
> On Switch2, bounce FastEthernet0/23 and 0/24 to get them out of the error-disabled state:
>
> ```
> Int po1
> Shutdown
> No shutdown
> ```

You should see the port channel come back up on both switches.

13.4 Load-balancing methods

At the beginning of the chapter, I said that a port channel allows traffic to flow simultaneously across both links. The port channel you just configured will allow traffic to simultaneously traverse FastEthernet0/23 and 0/24. But the way that traffic passes over those links is anything but indiscriminate.

To understand how a port channel decides which individual link to send traffic across, look at figure 13.2.

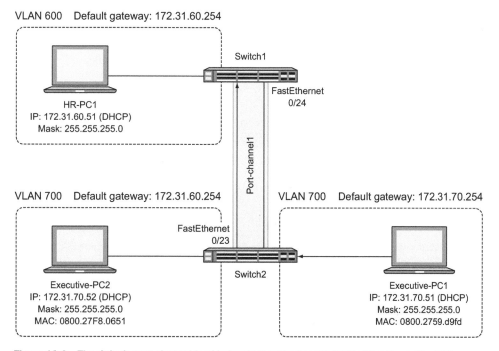

Figure 13.2   The default port channel load-balancing method sends traffic from Executive-PC1 across the FastEthernet0/23 link.

Notice that I've added an additional computer to VLAN 700. Don't worry about adding another computer to your topology. The purpose here is to just show you how port channels forward traffic.

By default, all port channels forward traffic based on the source MAC address of the frame. Notice that traffic from Executive-PC1—with a source MAC address of 0800.2759.d9fd—goes over FastEthernet0/23. You don't need to understand the algorithm IOS uses to make this decision, but you should know how to find out which port it will send traffic out of given a particular source MAC address.

Try it now

On Switch2, issue the following command to determine which physical port traffic from Executive-PC1 (0800.2759.d9fd) would traverse:

```
test etherchannel load-balance interface port-channel 1 mac
0800.2759.d9fd ffff.ffff.ffff
```

You should get the following output:

```
Switch2#test etherchannel load-balance interface port-channel 1 mac
    0800.2759.d9fd ffff.ffff.ffff
Would select Fa0/23 of Po1
```

The output indicates that traffic from Executive-PC1 would egress FastEthernet0/23 *every single time*. This might seem to defeat the entire purpose of the port channel, which is to allow you to use the bandwidth of both links simultaneously. But on closer inspection, you can see that the port channel does use both links.

Try it now

On Switch2, issue the following command to determine which physical port traffic from Executive-PC2 (0800.27F8.0651) would traverse:

```
test etherchannel load-balance interface port-channel 1 mac
0800.27F8.0651 ffff.ffff.ffff
```

You should see the following output:

```
Switch2#test etherchannel load-balance interface port-channel 1 mac
    0800.27F8.0651 ffff.ffff.ffff
Would select Fa0/24 of Po1
```

Traffic from Executive-PC2 would traverse the other link, FastEthernet0/24, as shown in figure 13.3.

This is exactly how the port channel uses both links simultaneously: by performing load balancing (or, more accurately, load sharing) based on the source MAC address.

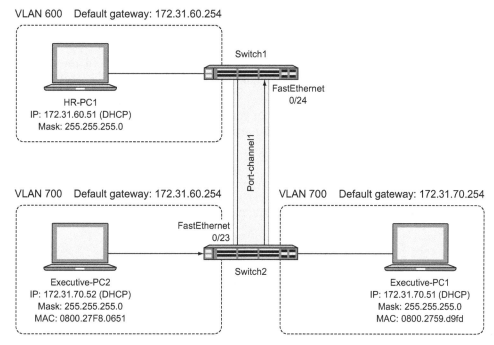

Figure 13.3   The default port channel load-balancing method sends traffic from Executive-PC2 across the FastEthernet0/24 link.

As a general rule, you won't change the default load-balancing method, even though you can. If you ever run into any unexpected behavior, or if you get unexpected output, you can verify the configured load-balancing method.

Try it now

On Switch1 and Switch2, verify the current load-balancing method with the following command:

```
Show etherchannel load-balance
```

You should see the following:

```
Switch2#show etherchannel load-balance
EtherChannel Load-Balancing Configuration:
        src-mac

EtherChannel Load-Balancing Addresses Used Per-Protocol:
Non-IP: Source MAC address
  IPv4: Source MAC address
  IPv6: Source MAC address
```

That lone `src-mac` in the output is short for "source MAC"—the currently configured load-balancing method. Keep in mind that the methods don't have to match on both switches. Mismatched load-balancing methods won't necessarily cause any problems, but they can, depending on the particulars of the network. In the worst case, you wouldn't be able to utilize the full bandwidth of the port channel, and network performance would suffer.

Again, I want to emphasize that you shouldn't change the load-balancing method under normal circumstances. But I also recognize that someone else might change it, so you need to know how to change it back to the default.

Try it now

On Switch1, set the load-balancing method to `src-mac`:

```
port-channel load-balance src-mac
```

That command might take you by surprise because it doesn't include the keywords `etherchannel` or `channel-group`. As usual, rely on the inline help to guide you when you can't remember the syntax of the command.

13.5   Commands in this chapter

Refer to table 13.1 for a refresher of this chapter's commands.

Table 13.1   Commands used in this chapter

Command	Configuration mode	Description
`interface range fa0/23-24`	Global	Selects FastEthernet0/23 and 0/24 for configuration
`channel-group 1 mode active`	Interface	Enables LACP on the selected port(s)
`show etherchannel summary`	N/A	Displays information on configured port channels
`no interface port-channel 1`	Global	Deletes the Port-channel 1 interface
`spanning-tree etherchannel guard misconfig`	Global	Enables EtherChannel Misconfiguration Guard
`channel-group 1 mode on`	Interface	Creates a static port channel using the selected port(s) as members
`test etherchannel load-balance interface port-channel 1 mac 0800.2759.d9fd ffff.ffff.ffff`	N/A	Displays which member interface traffic from 0800.2759.d9fd to the broadcast address will egress
`show etherchannel load-balance`	N/A	Displays the configured load-balancing method

Table 13.1 Commands used in this chapter

Command	Configuration mode	Description
`port-channel load-balance` `src-mac`	Global	Sets the load-balancing method to `src-mac`

13.6 *Hands-on lab*

In this lab, you'll re-create your port channel one more time using LACP, but this time you'll add an additional link. Follow these steps to complete the lab.

1 Delete the existing port channel on Switch1 and Switch2.
2 Connect FastEthernet0/22 on both switches.
3 Use LACP to create a port channel consisting of FastEthernet0/22, 0/23, and 0/24.

Making the network
scalable by connecting
routers and switches together

Right now, Switch1 routes IP traffic between two subnets: 172.31.60.0/24 in VLAN 600 and 172.31.70.0/24 in VLAN 700. This is a common and perfectly acceptable configuration. But there are times when you'll want to route inter-VLAN traffic using an additional device: a router.

In one case, you may run into a network that just doesn't have any routers or layer-3 switches. It's unlikely that such a network would be using VLANs to begin with, because there wouldn't already be any way to route between them. Hence, if you walk into an organization that needed VLANs set up, but all they have are some layer-2 switches and a router, then the only way to route traffic between VLANs is to use a router.

This specific use case for a router is becoming less and less common as layer-3 switches become more ubiquitous. But organizations of all sizes use routers heavily for other critical functions, including network connectivity between offices and connecting IP phones to the public switched telephone network (PSTN). That's why, as a Cisco network administrator, it's important that you have a clear and correct understanding of how these devices function.

In this chapter, I give you a gentle introduction to connecting and configuring routers to perform *inter-VLAN routing*. Later in the book, you'll learn about more advanced topics including routing over a *wide area network (WAN)* and configuring dynamic routing protocols.

Here are the basic steps you'll be performing in this chapter:

1 Connect the router to Switch1.
2 Create a VLAN trunk between Switch1 and Router1.
3 Configure Router1 to route between VLANs.

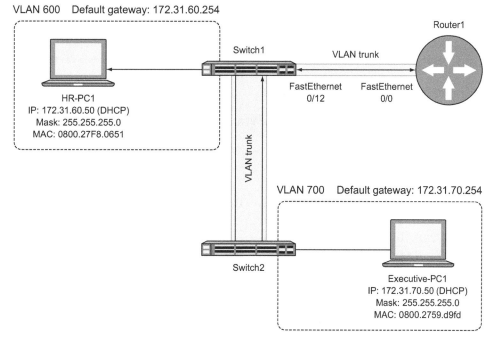

Figure 14.1 Router-on-a-stick configuration

14.1 *The router-on-a-stick configuration*

In this chapter, you're going to create what network folks colloquially call a *router-on-a-stick configuration*. The term *router-on-a-stick* might sound like a not-so-tasty snack idea from the ash heap of fast-food history. But as you can see in figure 14.1, it's just a way of describing how you'd physically connect a router to a switch.

Router1 is physically connected to Switch1 using a single Ethernet connection. This single connection is the *stick* part of the *router-on-a-stick* term. Also notice that there's a VLAN trunk configured between Switch1 and Router1. This trunk is what allows traffic from both VLAN 600 and 700 to reach Router1 so that it can perform inter-VLAN routing.

Above and beyond

You may hear someone refer to a physical Ethernet connection between devices as a layer-1 connection, referring to the Physical layer of the Open Systems Interconnect (OSI) model. The VLAN trunk operates at layer 2—the Data Link layer—the same layer where MAC addresses and the Address Resolution Protocol (ARP) function. I'm not going into the fine details of the OSI model in this book, but refer to https://www.manning.com/books/learn-cisco-network-administration-in-a-month-of-lunches for more information.

Recall that Switch1 has two switched virtual interfaces (SVIs): one for VLAN 600 with an IP of 172.31.60.254/24 and another for VLAN 700 with an IP of 172.31.70.254/24. Because Router1 will effectively replace Switch1 as the device that performs inter-VLAN routing between VLANs 600 and 700, you'll need to remove these SVIs from Switch1.

Try it now

On Switch1, remove the SVIs for VLANs 600 and 700:

```
no int vlan 600
no int vlan 700
```

Removing the SVIs not only removes the virtual interfaces; it also eliminates the corresponding IP addresses from existence. Recall that Executive-PC1 is configured to use 172.31.70.254 as its default gateway, whereas HR-PC1 is configured to use 172.31.60.254 as its default gateway. But as soon as you delete the SVIs for VLANs 600 and 700, those IP address cease to exist. The net effect is that devices in VLANs 600 and 700 can no longer communicate with each other. To remedy this, you'll connect and configure Router1 to do the job that Switch1 was doing until just now.

14.2 Connecting Router1

You should already have configured Router1 per the lab setup instructions of the online appendix. If you've done so, then Router1's FastEthernet0/0 interface will have an IP address of 192.168.1.201/24. You'll use this IP address to log into Router1 to configure it in a moment.

Try it now

Connect Router1's FastEthernet0/0 port to Switch1's FastEthernet0/12 port.
Power on Router1.
As you're waiting for Router1 to boot up, configure FastEthernet0/12 on Switch1 as an 802.1Q trunk port:

```
Interface f0/12
Switchport trunk encapsulation dot1q
Switchport mode trunk
```

To reiterate the earlier point, FastEthernet0/12 must be a trunk port so that traffic for VLANs 600 and 700 can traverse the single physical link going to Router1.

Try it now

Once Router1 has booted up, Telnet to it from Switch1:

```
telnet 192.168.1.201
```

Log in using the username "admin" and the password "cisco."

If you logged in successfully, you should see the `Router1#` prompt. You might be wondering how you're able to Telnet to Router1 from Switch1 before configuring the trunk on Router1. The answer lies in the output of the `show interfaces fa0/12 trunk` command on Switch1:

```
Switch1#show interfaces fa0/12 trunk

Port      Mode          Encapsulation  Status      Native vlan
Fa0/12    on            802.1q         trunking    1
```

Notice that the `Native vlan` is 1. Without getting into the gritty details of 802.1Q encapsulation, this means that Switch1 sends VLAN 1's traffic out as if FastEthernet0/12 were a normal access port in VLAN 1. To see why this is significant, take a look at the IP address of Switch1's VLAN 1 SVI:

```
Switch1#show ip interface Vlan 1 | i Internet
  Internet address is 192.168.1.101/24   192.168.1.101  YES  NVRAM  up    up
```

It's in the same subnet as the IP address of Router1's FastEthernet0/0 interface, which is 192.168.1.201/24. Router1's interface is effectively just like the network interface on a PC. It's not trunked and has only one IP address.

> **Try it now**
> On Router1, view the IP information for all interfaces:
>
> ```
> show ip interface brief
> ```

You should see only one IP address:

```
Router1#show ip interface brief
Interface        IP-Address       OK? Method Status                 Protocol
FastEthernet0/0  192.168.1.201    YES NVRAM  up                     up
FastEthernet0/1  unassigned       YES NVRAM  administratively down  down
```

What's missing here? In order for Router1 to act as the default gateway for the 172.31.60.0/24 (VLAN 600) and 172.31.70.0/24 (VLAN 700) subnets, it needs an IP address in each of these subnets. But you can't assign three different IP addresses to the FastEthernet0/0 interface. You could use the FastEthernet0/1 interface, but that would consume another port on Switch1. And instead of being a router on a stick, Router1 would be a router on two sticks. The solution is to configure a subinterface on Router1 for each VLAN and subnet.

14.3 Configuring subinterfaces

Conceptually, a subinterface on a router is similar to an SVI on a switch in that it's a virtual interface that resides in a single VLAN and can have its own IP address. But that's where the similarities end. Table 14.1 lists the subinterfaces you'll be configuring on Router1.

Table 14.1   Router1's (sub)interfaces, IP addresses, and corresponding VLANs

(Sub)interface	IP address	VLAN
FastEthernet0/0	192.168.1.201/24	1
FastEthernet0/0.600	172.31.60.254/24	600
FastEthernet0/0.700	172.31.70.254/24	700

Notice that the subinterfaces share the name of the physical parent interfaces. The name of each subinterface must be the name of the physical parent interface followed by a dot (.) and a unique number between 0 and 4294967295. It's important to note that the number of the subinterface has no inherent relationship to the VLAN. Instead, you have to specify the VLAN manually within the subinterface configuration.

Try it now

Create the subinterface FastEthernet0/0.600:

`Interface FastEthernet0/0.600`

Configure the subinterface to be a member of VLAN 600:

`encapsulation dot1Q 600`

Assign the IP address 172.31.60.254/24:

`ip address 172.31.60.254 255.255.255.0`

Add a friendly description:

`description VLAN 600 subinterface to Switch1 fa0/12`

Verify with a `show interface fa0/0.600`.

You should see the IP and VLAN information you just configured:

```
Router1#show int fa0/0.600
FastEthernet0/0.600 is up, line protocol is up
  Hardware is Gt96k FE, address is 0015.fa64.76d2 (bia 0015.fa64.76d2)
  Description: VLAN 600 subinterface to Switch1 fa0/12
  Internet address is 172.31.60.254/24
  MTU 1500 bytes, BW 100000 Kbit, DLY 100 usec,
     reliability 255/255, txload 1/255, rxload 1/255
  Encapsulation 802.1Q Virtual LAN, Vlan ID  600.
  ARP type: ARPA, ARP Timeout 04:00:00
  Last clearing of "show interface" counters never
```

Notice that the description you added to the configuration shows up as well. The description isn't necessary for the configuration, but you may find it helpful if you ever forget what the subinterface is for. You can use the `description` keyword on switch interfaces, too!

Creating a subinterface for VLAN 600 and assigning it an IP address provides a way for devices in VLAN 600 to route IP traffic to different subnets. But in order to perform inter-VLAN routing, Router1 also needs a subinterface in VLAN 700, along with a corresponding IP address for that subnet.

Try it now

Configure the subinterface for VLAN 700:

```
interface FastEthernet0/0.700
Encapsulation dot1q 700
Ip address 172.31.70.254 255.255.255.0
Description VLAN 700 subinterface to Switch1 fa0/12
```

Verify with a `show interface fa0/0.700`.

You should see the following:

```
Router1#show int fa0/0.700
FastEthernet0/0.700 is up, line protocol is up
  Hardware is Gt96k FE, address is 0015.fa64.76d2 (bia 0015.fa64.76d2)
  Description: VLAN 700 subinterface to Switch1 fa0/12
  Internet address is 172.31.70.254/24
  MTU 1500 bytes, BW 100000 Kbit, DLY 100 usec,
     reliability 255/255, txload 1/255, rxload 1/255
  Encapsulation 802.1Q Virtual LAN, Vlan ID  700.
  ARP type: ARPA, ARP Timeout 04:00:00
  Last clearing of "show interface" counters never
```

The next step is to verify that there is, in fact, a VLAN trunk between Router1 and Switch1.

Try it now

Issue the following commands on Router1 to verify that VLANs 600 and 700 are traversing the FastEthernet0/0 interface:

```
Show vlans 600
Show vlans 700
```

This is another area where routers and switches differ quite a bit. Notice that the output looks very unlike what you'd see when doing a `show vlan` on a switch. Here's what you should see:

```
Router1#show vlans 600

Virtual LAN ID:  600 (IEEE 802.1Q Encapsulation)

   vLAN Trunk Interface:   FastEthernet0/0.600
```

```
Protocols Configured:    Address:            Received:       Transmitted:
        IP               172.31.60.254          21                  0
      Other                                       0                  2
```

```
Router1#show vlans 700

Virtual LAN ID:  700 (IEEE 802.1Q Encapsulation)

  vLAN Trunk Interface:    FastEthernet0/0.700

    Protocols Configured:    Address:            Received:       Transmitted:
          IP                 172.31.70.254          191                64
        Other                                         0                16
```

I've truncated some of the output for brevity, but for each command you should see
the VLAN ID, the subinterface name, and the IP address. Don't worry if you don't see
anything greater than 0 under the `Received` or `Transmitted` column. You'll need
to generate some inter-VLAN traffic before those start going up. Recall that in chapter
8 you configured two DHCP scopes on Switch1, as shown in table 14.2.

Table 14.2   DHCP scopes, options, and lease times for each VLAN

VLAN	Subnet	Mask	Default gateway
600	172.31.60.0	255.255.255.0	172.31.60.254
700	172.31.70.0	255.255.255.0	172.31.70.254

You should recognize the default gateway IP addresses for each subnet. They're the
same addresses you just assigned to the subinterfaces on Router1. Hence, you should
be able to see that Executive-PC1 is using 172.31.70.254 as its default gateway.

Try it now
Issue an `ipconfig` on Executive-PC1.

The IP address may be different, but the default gateway IP should be the same as
shown:

```
PS C:\> ipconfig

Windows IP Configuration

Ethernet adapter Local Area Connection:

   Connection-specific DNS Suffix  . : benpiper.com
   Link-local IPv6 Address . . . . . : fe80::d8ae:58d6:2dc0:9450%11
   IPv4 Address. . . . . . . . . . . : 172.31.70.50
   Subnet Mask . . . . . . . . . . . : 255.255.255.0
   Default Gateway . . . . . . . . . : 172.31.70.254
```

Although it's not strictly necessary, you can save yourself some troubleshooting by making sure that you can ping Router1's FastEthernet0/0.700 interface.

Try it now

On Executive-PC1, ping 172.31.70.254.

If everything's configured right, you should get a response:

```
PS C:\> ping 172.31.70.254

Pinging 172.31.70.254 with 32 bytes of data:
Reply from 172.31.70.254: bytes=32 time=1ms TTL=255
Reply from 172.31.70.254: bytes=32 time=1ms TTL=255
Reply from 172.31.70.254: bytes=32 time=1ms TTL=255
Reply from 172.31.70.254: bytes=32 time=1ms TTL=255
```

This proves that the VLAN 700 connection between Switch1 and Router1 is working. But the purpose of the router is to perform routing between VLANs 600 and 700. A simple way to verify that inter-VLAN routing works is to ping a host in one VLAN from a host in a different VLAN.

Try it now

From Executive-PC1, ping HR-PC1 (172.31.60.50).

You should get a reply from HR-PC1:

```
PS C:\> ping 172.31.60.50

Pinging 172.31.60.50 with 32 bytes of data:
Reply from 172.31.60.50: bytes=32 time=1ms TTL=127
Reply from 172.31.60.50: bytes=32 time=1ms TTL=127
Reply from 172.31.60.50: bytes=32 time=2ms TTL=127
Reply from 172.31.60.50: bytes=32 time=1ms TTL=127
```

Pinging between hosts in different VLANs isn't particularly exciting. Even worse, the sheer amount of text-based output you have to look at can make your eyes glaze over, and forget about all the details that are happening under the hood. Figure 14.2 illustrates the details of what happens when you ping HR-PC1 from Executive-PC1.

In step 1, Executive-PC1 creates an IP packet with a ping request inside it. It encapsulates that packet inside an Ethernet frame addressed to Router1's MAC address—0015.fa64.76d2—and sends it out onto VLAN 700. Because Router1's FastEthernet0/0.700 subinterface is in VLAN 700, it receives the Ethernet frame.

In step 2, Router1 takes the IP packet and stuffs it into a new Ethernet frame addressed to HR-PC1's MAC address—0800.27f8.0651. It sends this frame out of its FastEthernet0/0.600 interface onto VLAN 600, where HR-PC1 receives it.

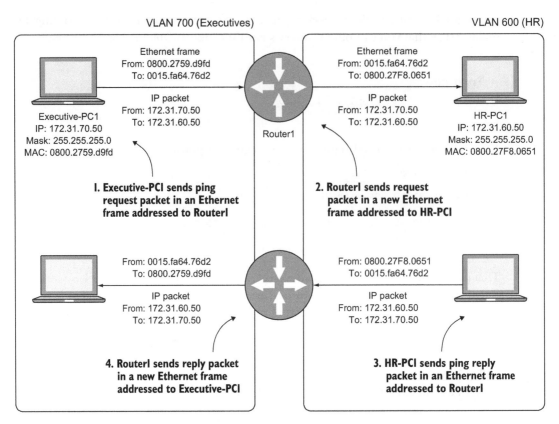

VLAN 700 (Executives)

VLAN 600 (HR)

Ethernet frame
From: 0800.2759.d9fd
To: 0015.fa64.76d2

IP packet
From: 172.31.70.50
To: 172.31.60.50

Ethernet frame
From: 0015.fa64.76d2
To: 0800.27F8.0651

IP packet
From: 172.31.70.50
To: 172.31.60.50

Executive-PC1
IP: 172.31.70.50
Mask: 255.255.255.0
MAC: 0800.2759.d9fd

Router1

HR-PC1
IP: 172.31.60.50
Mask: 255.255.255.0
MAC: 0800.27F8.0651

I. Executive-PCI sends ping request packet in an Ethernet frame addressed to Routerl

2. Routerl sends request packet in a new Ethernet frame addressed to HR-PCI

From: 0015.fa64.76d2
To: 0800.2759.d9fd

IP packet
From: 172.31.60.50
To: 172.31.70.50

From: 0800.27F8.0651
To: 0015.fa64.76d2

IP packet
From: 172.31.60.50
To: 172.31.70.50

4. Routerl sends reply packet in a new Ethernet frame addressed to Executive-PCI

3. HR-PCI sends ping reply packet in an Ethernet frame addressed to Routerl

Figure 14.2   Router1 routing between VLANs 600 and 700

In step 3, HR-PC1 creates an IP packet with a ping reply. It encapsulates the packet inside an Ethernet frame addressed to Router1's MAC address and sends it out onto VLAN 600.

In step 4, Router1 takes the IP packet containing the ping reply and encapsulates it inside a new Ethernet frame addressed to Executive-PC1's MAC address—0800.2759.d9fd.

That's a lot of things happening just to route an IP packet between two VLANs! Although figure 14.2 can help you understand the examples in this chapter, in the real world you're not always going to have such a nice diagram to visually represent how IP traffic flows from one VLAN to another. That's why it's important that you be able to quickly determine, based on boring text output, how a router will route traffic.

14.4   The IP routing table

In chapter 7, you briefly looked at the IP routing table on Switch1. Now it's time to learn how to interpret it.

Try it now
On Router1, issue a show ip route.

You should see the following:

```
Router1#sh ip route
Codes: C - connected, S - static, R - RIP, M - mobile, B - BGP
       D - EIGRP, EX - EIGRP external, O - OSPF, IA - OSPF inter area
       N1 - OSPF NSSA external type 1, N2 - OSPF NSSA external type 2
       E1 - OSPF external type 1, E2 - OSPF external type 2
       i - IS-IS, su - IS-IS summary, L1 - IS-IS level-1, L2 - IS-IS level-2
       ia - IS-IS inter area, * - candidate default, U - per-user static route
       o - ODR, P - periodic downloaded static route

Gateway of last resort is not set

     172.31.0.0/24 is subnetted, 2 subnets
C       172.31.60.0 is directly connected, FastEthernet0/0.600
C       172.31.70.0 is directly connected, FastEthernet0/0.700
C    192.168.1.0/24 is directly connected, FastEthernet0/0
```

The IP routing table describes each IP subnet the router knows about and which interface it must use to reach that subnet. The information in Router1's routing table should seem obvious. For example, Router1 knows that it can reach the 172.31.60.0/24 subnet out of the FastEthernet0/0.600 subinterface because the IP address you configured on that subinterface is in the 172.31.60.0/24 subnet. This is called a connected route because Router1 is directly connected to that subnet.

This seems obvious, but what if Router1 receives a packet for a subnet it knows nothing about? For example, if it receives a packet for 1.2.3.4, it has nowhere to send the packet because there's no corresponding route for it.

Try it now
On Executive-PC1, ping 1.2.3.4.

You should see a series of unsuccessful pings:

```
PS C:\> ping 1.2.3.4

Pinging 1.2.3.4 with 32 bytes of data:
Reply from 172.31.70.254: Destination host unreachable.
Reply from 172.31.70.254: Destination host unreachable.
Reply from 172.31.70.254: Destination host unreachable.
Reply from 172.31.70.254: Destination host unreachable.

Ping statistics for 1.2.3.4:
    Packets: Sent = 4, Received = 4, Lost = 0 (0% loss),
```

When a router receives a packet destined to a subnet for which it has no route, it will send a `Destination host unreachable` message back to the sender.

So far, you've been able to ping HR-PC1 from Executive-PC1. Now it's time to try a ping in the opposite direction, from HR-PC1 to Executive-PC1.

> **Try it now**
>
> From HR-PC1, try to ping Executive-PC1.

You should get successful ping replies:

```
PS C:\> ping 172.31.70.50

Pinging 172.31.70.50 with 32 bytes of data:
Reply from 172.31.70.50: bytes=32 time=1ms TTL=127
Reply from 172.31.70.50: bytes=32 time=1ms TTL=127
Reply from 172.31.70.50: bytes=32 time=2ms TTL=127
Reply from 172.31.70.50: bytes=32 time=1ms TTL=127

Ping statistics for 172.31.70.50:
    Packets: Sent = 4, Received = 4, Lost = 0 (0% loss),
Approximate round trip times in milli-seconds:
    Minimum = 1ms, Maximum = 2ms, Average = 1ms
```

Recall from chapter 9 that you implemented an ACL to block all IP traffic from the 172.31.60.0/24 subnet to the 172.31.70.0/24 subnet. You had applied that ACL to the VLAN 600 SVI on Switch1, but at the beginning of this chapter you deleted that SVI and assigned its IP (172.31.60.254) to the FastEthernet0/0.600 interface on Router1. The net effect of all this is that HR-PC1 now uses Router1, which has no access list in place. Let's fix that!

14.5   *Applying an ACL to a subinterface*

The way you create an ACL and apply it to an interface is almost exactly the same on a router as it is on a switch. You start by creating an ACL to deny all IP traffic from the 172.31.60.0/24 subnet to the 172.31.70.0/24 subnet.

> **Try it now**
>
> On Router1, create ACL 100 by issuing the following commands:
>
> ```
> access-list 100 deny ip 172.31.60.0 0.0.0.255 172.31.70.0 0.0.0.255
> access-list 100 permit ip any any
> ```
>
> Apply ACL 100 to the FastEthernet0/0.600 subinterface:
>
> ```
> int fa0/0.600
> ip access-group 100 in
> ```
>
> Verify with a `show access-list`.

You should see the new ACL:

```
Extended IP access list 100
    10 deny ip 172.31.60.0 0.0.0.255 172.31.70.0 0.0.0.255
    20 permit ip any any (23 matches)
```

Now that you've applied the ACL, you shouldn't be able to ping Executive-PC1 from HR-PC1 anymore.

Try it now
On HR-PC1, try to ping Executive-PC1 again.

You should see the following:

```
PS C:\> ping 172.31.70.50

Pinging 172.31.70.50 with 32 bytes of data:
Reply from 172.31.60.254: Destination net unreachable.
Reply from 172.31.60.254: Destination net unreachable.
Reply from 172.31.60.254: Destination net unreachable.
Reply from 172.31.60.254: Destination net unreachable.
```

Notice that the `Destination unreachable` message looks similar to the earlier message you got when trying to ping the 1.2.3.4 address. This error is the router's way of saying that it can't—or in this case, won't—send the IP packet along to its destination.

You don't need to become an expert at deciphering these error messages. Just remember that when you see one, it could indicate a missing route in the IP routing table or an access list blocking traffic.

14.6 Commands in this chapter

Refer to table 14.3 for a list of all the commands used in this chapter.

Table 14.3 Commands used in this chapter

Command	Configuration mode	Description
`interface fastethernet0/0.600`	Global	Creates the FastEthernet0/0.600 subinterface under the FastEthernet0/0 physical interface
`encapsulation dot1Q 600`	Interface	Places the selected subinterface in VLAN 600
`ip address 172.31.70.254 255.255.255.0`	Interface	Assigns 172.31.70.254/24 to the selected interface
`show vlans 600`	Global	Displays interfaces in VLAN 600 and their corresponding IP addresses
`show ip route`	Global	Displays the IP routing table

14.7 *Hands-on lab*

For today's lab, you're going to practice creating and applying ACLs on a router:

1 Create a new ACL to prevent devices in the Executives subnet from reaching the HR subnet.
2 Apply the ACL to the FastEthernet0/0.700 subinterface.
3 Try to ping HR-PC1 from Executive-PC1.
4 Remove the ACL from the FastEthernet0/0.700 interface.
5 Save your configuration.

Manually directing traffic using the IP routing table

Connecting two switches that are in the same physical location is easy. All you have to do is string a couple of Ethernet cables between them, configure the interfaces, and you're finished. But now imagine that your switches sit in separate offices hundreds of miles apart. How do you connect them?

In chapter 8 I said that you have a few options when it comes to connecting geographically separated sites. Private T1/E1 lines and MPLS virtual private networks (VPNs) are two popular methods. With both of these methods, the telecom carrier provides you physical connectivity between your sites. But it's still up to you to configure IP routing between those sites.

In the last chapter, you got a glimpse of how IP routing works when you set up your "router-on-a-stick" topology. Figure 15.1 illustrates the topology you have right now.

Recall that you didn't have to explicitly tell Router1 how to route between IP subnets. All you had to do was create a couple of subinterfaces, configure an IP address on each one, and the router took care of the rest.

But that's with just one router. When you connect geographically separated sites, you'll have multiple routers. Take a look at figure 15.2; you'll reconfigure your network to look like this in this chapter.

You're going to place Router1 between the two switches and configure it to route IP traffic between them. What may not be readily obvious from the diagram, however, is that Switch1 and Switch2 also will function as routers. Recall from chapter 7 that each layer-3 switch has a virtual router inside it. Another thing that may

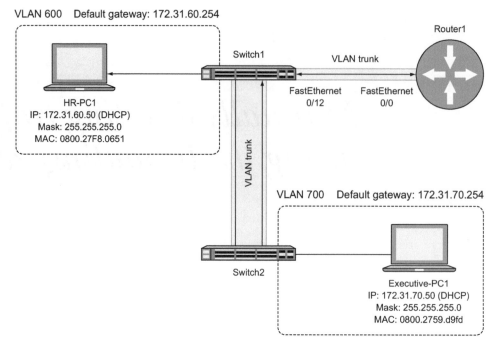

Figure 15.1   The router-on-a-stick physical topology

not be clear at the moment is the addition of two new *transit subnets*—10.0.12.0/30 between Switch1 and Router1 and 10.0.21.0/30 between Router1 and Switch2. I'll discuss transit subnets later in the chapter.

Here are the basic steps you'll perform in this chapter:

1 Connect Router1 to Switch2 and delete the existing subinterfaces on Router1.
2 Configure the interfaces between Router1 and Switch2.
3 Create a new subinterface between Router1 and Switch1.
4 Configure default gateways for the Executive and HR subnets.
5 Create a DHCP pool for the Executives subnet on Switch2.
6 Configure static IP routes on Switch1, Switch2, and Router1.

Let's get started!

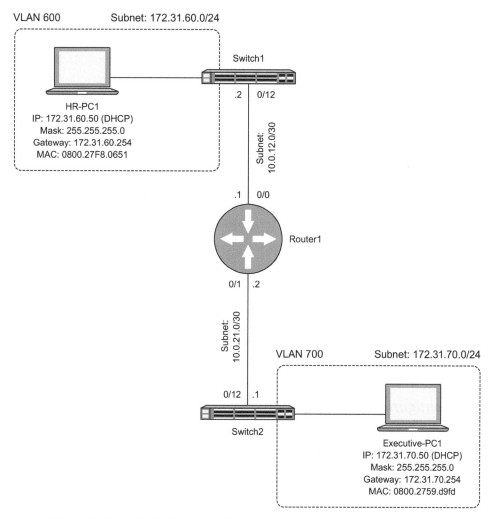

Figure 15.2 Switch1 and Switch2 connected via Router1

15.1 *Connecting Router1 to Switch2*

To refresh your memory, in chapter 14 you configured two subinterfaces on Router1: FastEthernet0/0.600 and FastEthernet0/0.700. Because you're no longer going to use the router-on-a-stick configuration, you'll need to delete those.

Try it now

Go ahead and connect Router1's FastEthernet0/1 interface to Switch2's FastEthernet0/12 interface.

PN 921 5441

(continued)

Execute the following commands to remove both subinterfaces from Router1:

```
no interface fa0/0.600
no interface fa0/0.700
```

As you execute these commands, you'll see this message: `Not all config may be removed and may reappear after reactivating the sub-interface.` This is normal.

Verify that both subinterfaces are in a `deleted` status by doing a `show ip interface brief`.

You should see both subinterfaces as `deleted`:

```
Router1#show ip interface brief
Interface            IP-Address      OK? Method Status                 Protocol
FastEthernet0/0      192.168.1.201   YES NVRAM  up                           up
FastEthernet0/0.600  unassigned      YES NVRAM  deleted                    down
FastEthernet0/0.700  unassigned      YES NVRAM  deleted                    down
FastEthernet0/1      unassigned      YES NVRAM  administratively down down
```

Notice that the FastEthernet0/1 interface, which is now connected to Switch2, doesn't have an IP address and is administratively down. In order for Router1 to route traffic to and from Switch2, you must configure a transit subnet between them.

15.2 *Configuring transit subnets*

A transit subnet's sole purpose is to carry IP traffic between two and only two devices in the same broadcast domain. What makes a transit subnet special is its relatively small size. Recall from chapter 7 that a subnet mask determines how big a subnet is. You need two transit subnets, one between Switch1 and Router1 and another between Router1 and Switch2. Each subnet needs only enough addresses for two devices. Those subnets are listed in table 15.1.

Table 15.1 Transit subnets; by using a subnet mask of 255.255.255.252, each transit subnet is big enough for only two devices.

Subnet	Subnet mask	Number of usable addresses
10.0.12.0	255.255.255.252	2
10.0.21.0	255.255.255.252	2

You have two different ways to configure a transit subnet between a router and a switch. You can assign the transit IP addresses directly to the physical interfaces of the router and switch. Or you can assign the transit IP addresses to a subinterface on the router and a transit VLAN SVI on the switch. I'm going to show you both ways, starting with the former.

15.2.1 *Assigning transit IP addresses directly to physical interfaces*

The process for assigning a transit IP to a physical interface on a router is slightly different than it is on a switch. As you perform the exercises, I'll point out where they differ.

Try it now

Configure Router1's FastEthernet0/1 interface with an IP address of 10.0.21.2 and a subnet mask of 255.255.255.252:

```
int fa0/1
description To Switch1 Fa0/12
ip address 10.0.21.2 255.255.255.252
no shutdown
```

You should see the interface come up:

```
*Jun 14 21:36:47.571: %LINK-3-UPDOWN: Interface FastEthernet0/1, changed
    state to up
*Jun 14 21:36:48.571: %LINEPROTO-5-UPDOWN: Line protocol on Interface
    FastEthernet0/1, changed state to up
```

Next, you'll need to configure the transit subnet on Switch2. By default, you can't assign an IP address directly to a switch port. You have to issue the no switchport command to turn the port into what's called a *routed interface*. As the term suggests, a routed interface behaves just like an interface on a router.

Try it now

On Switch2, enable IP routing (you enabled it on Switch1 earlier):

```
ip routing
```

Configure FastEthernet0/12 as a routed interface:

```
int fa0/12
no switchport
```

Assign it an IP address of 10.0.21.1 with a subnet mask of 255.255.255.252:

```
ip address 10.0.21.1 255.255.255.252
```

Verify with a show ip int fa0/12.

You should see the following:

```
Switch2#show ip int fa0/12
FastEthernet0/12 is up, line protocol is up
  Internet address is 10.0.21.1/30
  Broadcast address is 255.255.255.255
```

Notice that IOS lists the address as 10.0.21.1/30 instead of giving you the dotted-decimal subnet mask of 255.255.255.252. Explaining the relationship between the subnet mask and the *slash notation* involves a lot of binary math and is beyond the scope of this chapter. Just know that if you see the address listed as shown here, you've configured the IP address and subnet mask correctly.

Next, it's always a good idea to verify that Switch2 can ping Router1's new IP address.

Try it now

On Switch2, ping 10.0.21.2:

```
Switch2#ping 10.0.21.2
```

You should get a response:

```
Type escape sequence to abort.
Sending 5, 100-byte ICMP Echos to 10.0.21.2, timeout is 2 seconds:
!!!!!
Success rate is 100 percent (5/5), round-trip min/avg/max = 1/203/1007 ms
```

One of the advantages of this method is that it's quicker and doesn't require you to create a VLAN for each transit subnet. The downside, however, is that the Cisco uninitiated may have difficulty understanding the configuration.

15.2.2 *Assigning transit IP addresses to subinterfaces and SVIs*

Next, you'll create a transit subnet between Switch1 and Router1, but this time you're going to do it a little differently. On Switch1, you'll create a new VLAN and SVI, to which you'll assign one of the transit IPs.

Try it now

Configure a transit VLAN 999 and assign a transit IP address of 10.0.12.1 to its SVI:

```
Switch1(config)#vlan 999
Switch1(config-vlan)#name Transit
Switch1(config-vlan)#exit
Switch1(config)#interface vlan999
Switch1(config-if)#ip address 10.0.12.1 255.255.255.252
```

Make sure FastEthernet0/12 is configured as a trunk port:

```
Switch1(config)#interface fa0/12
Switch1(config-if)#description To Router1 Fa0/1
Switch1(config-if)#switchport trunk encapsulation dot1q
Switch1(config-if)#switchport mode trunk
```

Verify with a show ip interface vlan999.

You should see the following:

```
Show ip interface vlan999
Switch1#show ip interface vlan999
Vlan999 is up, line protocol is up
  Internet address is 10.0.12.1/30
  Broadcast address is 255.255.255.255
```

The next step is to configure a subinterface in VLAN 999 on Router1.

> **Try it now**
> On Router1, create the subinterface FastEthernet0/0.999 and place it in VLAN 999:
>
> ```
> Router1(config)#int fa0/0.999
> Router1(config-subif)#encapsulation dot1Q 999
> ```
>
> Assign the subinterface an IP address of 10.0.12.2:
>
> ```
> Router1(config-subif)#ip address 10.0.12.2 255.255.255.252
> ```
>
> Verify with a show ip int brief.

You should see the new subinterface along with its new IP address:

```
Router1#sh ip int brief
Interface               IP-Address      OK?  Method  Status   Protocol
FastEthernet0/0         192.168.1.201   YES  manual  up       up
FastEthernet0/0.600     unassigned      YES  manual  deleted  down
FastEthernet0/0.700     unassigned      YES  manual  deleted  down
FastEthernet0/0.999     10.0.12.2       YES  manual  up       up
FastEthernet0/1         10.0.21.2       YES  manual  up       up
```

Once again, it's always a good idea to ping Switch1 to verify IP connectivity:

```
Router1#ping 10.0.12.1

Type escape sequence to abort.
Sending 5, 100-byte ICMP Echos to 10.0.12.1, timeout is 2 seconds:
.!!!!
Success rate is 80 percent (4/5), round-trip min/avg/max = 1/3/4 ms
```

As I alluded to a moment ago, this method might be the way to go if you want to make your configuration clearer to those who aren't as familiar with IOS. Naming a VLAN "Transit" or something similar makes it hard to miss.

15.3 *Removing the trunk link between switches*

To simulate geographic distance between your switches, you'll need to remove the VLAN trunk link between them, which right now is just a port channel. To do this, you don't have to physically disconnect the Ethernet cables between the FastEthernet0/22, 0/23, and 0/24 ports—although you can if you want to. Instead, you can shut down the port channel interface itself.

Try it now

Shut down the Port-channel1 interface on Switch1:

```
interface Port-channel1
shutdown
```

15.4 *Configuring default gateways*

In the last chapter, you configured two subinterfaces on Router1 with the default gateway IP addresses for both the HR and Executives subnets. At the beginning of this chapter, you removed both of those subinterfaces. As it stands, devices in the Executives subnet (172.31.70.0/24) and HR subnet (172.31.60.0/24) don't have a default gateway.

Refer to figure 15.3. Switch1 will act as the default gateway for the HR subnet, whereas Switch2 will act as the default gateway for the Executives subnet.

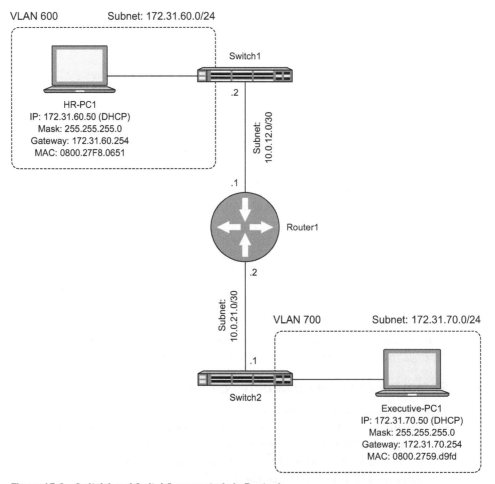

Figure 15.3   Switch1 and Switch2 connected via Router1

> **Try it now**
>
> On Switch2, create the VLAN 700 SVI and assign it an IP address of 172.31.70.254/24:
>
> ```
> Switch2(config)#int vlan700
> Switch2(config-if)#ip address 172.31.70.254 255.255.255.0
> ```
>
> On Switch1, re-create the VLAN 600 SVI and assign it an IP address of 172.31.60.254/24:
>
> ```
> Switch1(config)#int vlan600
> Switch1(config-if)#ip address 172.31.60.254 255.255.255.0
> ```

15.5 *Creating a DHCP pool for the Executives subnet*

Previously, you configured two DHCP scopes on Switch1: one for the HR subnet and one for the Executives subnet. But now that the Executives VLAN doesn't have a VLAN trunk over to Switch1, devices in that VLAN won't be able to pick up DHCP addresses from it. You have to configure a DCHP server on Switch2.

> **Try it now**
>
> Create a DHCP pool for the Executives subnet:
>
> ```
> ip dhcp pool Executives
>  network 172.31.70.0 255.255.255.0
>  dns-server 192.168.100.10 192.168.100.11
>  default-router 172.31.70.254
>  domain-name benpiper.com
>  lease 7
> ```
>
> Exclude some IP addresses to keep them available for static assignment:
>
> ```
> ip dhcp excluded-address 172.31.70.251 172.31.70.254
> ip dhcp excluded-address 172.31.70.1 172.31.70.49
> ```
>
> Go to Executive-PC1 and make sure it gets an IP address. Issue an `ipconfig /renew` if needed.

You should see the updated IP address information:

```
PS C:\> ipconfig /renew

Windows IP Configuration

Ethernet adapter Local Area Connection:

   Connection-specific DNS Suffix  . : benpiper.com
   Link-local IPv6 Address . . . . . : fe80::d8ae:58d6:2dc0:9450%11
   IPv4 Address. . . . . . . . . . . : 172.31.70.50
   Subnet Mask . . . . . . . . . . . : 255.255.255.0
   Default Gateway . . . . . . . . . : 172.31.70.254
```

Although it has a valid IP address, Executive-PC1 still can't ping HR-PC1:

```
PS C:\> ping 172.31.60.51

Pinging 172.31.60.51 with 32 bytes of data:
Reply from 172.31.70.254: Destination host unreachable.
Reply from 172.31.70.254: Destination host unreachable.
Reply from 172.31.70.254: Destination host unreachable.
Reply from 172.31.70.254: Destination host unreachable.
```

The reason this doesn't work is that Executive-PC1's default gateway—Switch2—doesn't know anything about the 172.31.60.0/24 subnet.

Try it now
See for yourself! On Switch2, issue a `show ip route`.

You should see the following:

```
Switch2#sh ip route
Codes: L - local, C - connected, S - static, R - RIP, M - mobile, B - BGP
       D - EIGRP, EX - EIGRP external, O - OSPF, IA - OSPF inter area
       N1 - OSPF NSSA external type 1, N2 - OSPF NSSA external type 2
       E1 - OSPF external type 1, E2 - OSPF external type 2
       i - IS-IS, su - IS-IS summary, L1 - IS-IS level-1, L2 - IS-IS level-2
       ia - IS-IS inter area, * - candidate default, U - per-user static route
       o - ODR, P - periodic downloaded static route, H - NHRP, l - LISP
       + - replicated route, % - next hop override

Gateway of last resort is not set

      10.0.0.0/8 is variably subnetted, 2 subnets, 2 masks
C        10.0.21.0/30 is directly connected, FastEthernet0/12
L        10.0.21.1/32 is directly connected, FastEthernet0/12
      172.31.0.0/16 is variably subnetted, 2 subnets, 2 masks
C        172.31.70.0/24 is directly connected, Vlan700
L        172.31.70.254/32 is directly connected, Vlan700
      192.168.1.0/24 is variably subnetted, 2 subnets, 2 masks
C        192.168.1.0/24 is directly connected, Vlan1
L        192.168.1.102/32 is directly connected, Vlan1
```

You can see the transit (10.0.21.0/30) and Executives subnets (172.31.70.0/24), but without an entry for the HR subnet (172.31.60.0/24), Switch2 has no idea where to send the ping packet from Executive-PC1! To remedy this you have to create a static IP route consisting of three pieces of information: the destination subnet, the subnet mask, and the next hop.

The *next hop* is the IP address of the device that Switch2 should send the packet to. In this case, that would be the IP address you assigned to Router1's FastEthernet0/1 interface earlier (10.0.21.2).

Try it now

Add a static route for the 172.31.60.0/24 subnet with 10.0.21.2 (Router1) as the next hop:

```
Switch2(config)#ip route 172.31.60.0 255.255.255.0 10.0.21.2
```

Verify with a `show ip route`.

You should see a new entry for the HR subnet:

```
Switch2#sh ip route
Codes: L - local, C - connected, S - static, R - RIP, M - mobile, B - BGP
       D - EIGRP, EX - EIGRP external, O - OSPF, IA - OSPF inter area
       N1 - OSPF NSSA external type 1, N2 - OSPF NSSA external type 2
       E1 - OSPF external type 1, E2 - OSPF external type 2
       i - IS-IS, su - IS-IS summary, L1 - IS-IS level-1, L2 - IS-IS level-2
       ia - IS-IS inter area, * - candidate default, U - per-user static route
       o - ODR, P - periodic downloaded static route, H - NHRP, l - LISP
       + - replicated route, % - next hop override

Gateway of last resort is not set

      10.0.0.0/8 is variably subnetted, 2 subnets, 2 masks
C        10.0.21.0/30 is directly connected, FastEthernet0/12
L        10.0.21.1/32 is directly connected, FastEthernet0/12
      172.31.0.0/16 is variably subnetted, 3 subnets, 2 masks
S        172.31.60.0/24 [1/0] via 10.0.21.2
C        172.31.70.0/24 is directly connected, Vlan700
L        172.31.70.254/32 is directly connected, Vlan700
      192.168.1.0/24 is variably subnetted, 2 subnets, 2 masks
C        192.168.1.0/24 is directly connected, Vlan1
L        192.168.1.102/32 is directly connected, Vlan1
```

The S indicates that this is a static route. Let's try that ping again.

Try it now

From Executive-PC1, try to ping 172.31.60.51 again.

```
PS C:\> ping 172.31.60.51

Pinging 172.31.60.51 with 32 bytes of data:
Request timed out.
Request timed out.
Request timed out.
Request timed out.
```

The ping still doesn't work. On Switch1, notice that a `show ip route` doesn't show the Executives subnet (172.31.70.0/24):

```
Switch1#show ip route
Codes: L - local, C - connected, S - static, R - RIP, M - mobile, B - BGP
       D - EIGRP, EX - EIGRP external, O - OSPF, IA - OSPF inter area
       N1 - OSPF NSSA external type 1, N2 - OSPF NSSA external type 2
       E1 - OSPF external type 1, E2 - OSPF external type 2
       i - IS-IS, su - IS-IS summary, L1 - IS-IS level-1, L2 - IS-IS level-2
       ia - IS-IS inter area, * - candidate default, U - per-user static route
       o - ODR, P - periodic downloaded static route, H - NHRP, l - LISP
       + - replicated route, % - next hop override

Gateway of last resort is not set

      10.0.0.0/8 is variably subnetted, 2 subnets, 2 masks
C        10.0.12.0/30 is directly connected, Vlan999
L        10.0.12.1/32 is directly connected, Vlan999
      172.31.0.0/16 is variably subnetted, 2 subnets, 2 masks
C        172.31.60.0/24 is directly connected, Vlan600
L        172.31.60.254/32 is directly connected, Vlan600
      192.168.1.0/24 is variably subnetted, 2 subnets, 2 masks
C        192.168.1.0/24 is directly connected, Vlan1
L        192.168.1.101/32 is directly connected, Vlan1
```

To fix this, you'll need to add a static route for the Executives subnet.

> **Try it now**
>
> Add the static route for the Executives subnet (172.31.70.0/24):
>
> `Switch1(config)#ip route 172.31.70.0 255.255.255.0 10.0.12.2`
>
> Verify by doing another `show ip route`.

You should now see the subnet listed as a static route:

```
Switch1#sh ip route
Codes: L - local, C - connected, S - static, R - RIP, M - mobile, B - BGP
       D - EIGRP, EX - EIGRP external, O - OSPF, IA - OSPF inter area
       N1 - OSPF NSSA external type 1, N2 - OSPF NSSA external type 2
       E1 - OSPF external type 1, E2 - OSPF external type 2
       i - IS-IS, su - IS-IS summary, L1 - IS-IS level-1, L2 - IS-IS level-2
       ia - IS-IS inter area, * - candidate default, U - per-user static route
       o - ODR, P - periodic downloaded static route, H - NHRP, l - LISP
       + - replicated route, % - next hop override

Gateway of last resort is not set

      10.0.0.0/8 is variably subnetted, 2 subnets, 2 masks
C        10.0.12.0/30 is directly connected, Vlan999
L        10.0.12.1/32 is directly connected, Vlan999
      172.31.0.0/16 is variably subnetted, 3 subnets, 2 masks
C        172.31.60.0/24 is directly connected, Vlan600
```

```
L         172.31.60.254/32 is directly connected, Vlan600
S         172.31.70.0/24 [1/0] via 10.0.12.2
      192.168.1.0/24 is variably subnetted, 2 subnets, 2 masks
C         192.168.1.0/24 is directly connected, Vlan1
L         192.168.1.101/32 is directly connected, Vlan1
```

Try it now
From Executive-PC1, try to ping HR-PC1 again:

```
ping 172.31.60.51
```

The ping still doesn't work:

```
PS C:\> ping 172.31.60.51

Pinging 172.31.60.51 with 32 bytes of data:
Request timed out.
Request timed out.
Request timed out.
Request timed out.
```

The reason it still doesn't work is that Router1 doesn't know about the Executives and HR subnets. Remember that all traffic between the HR and Executives subnets must pass through Router1. To fix this, you'll need to tell Router1 about both subnets.

Try it now
On Router1, do a `show ip route`.

You should see that Router1 doesn't know about either subnet:

```
Router1#show ip route
Codes: C - connected, S - static, R - RIP, M - mobile, B - BGP
       D - EIGRP, EX - EIGRP external, O - OSPF, IA - OSPF inter area
       N1 - OSPF NSSA external type 1, N2 - OSPF NSSA external type 2
       E1 - OSPF external type 1, E2 - OSPF external type 2
       i - IS-IS, su - IS-IS summary, L1 - IS-IS level-1, L2 - IS-IS level-2
       ia - IS-IS inter area, * - candidate default, U - per-user static route
       o - ODR, P - periodic downloaded static route

Gateway of last resort is not set

     10.0.0.0/30 is subnetted, 2 subnets
C       10.0.12.0 is directly connected, FastEthernet0/0.999
C       10.0.21.0 is directly connected, FastEthernet0/1
C    192.168.1.0/24 is directly connected, FastEthernet0/0
```

It has the transit subnets in its routing table because those are its *connected networks*—that is, it has IP addresses in both subnets. But it doesn't have IP addresses in the

Executives or HR subnet, so it doesn't know about them. To fix this, you must add static routes for both subnets. Remember, Router1 has to know about both subnets so it can not only pass the ping request from Executive-PC1 to HR-PC1 but also pass the reply in the opposite direction.

Try it now

On Router1, add a static route for 172.31.60.0/24, using Switch1's transit IP address (10.0.12.1) as the next hop:

```
Router1(config)#ip route 172.31.60.0 255.255.255.0 10.0.12.1
```

Add another static route for 172.31.70.0/24, using Switch2's transit IP address (10.0.21.1) as the next hop:

```
Router1(config)#ip route 172.31.70.0 255.255.255.0 10.0.21.1
```

Verify with a show ip route.

You should now see both subnets listed as static routes in the routing table:

```
Router1#show ip route
Codes: C - connected, S - static, R - RIP, M - mobile, B - BGP
       D - EIGRP, EX - EIGRP external, O - OSPF, IA - OSPF inter area
       N1 - OSPF NSSA external type 1, N2 - OSPF NSSA external type 2
       E1 - OSPF external type 1, E2 - OSPF external type 2
       i - IS-IS, su - IS-IS summary, L1 - IS-IS level-1, L2 - IS-IS level-2
       ia - IS-IS inter area, * - candidate default, U - per-user static route
       o - ODR, P - periodic downloaded static route

Gateway of last resort is not set

     172.31.0.0/24 is subnetted, 2 subnets
S       172.31.60.0 [1/0] via 10.0.12.1
S       172.31.70.0 [1/0] via 10.0.21.1
     10.0.0.0/30 is subnetted, 2 subnets
C       10.0.12.0 is directly connected, FastEthernet0/0.999
C       10.0.21.0 is directly connected, FastEthernet0/1
C    192.168.1.0/24 is directly connected, FastEthernet0/0
```

Now you should be able to ping both subnets from Router1.

Try it now

From Router1, ping HR-PC1 (172.31.60.51) and Executive-PC1 (172.31.70.50):

```
Router1#ping 172.31.60.51
Router1#ping 172.31.70.50
```

You should get responses from both machines:

```
Type escape sequence to abort.
Sending 5, 100-byte ICMP Echos to 172.31.60.51, timeout is 2 seconds:
!!!!!
Success rate is 100 percent (5/5), round-trip min/avg/max = 1/2/4 ms
Router1#ping 172.31.70.50

Type escape sequence to abort.
Sending 5, 100-byte ICMP Echos to 172.31.70.50, timeout is 2 seconds:
!!!!!
Success rate is 100 percent (5/5), round-trip min/avg/max = 1/2/4 ms
```

Perfect! Now you have IP routing fully configured between Executive-PC1 and HR-PC1. Now it's time to try pinging HR-PC1 from Executive-PC1 again.

Try it now

From HR-PC1, try to ping Executive-PC1 again:

```
ping 172.31.60.51
```

```
PS C:\> ping 172.31.60.51
Pinging 172.31.60.51 with 32 bytes of data:
Request timed out.
Request timed out.
Request timed out.
Request timed out.
```

Uh-oh! It still fails! Even though IP routing works, the ping fails because of an ACL you configured in chapter 9. It's time to get rid of that.

Try it now

On Switch1, remove the inbound ACL 101 from FastEthernet0/20, which is the interface connected to HR-PC1:

```
Switch1(config)#int fa0/20
Switch1(config-if)#no ip access-group 101 in
```

On Executive-PC1, try pinging 172.31.60.51 again.

Now it works:

```
PS C:\> ping 172.31.60.51

Pinging 172.31.60.51 with 32 bytes of data:
Reply from 172.31.60.51: bytes=32 time=1ms TTL=125
Reply from 172.31.60.51: bytes=32 time=1ms TTL=125
Reply from 172.31.60.51: bytes=32 time=1ms TTL=125
Reply from 172.31.60.51: bytes=32 time=1ms TTL=125
```

```
Ping statistics for 172.31.60.51:
    Packets: Sent = 4, Received = 4, Lost = 0 (0% loss),
Approximate round trip times in milli-seconds:
    Minimum = 1ms, Maximum = 1ms, Average = 1ms
```

That's a lot of work to route between two subnets! Although it was a bit time-consuming, static routing is usually a one-and-done kind of deal. It's not unusual for an organization to use static routing to connect multiple offices when there are only a small number of sites.

But static routing isn't without its drawbacks. A company I used to work for used static routing to connect four offices around the country. But when the company was acquired by a much larger company that had hundreds of subnets, static routes could no longer cut it. Fortunately, I had another option: dynamic routing protocols.

A dynamic routing protocol allows each router in a network to automatically advertise all the subnets it knows about. Each router propagates information about those subnets throughout the network until every other router knows about every subnet. In short, it automates the process of adding routes to the IP routing table so that you don't have to.

Although the concept is simple, configuring dynamic routing protocols confuses many people. In the next chapter, I'll give you a rundown of the most popular protocols and show you how to replace the static configuration you performed in this chapter with a robust, dynamic configuration—just like one you'd use in a production environment!

15.6 *Commands in this chapter*

Refer to table 15.2 for a list of all the commands used in this chapter.

Table 15.2 Commands used in this chapter

Command	Configuration mode	Description
ip routing	Global	Enables IP routing
no switchport	Interface	Changes the selected interface from a switch port into a routed interface
show ip interface fa0/12	N/A	Displays the IP information for FastEthernet0/12

15.7 *Hands-on lab*

For this lab, you're going to remove the static routes from Router1, Switch1, and Switch2. This will set you up for the next chapter, where you'll configure dynamic routing.

Issue the following commands in global configuration mode:

1 On Switch1: no ip route 172.31.70.0 255.255.255.0 10.0.12.2
2 On Switch2: no ip route 172.31.60.0 255.255.255.0 10.0.21.2
3 On Router1: no ip route 172.31.60.0 255.255.255.0 10.0.12.1 and no ip route 172.31.70.0 255.255.255.0 10.0.21.1

A dynamic routing protocols crash course

16

In the last chapter, you had to manually configure static routes to enable IP connectivity throughout your network. In this chapter, you're going to automate this process by configuring two of the most popular dynamic routing protocols: Cisco's very own Enhanced Interior Gateway Routing Protocol (EIGRP) and Open Shortest Path First (OSPF). But before you learn how these two protocols work and how to configure them, it helps to understand why they exist in the first place.

Network nerds sometimes refer to dynamic routing protocols as interior gateway protocols (IGPs). For brevity, I'll use this acronym throughout the rest of the chapter. IGPs automate the process of advertising subnets to other routers in the network. Although this may not sound particularly exciting, it can save you a lot of work.

IGPs do other things as well. If there are multiple paths or routes to a subnet, an IGP will choose the best one—the best usually being the shortest and fastest path. An IGP can also automatically route around link failures if another path is available. The downside to IGPs is that they're more complicated to configure, as you'll find out in this chapter.

To illustrate these features, you'll be configuring the topology shown in figure 16.1.

Notice that you'll end up with redundant connections between Switch1 and Switch2. You already have the connection via Router1. Later in the chapter you'll add an additional connection directly between Switch1 and Switch2. Unlike in previous chapters, the direct connection between the switches won't be a VLAN trunk. Instead, you'll set up the respective interfaces on Switch1 and Switch2 as routed

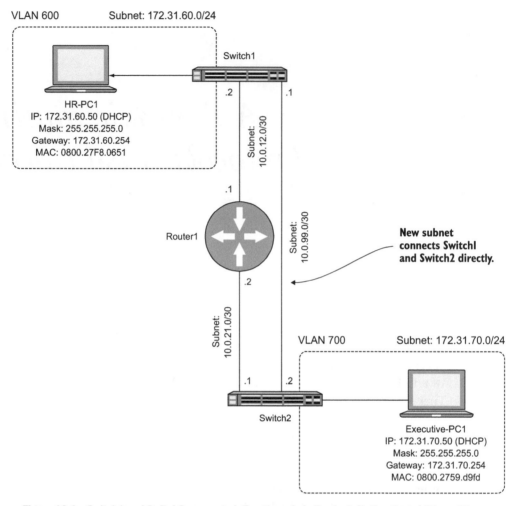

Figure 16.1   Switch1 and Switch2 connected directly and via Router1. Notice the addition of the 10.0.99.0/30 subnet between Switch1 and Switch2.

interfaces so that those switches act as directly connected routers. The two IGPs you'll configure—EIGRP and OSPF—will decide how to route IP traffic between VLANs 600 and 700.

Although EIGRP and OSPF can run simultaneously, that's an advanced configuration beyond the scope of this book. So you'll start by configuring EIGRP first, seeing how it works, and then you'll tear down that configuration and set up OSPF. Let's get started!

16.1   *Understanding router IDs*

As you add routers and subnets to a network, it becomes more difficult to keep track of what's where. You need a way to uniquely identify each device on the network. One way to do this is to assign friendly hostnames like Router and Switch2. But IGPs don't identify routers based on hostnames. Instead, they use a *router ID*, or *RID*.

An RID looks just like an IP address, even though it's technically not. When you configure an IGP on a router, it will take the router's highest IP address (going from left to right) and assign it as the RID. Take a look at the IP addresses on Router1:

```
Router1#show ip interface brief
Interface           IP-Address      OK? Method Status     Protocol
FastEthernet0/0     192.168.1.201   YES NVRAM  up         up
FastEthernet0/0.999 10.0.12.2       YES NVRAM  up         up
FastEthernet0/1     10.0.21.2       YES NVRAM  up         up
```

The router ID would be 192.168.1.201 because that's the highest RID on any of the up interfaces. The problem with this is that you may not remember that 192.168.1.201 is Router1. It's not intuitive. But changing the IP address on Router1, let alone all the other devices in your network, is a hassle. Fortunately, you don't have to. Instead, you can assign a brand-new IP address to a special type of interface called a loopback interface.

16.1.1 *Configuring loopback interfaces*

Up to this point, every IP address you've configured has been on an interface, whether a physical interface or an SVI. But there's another type of virtual interface called a loopback interface. You can assign an IP address to a loopback interface, but unlike a physical interface or an SVI, a loopback isn't tied to any physical interface or VLAN, and it's always up (unless you administratively shut it down). If you're familiar with the loopback adapter in a PC, it's basically the same thing. You can configure as many loopback interfaces as you need.

Here's the best part about loopbacks when it comes to routing protocols: when you enable EIGRP or OSPF, it will use the loopback IP address as the router ID, even if there's a higher IP address on a physical interface or SVI. If you have multiple loopback interfaces, it will use the highest IP address out of all the loopbacks. This way you can implicitly set the router ID by configuring a loopback.

You want to have all your loopbacks configured before configuring your IGP. Once the IGP starts up, it will lock in the router ID until the device reboots or you restart the IGP, even if you change or delete your loopback IP addresses.

Try it now

Log into Switch1, Switch2, and Router1. Configure the Loopback1 interface for each device as follows.

```
Switch1:
interface loopback1
ip address 1.1.1.1 255.255.255.255
```

(continued)

```
Switch2:
interface loopback1
ip address 2.2.2.2 255.255.255.255

Router1:
interface loopback1
ip address 12.12.12.12 255.255.255.255
```

On all devices:

Verify the loopback IP addresses with a `show ip interface brief`. Remember that loopback interfaces always begin with the word `Loopback`.

The 255.255.255.255 subnet mask may look a little weird. Recall that the subnet mask marks the boundaries of each subnet. In this case, the subnet mask specifies that each loopback IP address is the only IP address in the subnet. Don't worry if that sounds strange. The point is that by using the unusual mask, you're conserving IP addresses.

One final note on loopbacks: they're optional, but I recommend configuring them anyway, especially if your organization tends to assign ambiguous names to Cisco devices. Loopbacks can serve as a good unique identifier, even if it's just for your own personal use. Once you get your loopbacks set up, you're ready to start configuring EIGRP.

16.2 *Configuring EIGRP*

Configuring EIGRP is simple, but the commands you'll use aren't intuitive. Many folks find them downright confusing, so I'll spend some time explaining them shortly.

At a high level, there are two things you must to do configure EIGRP on each router in your network. First, you have to tell EIGRP which subnets to use to communicate with other routers, or *neighbors*, running EIGRP. Second, you also have to tell EIGRP which subnets you want it to advertise to those neighbors. Take a look at figure 16.2.

Switch1, Switch2, and Router1 will all be running EIGRP with each other. To start with, you'll enable EIGRP on only two subnets: 10.0.12.0/30 between Switch1 and Router1 and 10.0.21.0/30 between Router1 and Switch2.

Try it now

On Switch1, execute the following configuration commands to enable EIGRP:

```
Switch1(config)# router eigrp 7
Switch1(config-router)# network 10.0.12.1 0.0.0.0
```

The `router eigrp 7` command gets you into router configuration mode for EIGRP. The 7 indicates the EIGRP *autonomous system (AS)* number. The AS number is arbitrary

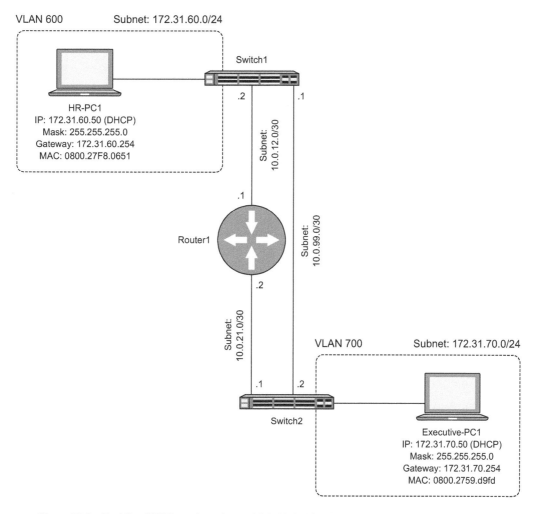

Figure 16.2 **Enabling EIGRP on the subnets 10.0.12.0/30, 10.0.99.0/30, 10.0.21.0/30, 172.31.60.0/24, and 172.31.70.0/24**

and has no significance by itself, but all EIGRP routers that you want to share routes must share the same AS number. Just as a router ID uniquely identifies a router, an AS number uniquely identifies the group of EIGRP routers that share routes.

The last part of the `network 10.0.12.1 0.0.0.0` command is a wildcard mask. The `network` command confuses many people because it does two different things. First, it enables EIGRP on Switch1's 10.0.12.1 interface, causing it to speak EIGRP with Router1. Second, it causes EIGRP to advertise the subnet that the IP address is a part of. Because 10.0.12.1 is part of the 10.0.12.0/30 subnet, EIGRP advertises that subnet. Next, you'll configure EIGRP to advertise the 172.31.60.0/24 network.

This command enables EIGRP on any interface that has an IP address between 172.31.60.0 and 172.31.60.255. Recall from chapter 9 that a wildcard mask is an inverted subnet mask. A wildcard mask of 0.0.0.255 is equivalent to a subnet mask of 255.255.255.0. Hence, the first three octets in the statement have to match the IP address of an interface, but the last octet can be any number between 0 and 255. Switch1's VLAN 600 SVI has an IP address of 172.31.60.254, so IOS enables EIGRP on the VLAN 600 SVI. As part of the deal, IOS also advertises the 172.31.60.0/24 subnet to other EIGRP routers. At this point, you've read a lot more than you've typed, so it's time to see EIGRP in action!

Your screen should fill with some rather lengthy output:

```
Switch1#show ip protocols
*** IP Routing is NSF aware ***

Routing Protocol is "eigrp 7"
  Outgoing update filter list for all interfaces is not set
  Incoming update filter list for all interfaces is not set
  Default networks flagged in outgoing updates
  Default networks accepted from incoming updates
  EIGRP-IPv4 Protocol for AS(7)
    Metric weight K1=1, K2=0, K3=1, K4=0, K5=0
    NSF-aware route hold timer is 240
    Router-ID: 1.1.1.1
    Topology : 0 (base)
      Active Timer: 3 min
      Distance: internal 90 external 170
      Maximum path: 4
      Maximum hopcount 100
      Maximum metric variance 1

  Automatic Summarization: disabled
  Maximum path: 4
  Routing for Networks:
    10.0.12.1/32
    172.31.60.0/24
  Routing Information Sources:
    Gateway         Distance      Last Update
  Distance: internal 90 external 170
```

Notice that the Router-ID is 1.1.1.1. You should recognize that as the Loopback0 IP address you configured moments ago. Also take a look at the two subnets under the `Routing for Networks` section. These should match up with what you just indicated with the `network` statement. Something that you may find odd is that this output doesn't tell you which interfaces EIGRP is enabled on. To get that information, you'll need a different command.

Try it now

On Switch1, execute the following command to see which interfaces EIGRP is enabled on:

```
show ip eigrp interfaces
```

Follow this with

```
show ip interface brief | i up
```

You should see the following:

```
Switch1#show ip eigrp interfaces
EIGRP-IPv4 Interfaces for AS(7)
            Xmit Queue    PeerQ      Mean   Pacing Time   Multicast    Pending
Interface   Peers  Un/Reliable Un/Reliable SRTT Un/Reliable Flow Timer Routes
Vl600        0     0/0         0/0          0    0/0          0           0
Vl999        0     0/0         0/0          0    0/0          0           0


Switch1#show ip int br | i up
Vlan1                  192.168.1.101    YES NVRAM  up        up
Vlan600                172.31.60.254    YES NVRAM  up        up
Vlan999                10.0.12.1        YES NVRAM  up        up
FastEthernet0/12       unassigned       YES unset  up        up
Loopback1              1.1.1.1          YES NVRAM  up        up
```

Hopefully, everything you've learned in previous chapters is starting to come together in your mind. EIGRP is enabled on the SVIs for VLANs 600 and 999, which have IP addresses in the 172.31.60.0/24 and 10.0.12.0/30 subnets, respectively. This isn't immediately obvious from either of the outputs. The information is scattered and you have to put it together, which is why I had you execute both commands in sequence. Now that you have EIGRP configured on Switch1, it's time to set up its neighbor, Router1.

Try it now

On Router1, issue the following configuration commands:

```
router eigrp 7
network 10.0.12.2 0.0.0.0
network 10.0.21.2 0.0.0.0
```

You should immediately see the following console message:

```
%DUAL-5-NBRCHANGE: IP-EIGRP(0) 7: Neighbor 10.0.12.1 (FastEthernet0/0.999) is
    up: new adjacency
```

By the way, DUAL is an acronym for the *Diffusing Update Algorithm* that EIGRP uses to calculate the best path to a destination. You don't need to understand how this algorithm works, but linking DUAL and EIGRP in your mind can be helpful, as you'll see in a moment.

When two EIGRP routers begin talking to each other, they form an *adjacency* and begin exchanging routes. At this point, Router1 should have a route to the 172.31.60.0/24 subnet.

Try it now

Do a show ip route eigrp to view the routes learned via EIGRP.

You should see only one EIGRP route:

```
Router1#show ip route eigrp
     172.31.0.0/24 is subnetted, 1 subnets
D       172.31.60.0 [90/28416] via 10.0.12.1, 01:52:49, FastEthernet0/0.999
```

Notice the new route designated by a D (another reference to DUAL). It's to the 172.31.60.0/24 network. The next hop is 10.0.12.1, the transit IP address of Switch1's interface connected to Router1. If you see this route, you're ready to finish your configuration with Switch2.

Try it now

On Switch2, issue the following commands:

```
router eigrp 7
network 10.0.21.1 0.0.0.0
network 172.31.70.0 0.0.0.255
```

This time, verify with a show ip eigrp neighbors.

You should see the adjacency with Router1's 10.0.21.2 transit IP address:

```
Switch2#show ip eigrp neighbors
EIGRP-IPv4 Neighbors for AS(7)
H   Address         Interface        Hold Uptime    SRTT    RTO  Q   Seq
                                     (sec)          (ms)         Cnt Num
0   10.0.21.2       Fa0/12           15  00:01:22   1       100  0   9
```

Now it's time for the real test. If everything works correctly, you should be able to see two EIGRP routes for the 172.31.60.0/24 and 10.0.12.0/30 networks.

The output on Switch2 will be a little more verbose than what you saw on Router1:

```
Switch2#show ip route eigrp
Codes: L - local, C - connected, S - static, R - RIP, M - mobile, B - BGP
       D - EIGRP, EX - EIGRP external, O - OSPF, IA - OSPF inter area
       N1 - OSPF NSSA external type 1, N2 - OSPF NSSA external type 2
       E1 - OSPF external type 1, E2 - OSPF external type 2
       i - IS-IS, su - IS-IS summary, L1 - IS-IS level-1, L2 - IS-IS level-2
       ia - IS-IS inter area, * - candidate default, U - per-user static route
       o - ODR, P - periodic downloaded static route, H - NHRP, l - LISP
       + - replicated route, % - next hop override

Gateway of last resort is not set

      10.0.0.0/8 is variably subnetted, 3 subnets, 2 masks
D        10.0.12.0/30 [90/30720] via 10.0.21.2, 00:03:37, FastEthernet0/12
      172.31.0.0/16 is variably subnetted, 3 subnets, 2 masks
D        172.31.60.0/24 [90/30976] via 10.0.21.2, 00:03:37, FastEthernet0/12
```

Based on this output, Switch2 and the devices in the Executives subnet (172.31.70.0/24) should be able to reach the devices in the HR subnet (172.31.60.0/24). In earlier chapters, you would test connectivity by pinging from one PC to another. But now I'm going to show you a more convenient way.

If all is well, you should have a successful ping:

```
Switch2#ping 172.31.60.254 source 172.31.70.254
Type escape sequence to abort.
Sending 5, 100-byte ICMP Echos to 172.31.60.254, timeout is 2 seconds:
Packet sent with a source address of 172.31.70.254
!!!!!
Success rate is 100 percent (5/5), round-trip min/avg/max = 1/5/9 ms
```

At the risk of seeming obvious, the command sources a ping from Switch2's 172.31.70.254 address and sends it to 172.31.60.254. This is an effective way to ensure that you have full IP connectivity between the two subnets.

16.2.1 *Choosing the best path*

One big advantage of using an IGP is that it can automatically adjust to route traffic over the best path, if multiple paths exist. To see this in action, you'll connect an

Ethernet cable directly between Switch1 and Switch2 and assign new IP addresses to each interface.

> ### Try it now
>
> Connect an Ethernet cable directly between FastEthernet0/24 interfaces on Switch1 and Switch2.
>
> Convert the interfaces to routed interfaces and assign IP addresses as follows.
>
> On Switch1:
>
> ```
> interface fa0/24
> No switchport
> Ip address 10.0.99.1 255.255.255.252
> No shutdown
> ```
>
> On Switch2:
>
> ```
> Interface fa0/24
> No switchport
> Ip address 10.0.99.2 255.255.255.252
> No shutdown
> ```

Keep in mind that you haven't yet enabled EIGRP on these new interfaces, so as far as EIGRP is concerned, there's only one path between Switch1 and Switch2. To prove this to yourself, run a traceroute.

> ### Try it now
>
> On Switch2, execute the following command:
>
> ```
> traceroute 172.31.60.254
> ```

The output should indicate that traffic takes the path through Router1 instead of going directly to Switch1:

```
Switch2#traceroute 172.31.60.254
Type escape sequence to abort.
Tracing the route to 172.31.60.254
VRF info: (vrf in name/id, vrf out name/id)
  1 10.0.21.2 9 msec 0 msec 0 msec
  2 10.0.12.1 0 msec *  0 msec
```

The traceroute goes to 10.0.21.2 (Router1) and then to 10.0.12.1 (Switch2)—two *hops*. By default, EIGRP selects the best path based in part on the number of hops. The fewer hops to get to a destination, the shorter the path. Clearly, a direct connection between Switch1 and Switch2 is shorter than one going from Switch2 to Router1 to Switch1. But to get EIGRP to even consider the new path, you need to explicitly reconfigure EIGRP on Switch1 and Switch2.

Try it now

On Switch1, issue the following commands to enable EIGRP on the new transit subnet:

```
Switch1(config-if)#router eigrp 7
Switch1(config-router)#network 10.0.99.1 0.0.0.0
```

On Switch2:

```
Switch2(config-if)#router eigrp 7
Switch2(config-router)#network 10.0.99.2 0.0.0.0
```

Remember that the 7 indicates the AS number, which must be the same on all EIGRP routers in the topology.

While still on Switch2, issue a show ip eigrp neighbors.

You should see something similar to the following:

```
Switch2#show ip eigrp neighbors
EIGRP-IPv4 Neighbors for AS(7)
H   Address        Interface      Hold Uptime    SRTT    RTO     Q    Seq
                                  (sec)          (ms)            Cnt  Num
1   10.0.99.1      Fa0/24         11 00:00:33    1598    5000    0    9
0   10.0.21.2      Fa0/12         13 00:37:55    1       100     0    13
```

Switch2 now has two adjacencies, one with Switch1 and another with Router1. Because the best path to the 172.31.60.0/24 network is directly through Switch1, rather than Router1, EIGRP should have changed the route to reflect the new connection.

Try it now

On Switch2, run another show ip route eigrp.

You should see that EIGRP has updated the route as follows:

```
Switch2#show ip route eigrp
Codes: L - local, C - connected, S - static, R - RIP, M - mobile, B - BGP
       D - EIGRP, EX - EIGRP external, O - OSPF, IA - OSPF inter area
       N1 - OSPF NSSA external type 1, N2 - OSPF NSSA external type 2
       E1 - OSPF external type 1, E2 - OSPF external type 2
       i - IS-IS, su - IS-IS summary, L1 - IS-IS level-1, L2 - IS-IS level-2
       ia - IS-IS inter area, * - candidate default, U - per-user static
    route
       o - ODR, P - periodic downloaded static route, H - NHRP, l - LISP
       + - replicated route, % - next hop override

Gateway of last resort is not set

      10.0.0.0/8 is variably subnetted, 5 subnets, 2 masks
D        10.0.12.0/30 [90/28416] via 10.0.99.1, 00:02:11, FastEthernet0/24
      172.31.0.0/16 is variably subnetted, 3 subnets, 2 masks
D        172.31.60.0/24 [90/28416] via 10.0.99.1, 00:02:11, FastEthernet0/24
```

The best path to 172.31.60.0/24 is now via 10.0.99.1 (Switch1). To truly appreciate what just happened, another traceroute is in order.

> **Try it now**
>
> On Switch2, run another traceroute:
>
> ```
> traceroute 172.31.60.254
> ```

This time, you should see only one hop:

```
Switch2#traceroute 172.31.60.254
Type escape sequence to abort.
Tracing the route to 172.31.60.254
VRF info: (vrf in name/id, vrf out name/id)
  1 10.0.99.1 0 msec *  0 msec
```

Bingo! The traceroute goes straight from Switch2 to Switch1.

16.2.2 Routing around failures

One of the biggest selling points of IGPs in general is their ability to automatically route around link failures. EIGRP can detect and respond to a failure quickly, sometimes even within milliseconds. To demonstrate this, you'll simulate a connection failure between Switch1 and Switch2's direct link.

> **Try it now**
>
> Physically disconnect one end of the cable between Switch1 and Switch2's FastEthernet0/24 ports. Alternatively, shut down the interface on one of the ports.
>
> Do a `show ip route eigrp`.

Like magic, EIGRP changes the route to go through Router1:

```
Switch2#show ip route eigrp
Codes: L - local, C - connected, S - static, R - RIP, M - mobile, B - BGP
       D - EIGRP, EX - EIGRP external, O - OSPF, IA - OSPF inter area
       N1 - OSPF NSSA external type 1, N2 - OSPF NSSA external type 2
       E1 - OSPF external type 1, E2 - OSPF external type 2
       i - IS-IS, su - IS-IS summary, L1 - IS-IS level-1, L2 - IS-IS level-2
       ia - IS-IS inter area, * - candidate default, U - per-user static route
       o - ODR, P - periodic downloaded static route, H - NHRP, l - LISP
       + - replicated route, % - next hop override

Gateway of last resort is not set

      10.0.0.0/8 is variably subnetted, 3 subnets, 2 masks
D        10.0.12.0/30 [90/30720] via 10.0.21.2, 00:00:05, FastEthernet0/12
      172.31.0.0/16 is variably subnetted, 3 subnets, 2 masks
D        172.31.60.0/24 [90/30976] via 10.0.21.2, 00:00:05, FastEthernet0/12
```

16.2.3 *EIGRP recap*

There's enough information about EIGRP to fill hundreds of pages and take hours of your time, and what I've covered is just the basics. To get a basic, minimal EIGRP configuration up and running, you need to do the following:

1. Decide which devices will participate in the EIGRP autonomous system (AS).
2. Decide on an AS number that all devices will use.
3. Decide which subnets EIGRP will advertise.
4. Issue the appropriate EIGRP commands covered in this section.

Before moving on to OSPF, I want to give you some pointers on when you might prefer EIGRP. As I alluded to at the beginning of the chapter, EIGRP started out as a Cisco-proprietary protocol, which means it originally didn't work with non-Cisco devices. In recent years, Cisco has opened up EIGRP so that other vendors can develop their own implementations of the protocol. Even so, if your network has non-Cisco routers or switches, my advice is to steer clear of EIGRP.

Another thing to consider is your network's size. Cisco designed EIGRP for use on networks of up to about 500 routers. If your organization has or eventually will have more than that, EIGRP isn't your best choice. Instead, you need another IGP called Open Shortest Path First (OSPF), which you'll learn how to configure in the next section. But first, you need to blow away your EIGRP configuration.

> **Try it now**
>
> Reconnect the direct link between Switch1 and Switch2 that you disconnected or shut down earlier.
>
> Execute the following configuration command to disable EIGRP on Switch1, Switch2, and Router1:
>
> ```
> no router eigrp 7
> ```

16.3 *Open Shortest Path First*

OSPF accomplishes the same thing as EIGRP, but it's designed to be more scalable for very large networks. Configuring OSPF is much the same as configuring EIGRP but with one small difference.

> **Try it now**
>
> On Switch2, issue the following commands to configure OSPF:
>
> ```
> router ospf 1
> network 10.0.21.1 0.0.0.0 area 0
> network 172.31.70.0 0.0.0.255 area 0
> network 10.0.99.2 0.0.0.0 area 1
> ```

(continued)

The `network` command has an extra parameter, `area`, followed by a number. I'll explain this OSPF-specific parameter in a moment. But first, verify your configuration with a `show ip protocols`.

You should get the following output:

```
Switch2#show ip protocols
*** IP Routing is NSF aware ***

Routing Protocol is "ospf 1"
  Outgoing update filter list for all interfaces is not set
  Incoming update filter list for all interfaces is not set
  Router ID 2.2.2.2
  It is an area border router
  Number of areas in this router is 2. 2 normal 0 stub 0 nssa
  Maximum path: 4
  Routing for Networks:
    10.0.21.1 0.0.0.0 area 0
    10.0.99.2 0.0.0.0 area 1
    172.31.70.0 0.0.0.255 area 0
  Routing Information Sources:
    Gateway          Distance      Last Update
    1.1.1.1               110      00:00:08
    12.12.12.12           110      00:00:08
  Distance: (default is 110)
```

One of the ways OSPF achieves scalability is through the use of *areas*. I'm not going to get into the technical details of what areas are or how they work, but to get OSPF up and running, you need to have at least one network in *area 0*, also known as the *backbone area*.

Here's what you need to remember about areas: OSPF is designed to keep traffic within the same area, even if there's a better path through another area. In the preceding configuration, you placed the direct connection between Switch1 and Switch2 into area 1 while keeping the other subnets in area 0. Refer to figure 16.3 to get the full picture of what your setup will look like when you've finished.

Because the path through Router1 will lie completely within area 0, OSPF will prefer this path, even though a better path is available. Let's continue with the configuration.

Try it now

Configure OSPF on Router1 using the following set of commands:

```
router ospf 1
network 10.0.12.2 0.0.0.0 area 0
network 10.0.21.2 0.0.0.0 area 0
```

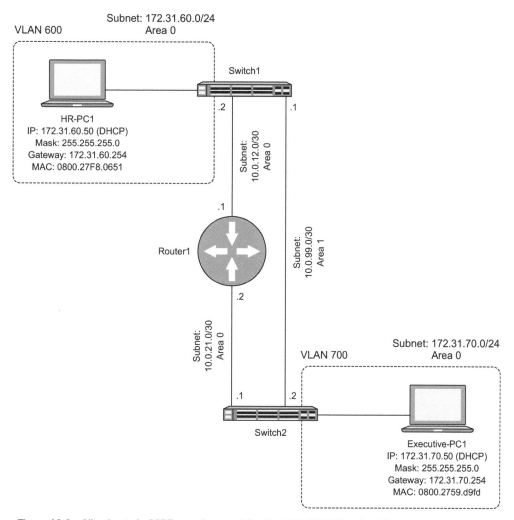

Figure 16.3 All subnets in OSPF area 0, except for the 10.0.99.0/30 subnet between Switch1 and Switch2

By the way, the 1 in `router ospf 1` indicates the OSPF process number, which is a way of uniquely identifying an OSPF instance on a router. It's not something you really need to think about. You just have to remember to include it when configuring OSPF. Unlike an EIGRP AS number, the OSPF process number doesn't have to match on all your routers. But it's a good idea to stick with the same number for consistency.

You should see the following output:

```
%OSPF-5-ADJCHG: Process 1, Nbr 2.2.2.2 on FastEthernet0/1 from LOADING to
    FULL, Loading Done
```

The console message indicates that Router1 has formed an adjacency with 2.2.2.2, meaning that they've exchanged routes and are fully in sync. You should recognize

2.2.2.2 as the IP address of Switch2's loopback interface. Like EIGRP, OSPF takes the highest loopback IP address and makes it the router ID. Unlike EIGRP, OSPF makes heavy use of the router ID in its various outputs.

Try it now

On Router1, view the OSPF routes in the IP routing table:

```
Show ip route ospf
```

Then view the details of the route for the 172.31.70.0 network:

```
Show ip route 172.31.70.0
```

Here's what you should see:

```
Router1#show ip route ospf
     172.31.0.0/24 is subnetted, 1 subnets
O       172.31.70.0 [110/2] via 10.0.21.1, 00:18:20, FastEthernet0/1
```

Notice that IOS marks the route with an O for OSPF. Other than that, the route looks nearly identical to the route that you saw when you configured EIGRP. But when you view the route details, some more differences become apparent:

```
Router1#show ip route 172.31.70.0
Routing entry for 172.31.70.0/24
  Known via "ospf 1", distance 110, metric 2, type intra area
  Last update from 10.0.21.1 on FastEthernet0/1, 00:18:37 ago
  Routing Descriptor Blocks:
  * 10.0.21.1, from 2.2.2.2, 00:18:37 ago, via FastEthernet0/1
      Route metric is 2, traffic share count is 1
```

In the `Routing Descriptor Blocks` section you can see another reference to 2.2.2.2. This makes it easy to tell which device is advertising this route. In this case, it's Switch2.

The final step is to configure Switch1.

Try it now

Configure OSPF on Switch1 using the following commands:

```
router ospf 1
Network 10.0.12.1 0.0.0.0 area 0
Network 172.31.60.0 0.0.0.255 area 0
Network 10.0.99.1 0.0.0.0 area 1
```

Verify with a show ip ospf neighbor.

You should see two adjacencies, one with Router1 and another with Switch2:

```
Switch1#show ip ospf neighbor

Neighbor ID     Pri   State      Dead Time   Address     Interface
12.12.12.12      1    FULL/DR    00:00:30    10.0.12.2   Vlan999
2.2.2.2          1    FULL/DR    00:00:30    10.0.99.2   FastEthernet0/24
```

See how easy it is to tell which device is which? This is one of the reasons I prefer OSPF over EIGRP, especially in large networks. If you see both adjacencies, your OSPF configuration is complete. Now it's time to test it!

> **Try it now**
>
> On Switch2, issue a `show ip route ospf` followed by a `traceroute 172.31.60.254`.

You should see the following:

```
Switch2#show ip route ospf
Gateway of last resort is not set

      10.0.0.0/8 is variably subnetted, 5 subnets, 2 masks
O        10.0.12.0/30 [110/2] via 10.0.21.2, 00:04:33, FastEthernet0/12
      172.31.0.0/16 is variably subnetted, 3 subnets, 2 masks
O        172.31.60.0/24 [110/3] via 10.0.21.2, 00:03:37, FastEthernet0/12

Switch2#traceroute 172.31.60.254
Type escape sequence to abort.
Tracing the route to 172.31.60.254
VRF info: (vrf in name/id, vrf out name/id)
  1 10.0.21.2 8 msec 0 msec 0 msec
  2 10.0.12.1 0 msec *  0 msec
```

To get to the 172.31.60.0/24 network, a packet goes to 10.0.21.2 (Router1) and then 10.0.12.1 (Switch1). What all three subnets have in common is that they're all in area 0. Remember that OSPF prefers to keep traffic within the same area whenever possible.

But suppose that the path via Router1 goes down. OSPF should adjust accordingly and reroute traffic over the direct link between Switch1 and Switch2. Let's try it!

> **Try it now**
>
> On Switch2, shut down the FastEthernet0/12 link facing Router1:
>
> ```
> Interface fa0/12
> Shutdown
> ```
>
> You should see the following OSPF message:
>
> ```
> %OSPF-5-ADJCHG: Process 1, Nbr 12.12.12.12 on FastEthernet0/12 from FULL
> to DOWN, Neighbor Down: Interface down or detached
> ```

(continued)

Execute another show ip route ospf followed by a traceroute 172.31.60.254.

You should see a different route with Switch1 as the next hop:

```
Switch2#show ip route ospf
Gateway of last resort is not set

      10.0.0.0/8 is variably subnetted, 3 subnets, 2 masks
O IA    10.0.12.0/30 [110/2] via 10.0.99.1, 00:00:28, FastEthernet0/24
      172.31.0.0/16 is variably subnetted, 3 subnets, 2 masks
O IA    172.31.60.0/24 [110/2] via 10.0.99.1, 00:00:28, FastEthernet0/24
Switch2#traceroute 172.31.60.254
Type escape sequence to abort.
Tracing the route to 172.31.60.254
VRF info: (vrf in name/id, vrf out name/id)
  1 10.0.99.1 9 msec *  0 msec
```

The IP routing table lists the route as O IA, which means OSPF *inter-area*. This indicates that to get to the 172.31.60.0/24 network, traffic must jump between OSPF areas 0 and 1, hence the term *inter-area*.

16.4   Commands used in this chapter

Refer to table 16.1 for a list of all the commands used in this chapter.

Table 16.1   Commands used in this chapter

Command	Configuration mode	Description
Interface loopback0	Global	Creates a loopback interface named loopback0.
Router eigrp 7	Global	Enters router configuration mode for EIGRP AS 7.
Network 10.1.1.1 0.0.0.0	EIGRP router	Enables EIGRP on any interface with an IP address of 10.1.1.1. Also advertises the subnet of the interface.
Show ip eigrp neighbor	N/A	Displays adjacent EIGRP neighbors.
Router ospf 1	Global	Enter router configuration mode for OSPF process 1.
Network 10.1.1.1 0.0.0.0 area 0	OSPF router	Enables OSPF on any interface with an IP address of 10.1.1.1. Also advertises the subnet of the interface into area 0.
Show ip ospf neighbor	N/A	Displays adjacent OSPF neighbors.
Show ip protocols	N/A	Displays information about active routing protocols on the router.

16.5 *Hands-on lab*

For today's hands-on lab, place the 10.0.99.0/30 subnet into OSPF area 0. You have a couple of ways to achieve this, so use the method that seems best to you. If you're successful, OSPF will prefer the direct path between Switch1 and Switch2. Once you've done that, add Switch1's loopback (1.1.1.1) and Switch2's loopback (2.2.2.2) to area 0.

Tracking down devices 17

In this chapter, you'll learn how to use the command line to track down devices throughout your network. To be clear, I'm not just talking about figuring out the general geographic location of a device. I'm talking about tracking down a device to the specific switch or router and port it's connected to. Although this isn't something you'll have to do very often, when the need arises, knowing how to track down that elusive printer or virus-laden PC can make you a hero.

17.1 Device-tracking scenarios

I won't discuss every possible scenario in which you'll find it necessary to track down a specific device. But drawing from my own experience, two basic scenarios come to mind.

Many organizations use a network-monitoring package like WhatsUp Gold to track network bandwidth utilization and uptime. When the network begins to slow, your manager may turn to the network administrator (you) to find out who the *top talkers* are—those devices that historically use up the most bandwidth. Most of the time, knowing the IP addresses of these top talkers is enough to figure out where they are, especially if they're servers in a data center where things don't move around very much. But occasionally you may encounter a mysterious device—nobody knows where or what it is!

Another situation involves tracking down a printer in a remote office with no IT staff. The story usually goes like this: someone needs to move a printer to a different location within the office, which entails moving it to a different switch port. All you need to do is reconfigure the new switch port the same as the current one. The problem is that you don't know which port the printer's currently plugged into, so you can't find out the VLAN or speed and duplex information.

You might be rolling your eyes and thinking that the real problem with these scenarios is a failure to properly document the network, and that's true. Unfortunately, poor or nonexistent network documentation is more common than you might think. I'd say that in most organizations without a full-time network administrator, having no network documentation is the rule rather than the exception.

Because of that, learning how to track down devices isn't just a tangential, nice-to-have skill. It's critical in order to be able to document your network. Fortunately, you don't have to hop on a plane and visit remote offices and data centers—at least not to do this. Instead, you can easily track down devices from the IOS command line, usually in just a matter of minutes or less.

17.2 Steps to tracking down a device

Before getting started, it may help to keep in mind the high-level process you'll go through anytime you track down a device, which I'll call the *target device*.

17.2.1 Get the IP address

Almost every end-user device on your network—whether it's a printer, server, PC, IP phone, or something else—has an IP address. It's possible that you'll need to track down a device in an office far, far away and have no idea what its IP address is. How you obtain the IP address for such a device can vary widely depending on what the device is. Unless it's a PC or server that you can run an `ifconfig` or `ipconfig` against, finding out the IP address is beyond the scope of this book.

17.2.2 Trace the device to the last hop

The last hop is the last device that an IP packet passes through as it reaches its destination. As you'll recall from the last chapter, this can be a router or a layer-3 switch.

17.2.3 Get the MAC address

Once you get to the last-hop device, whether it's a switch or a router, you can query the device's ARP table to find the MAC address of the device. Recall from chapter 2 that ARP is the function that maps an IP address to a MAC address. Once you have the MAC address, you can track it down to a single port.

In this chapter, I'm going to track down two devices—a server and a printer—to show you how it's done. If you want to follow along with me, which I highly recommend, follow the "Try it now" exercises throughout.

> **Try it now**
> Pick two devices in your network and write down their IP addresses.

17.3 *Example 1—Tracking down a network printer*

The first device I'll track down is a network printer with the IP address 172.31.60.50. Even though I already know physically where this printer is (it's sitting right behind me) and even which VLAN it's in, I'll pretend I don't. As far as I'm concerned, the only devices I know about are those listed in table 17.1. Let's get started!

Table 17.1   Interfaces and IP addresses for Switch1, Switch2, and Router1

Device	Interface	IP address
Switch1	FastEthernet0/12	10.0.12.1/30
Switch1	FastEthernet0/24	10.0.99.1/30
Switch2	FastEthernet0/12	10.0.21.1/30
Switch2	FastEthernet0/24	10.0.99.2/30
Router1	FastEthernet0/0.999	10.0.12.2/30
Router1	FastEthernet0/1	10.0.21.2/30

17.3.1 *Tracing to the last hop using traceroute*

It doesn't usually matter where you run traceroute from. But as a rule of thumb, you're better off starting out on a router that lies somewhere near the nexus of the network. In my lab network, that would be Router1. There are a couple of reasons for this. First, as a network administrator, you're more likely to be familiar with the devices that lie at the heart of your network. Second, those central routers often have visibility into most if not all of the network—specifically, they're running dynamic routing protocols and know all of the routes to the various subnets across your network. I'll start on Router1 looking for the printer with an IP address of 172.31.60.50.

Try it now

Run a traceroute to the IP address of your first target device:

```
traceroute 172.31.60.50
```

Here's the output I see:

```
Router1#traceroute 172.31.60.50

Type escape sequence to abort.
Tracing the route to 172.31.60.50

 1 10.0.12.1 4 msec 0 msec 4 msec
 2 172.31.60.50 4 msec 4 msec 0 msec
```

The last IP address (172.31.60.50) is the target device, which I know isn't a router or switch, so I'm going to ignore that. Instead, I'm interested in the last hop, 10.0.12.1.

Example 1—Tracking down a network printer **235**

In a perfect world, I'd have a clean-looking network diagram that tells me exactly what this device is. Ideally, I should be able to log right into this last-hop device and continue my search. Unfortunately, this world is far from perfect, so I have to take a detour to figure out what this device is. For that, it's IOS to the rescue!

Try it now

On Router1, do a `show ip route` against the IP address of the last hop:

```
show ip route 10.0.12.1
```

You should get a few lines of output:

```
Router1#show ip route 10.0.12.1
Routing entry for 10.0.12.0/30
  Known via "connected", distance 0, metric 0 (connected, via interface)
  Routing Descriptor Blocks:
  * directly connected, via FastEthernet0/0.999
      Route metric is 0, traffic share count is 1
```

Notice that it says that the next hop is directly connected via FastEthernet0/0.999. This is telling me that the device I'm on (Router1) has an interface with an IP address in the same subnet as the last-hop device. Specifically, the interface is the subinterface FastEthernet0/0.999. Again, feigning complete and utter ignorance of the network, I need to find out what this interface is connected to.

17.3.2 Cisco Discovery Protocol

One of your best pals when tracking down a device is *Cisco Discovery Protocol (CDP)*. With some notable exceptions, all Cisco routers and switches have CDP enabled by default. As the name suggests, each device running CDP advertises itself and its capabilities to its directly connected neighbors. CDP advertisements contain the device hostname, platform, and IP addresses—more than enough information to help you figure out which devices are adjacent to the one you're working on.

Try it now

On Router1, run a `show cdp neighbors`.

You should see a list of connected devices, assuming they're Cisco devices that are running CDP:

```
Router1#show cdp neighbors
Capability Codes: R - Router, T - Trans Bridge, B - Source Route Bridge
                  S - Switch, H - Host, I - IGMP, r - Repeater

Device ID    Local Intrfce   Holdtme    Capability    Platform    Port ID
Switch2      Fas 0/1         139        R S I         WS-C3560-   Fas 0/12
Switch1      Fas 0/0         145        R S I         WS-C3560-   Fas 0/12
```

By the way, CDP is a Cisco-proprietary protocol, so don't expect it to show you information about non-Cisco devices. Notice that Switch1 is connected to the FastEthernet0/0 interface, which is the parent of the FastEthernet0/0.999 subinterface. The next stop, then, is Switch1.

Above and beyond

By default, CDP advertisements traverse VLAN 1, and you can't shut down VLAN 1 on a trunk interface. This is why the output shows the physical interface rather than the subinterface.

17.3.3 *Obtaining the MAC address of the device*

The next step is to jump on the last-hop device—which in my case is Switch1—and query the ARP table to get the MAC address of the printer.

Try it now

Do a `show arp` followed by the IP address of your target:

```
show arp 172.31.60.50
```

You should get some output that includes the MAC address:

```
Switch1#show arp 172.31.60.50
Protocol    Address         Age (min)   Hardware Addr    Type    Interface
Internet    172.31.60.50          2     0030.c1c3.80d0   ARPA    Vlan600
```

As you probably guessed, the `Hardware Addr` is the MAC address of the printer. But the `Interface` in that last column, Vlan600, might seem puzzling. Vlan600 isn't a physical interface. It's actually Switch1's SVI. To find out the physical interface where the printer is connected, you need to dig a bit deeper.

17.3.4 *Viewing the MAC address table*

Once you have the MAC address of the target device, you're ready to narrow its location to a specific port. To do that, you'll query the MAC address table.

Try it now

Do a `show mac address-table address` followed by the MAC address:

```
show mac address-table address 0030.c1c3.80d0
```

Alternatively, you can view all entries in the table by issuing a simple `show mac address-table`.

Example 1—Tracking down a network printer **237**

If you view just the entry for the single MAC address, you should see something like this:

```
Switch1#show mac address-table address 0030.c1c3.80d0
          Mac Address Table
-------------------------------------------

Vlan    Mac Address       Type        Ports
----    -----------       --------    -----
 600    0030.c1c3.80d0    STATIC      Fa0/5
Total Mac Addresses for this criterion: 1
```

The output gives you the VLAN, MAC address, and physical port where the MAC address is connected. It appears that the printer is connected directly to FastEthernet0/5, but to be sure, it's a good idea to check the port configuration:

```
Switch1#sh run int fa0/5
Building configuration...

Current configuration : 256 bytes
!
interface FastEthernet0/5
 switchport access vlan 600
 switchport mode access
 switchport port-security maximum 3
 switchport port-security
 switchport port-security aging time 10
 switchport port-security violation restrict
 spanning-tree portfast
End
```

This is clearly an access port in VLAN 600, and Port Security is enabled. Although there's nothing that screams "This is a printer!" it does at least look as if this is some sort of edge device. Let's dig deeper by taking a look at Port Security:

```
Switch1#sh port-security interface fa0/5
Port Security               : Enabled
Port Status                 : Secure-up
Violation Mode              : Restrict
Aging Time                  : 10 mins
Aging Type                  : Absolute
SecureStatic Address Aging  : Disabled
Maximum MAC Addresses       : 3
Total MAC Addresses         : 1
Configured MAC Addresses    : 0
Sticky MAC Addresses        : 0
Last Source Address:Vlan    : 0030.c1c3.80d0:600
Security Violation Count    : 0
```

Port Security has seen only one MAC address within the last 10 minutes, and it's that of the printer. Based on that, you can be reasonably certain that the printer is plugged into FastEthernet0/5 on Switch1!

I use the phrase "reasonably certain" because there could be another switch between Switch1 and the printer. Small non-Cisco switches like those you'd buy at the grocery store don't use CDP or form VLAN trunks, so they can be essentially invisible. But if you've narrowed your search to a single port with just a single MAC address hanging off it, then you've probably reached the end of the line.

17.4 *Example 2—Tracking down a server*

For my next trick, I'll locate a Linux server with an IP address of 172.31.70.51. Again, I'll pretend I don't know where this server is so that I can illustrate all the normal steps you'd go through. I'm going to repeat the same basic steps as before, but this time I'll curtail my explanations a bit. Also, there are no "Try it now" exercises in this section because you'll perform the steps in the hands-on lab.

17.4.1 *Tracing to the last hop using traceroute*

I'll start on Router1 again and run another traceroute, this time to the server's IP address. I get the familiar output:

```
Router1#traceroute 172.31.70.51

Type escape sequence to abort.
Tracing the route to 172.31.70.51

  1 10.0.21.1 4 msec 0 msec 0 msec
  2 172.31.70.51 4 msec 0 msec 0 msec
```

This time, the last hop is 10.0.21.1. Let's see where that device is:

```
Router1#show ip route 10.0.21.1
Routing entry for 10.0.21.0/30
  Known via "connected", distance 0, metric 0 (connected, via interface)
  Routing Descriptor Blocks:
  * directly connected, via FastEthernet0/1
      Route metric is 0, traffic share count is 1
```

This device, whatever it is, is directly connected to Router1's FastEthernet0/1 interface. Assuming it's a Cisco device and CDP is enabled on it, I should be able to execute a show cdp neighbors and find out what it is:

```
Router1#sh cdp neighbors
Capability Codes: R - Router, T - Trans Bridge, B - Source Route Bridge
                  S - Switch, H - Host, I - IGMP, r - Repeater

Device ID   Local Intrfce   Holdtme   Capability   Platform    Port ID
Switch2     Fas 0/1          164         R S I      WS-C3560-   Fas 0/12
Switch1     Fas 0/0          171         R S I      WS-C3560-   Fas 0/12
```

By the way, notice that Switch2 and Switch1 have an R under the Capability column, indicating that they're both functioning as routers. In this case, it looks like Switch2 is the last hop. But before jumping over there, I want to address a question that might be nagging you.

Example 2—Tracking down a server   **239**

You might be wondering how I'd proceed if Switch2 wasn't directly connected but was a few hops removed from Router1. In that case, I could Telnet or SSH directly to its IP address, 10.0.21.1. To illustrate, I'll go ahead and do that now:

```
Router1#telnet 10.0.21.1
Trying 10.0.21.1 ... Open

User Access Verification

Username: admin
Password:
Switch2#
```

Once I log into Switch2, I get the enable prompt, indicating that my login to Switch2 was successful. From here, I can continue my search for the server.

17.4.2 *Obtaining the MAC address of the device*

Because Switch2 is the last hop, it should have an ARP entry for my secret server:

```
Switch2#sh arp 172.31.70.51
Protocol    Address        Age (min)    Hardware Addr    Type    Interface
Internet    172.31.70.51          0     000c.295c.0254   ARPA    Vlan700
```

Sure enough, the MAC address of the server is 000c.295c.0254. And just as before, the interface is not a physical interface but an SVI.

17.4.3 *Viewing the MAC address table*

The final step is to find out which port this MAC address is hanging off:

```
Switch2#sh mac address-table address 000c.295c.0254
          Mac Address Table
-------------------------------------------

Vlan    Mac Address      Type       Ports
----    -----------      --------   -----
 700    000c.295c.0254   DYNAMIC    Fa0/22
Total Mac Addresses for this criterion: 1
```

According to the output, this MAC address is reachable off FastEthernet0/22. But that doesn't necessarily mean the server is connected directly to that port. There could be another switch, or even a series of switches, in between Switch2 and the server. Let's check the configuration of the port:

```
Switch2#show run interface fa0/22
Building configuration...

Current configuration : 34 bytes
!
interface FastEthernet0/22
End
```

The interface configuration section is blank, which means the port is using a default configuration. To find out whether it's operating as a VLAN trunk or access port, we'll need to dig a bit deeper:

```
Switch2#show int fa0/22 switchport | i Mode|Trunk
Administrative Mode: dynamic auto
Operational Mode: trunk
Administrative Trunking Encapsulation: negotiate
Operational Trunking Encapsulation: dot1q
Negotiation of Trunking: On
Access Mode VLAN: 1 (default)
Trunking Native Mode VLAN: 1 (default)
Trunking VLANs Enabled: ALL
Capture Mode Disabled
```

FastEthernet0/22 is an 802.1Q VLAN trunk, but that doesn't necessarily mean the device on the other end is a switch. Recall from chapter 10 that virtualization products like VMware ESXi and Microsoft Hyper-V also use 802.1Q trunks. You may sometimes even find an end-user device like a PC or IP phone connected to a trunk port. The bottom line is that you shouldn't assume that a trunk port gives you any definitive indication of what kind of device is connected on the other end.

At this point, it's inconclusive whether we've discovered the port the server's connected to. Let's investigate a bit more by looking at all MAC addresses on this port:

```
Switch2#show mac address-table interface fa0/22
          Mac Address Table
-------------------------------------------

Vlan    Mac Address       Type        Ports
----    -----------       --------    -----
 700    000c.295c.0254    DYNAMIC     Fa0/22
 700    000c.29d9.6546    DYNAMIC     Fa0/22
 700    001d.45cf.e817    DYNAMIC     Fa0/22
 700    00d0.b80d.6782    DYNAMIC     Fa0/22
 700    78e3.b50d.56e8    DYNAMIC     Fa0/22
 700    78e3.b510.acd2    DYNAMIC     Fa0/22
   1    001d.45cf.e817    DYNAMIC     Fa0/22
 600    001d.45cf.e817    DYNAMIC     Fa0/22
Total Mac Addresses for this criterion: 8
```

Not surprisingly, Switch2 knows about multiple MAC addresses in VLAN 700 that are reachable off this port. There's also one MAC that appears in VLANs 1, 600, and 700 simultaneously. This is a surefire indication that the device on the other end is a switch. If it's a Cisco switch, CDP should tell us:

```
Switch2#show cdp neighbors fa0/22
Capability Codes: R - Router, T - Trans Bridge, B - Source Route Bridge
                  S - Switch, H - Host, I - IGMP, r - Repeater, P - Phone,
                  D - Remote, C - CVTA, M - Two-port Mac Relay

Device ID    Local Intrfce    Holdtme    Capability    Platform     Port ID
Switch3      Fas 0/22         154              S I     WS-C3560-    Fas 0/21
```

Example 2—Tracking down a server **241**

It looks like another switch! By the way, notice that the Capability column doesn't indicate that Switch3 is a router. This is why its IP address didn't show up in the traceroute! Speaking of which, how do you manage it without knowing its management IP address? CDP can help you with that as well:

```
Switch2#show cdp neighbors fa0/22 detail
-----------------------
Device ID: Switch3
Entry address(es):
  IP address: 192.168.1.103
Platform: cisco WS-C3560-24TS,  Capabilities: Switch IGMP
Interface: FastEthernet0/22,  Port ID (outgoing port): FastEthernet0/21
Holdtime : 150 sec
[output truncated]
```

CDP provides the management IP address of the switch, 192.168.1.103. Let's Telnet to it:

```
Switch2#telnet 192.168.1.103
Trying 192.168.1.103 ... Open

User Access Verification

Username: admin
Password:
Switch3#
```

Bingo! We're one step closer to hunting down the elusive server! Let's check Switch3's MAC address table:

```
Switch3#show mac address-table address 000c.295c.0254
          Mac Address Table
-------------------------------------------

Vlan    Mac Address       Type        Ports
----    -----------       --------    -----
 700    000c.295c.0254    DYNAMIC     Fa0/10
Total Mac Addresses for this criterion: 1
```

It looks like the server is connected to the FastEthernet0/10 port on Switch3. Let's inspect the interface configuration:

```
Switch3#sh run int fa0/10
Building configuration...

Current configuration : 112 bytes
!
interface FastEthernet0/10
 description Linux server
 switchport access vlan 700
 switchport mode access
end
```

Got it! The Linux server is connected to FastEthernet0/10.

17.5   Commands used in this chapter

Now that you have a good understanding of how IP routing works and the relationship between IP and MAC addresses, the process of locating a device should be intuitive. You always start with the IP address, trace it down to the last hop, and then find its MAC address. Once you have its MAC address, you can easily determine the VLAN the device is in and which switch it's on. From there, locating the specific port is trivial.

As you walk through the hands-on lab, refer to the commands in table 17.2.

Table 17.2   Commands used in this chapter

Command	Configuration mode	Description
traceroute x.x.x.x	N/A	Displays the hops an IP packet goes through to reach its destination
show cdp neighbors	N/A	Displays hostname and interface information about directly connected Cisco devices
show arp x.x.x.x	N/A	Queries the ARP table and displays the MAC address of the specified IP address
show mac address-table	N/A	Displays the MAC address table

17.6   Hands-on lab

Use the steps you've learned in this chapter to locate the second target device you chose at the beginning of the chapter. Using the commands in table 17.2, try to figure out exactly which switch and port it's connected to.

Securing Cisco devices

If you work in a Windows Active Directory environment, you're accustomed to having a single *credential*—that is, a username and password—to log into almost everything. Sadly, many Cisco networks haven't adopted this "one credential to rule them all" approach. Instead, it's quite common to find that each device requires nothing more than a generic administrator password to log in and start making changes. In slightly more secure environments, the devices may require a unique username and password.

One downside of this setup is that when you want to give someone access to several devices, you have to manually configure a credential on each one. For example, a company I once worked for hired a contractor to configure a Cisco IP phone system. He needed to log into a few of our routers that were scattered across the country, so I created individual, privileged accounts just on those routers he needed access to. Cisco calls each of these accounts a *local user account*.

Although having local accounts on each device isn't ideal, it's a reality in many organizations. As a Cisco network administrator, you need to know not only how to create local accounts but, more importantly, how to lock down your Cisco devices to mitigate the damage if such a privileged account gets into the wrong hands.

One of the most effective ways to do this is to restrict Telnet and Secure Shell (SSH) access to certain IP addresses or subnets. For instance, if your organization has a dedicated subnet for the IT department, you can lock down access so that only devices in that subnet can Telnet or SSH to your Cisco devices.

In this chapter, you'll create a privileged user account on Switch1. You'll then configure SSH access and require a valid username and password to manage the switch. As a bonus, you'll also disable Telnet access, which is inherently insecure because it provides no encryption or authentication. Finally, you'll lock down management access to a range of subnets. Let's get started!

18.1 Creating a privileged user account

A *privileged user account* is one that doesn't require the user to explicitly enter the enable password in order to get into privileged enable mode. As soon as a privileged user logs in, IOS drops them into enable mode "automagically." In a moment, you'll create a new account on Switch1 using a name of your choice. You'll make this a privileged account by assigning a *privilege level* of 15, which is the highest possible. Although there are lower levels, you'll likely never see them in a production environment. I've never configured any privilege level other than 15 when creating a local account for administrative access.

> **Try it now**
>
> On Switch1, issue the following global configuration command, replacing `ben` and `cisco` with a username and password of your choice:
>
> ```
> username ben privilege 15 secret cisco
> ```

> **Above and beyond**
>
> Instead of using the `secret` keyword, you may occasionally see `password`. The difference is that `secret` triggers IOS to encrypt the password and store the encrypted version in the configuration. This makes it nearly impossible to discover a user's password by just parsing the running configuration. The `password` keyword stores the password in plain text, unencrypted, in the configuration. Unless you need to be able to see the password in the running configuration, always use the `secret` keyword.

18.1.1 Testing the account

As part of the initial lab setup, Switch1, Switch2, and Router1 have Telnet access enabled. In addition to having a Telnet server, IOS has its own built-in Telnet client. This can come in handy when you're on one device and want to test Telnet connectivity to another without having to load PuTTY. You can even use the built-in Telnet client to connect back to the device you're on! Although you wouldn't normally Telnet from Switch1 to Switch1, for example, this is an easy way to test your configuration.

> **Try it now**
>
> On Switch1, Telnet to Switch1's loopback0 address, which you configured back in chapter 16 (1.1.1.1):
>
> ```
> telnet 1.1.1.1
> ```
>
> When prompted, log in using the credentials you just created.

When you Telnet to Switch1, it prompts you for a username and password, like so:

```
Switch1#telnet 1.1.1.1
Trying 1.1.1.1 ... Open

User Access Verification

Username: ben
Password:
Switch1#
```

You're in! It's not obvious that you're actually Telnetting from Switch1 to Switch1 because the prompt looks exactly the same as before. Fortunately, there's a way to figure out how you're connected.

> **Try it now**
> Issue the command show users.

You should see the following:

```
Switch1#show users
     Line       User        Host(s)      Idle       Location
    0 con 0                  1.1.1.1      00:00:00
*   1 vty 0     ben          idle         00:00:00 1.1.1.1

   Interface   User        Mode         Idle       Peer Address
```

Under the `Line` column it says `vty  0`. VTY stands for *Virtual TeletYpe*, and a VTY line is how IOS keeps track of individual Telnet and SSH sessions into the device. The asterisk at the beginning of the line indicates the VTY line you're connected to. If you were to Telnet in again from the current session, you'd see a second connection.

> **Try it now**
> From Switch1, Telnet into Switch1 again:
> ```
> telnet 1.1.1.1
> ```
> Log in using the same credentials as before.
> Once you're in, issue another show users.

You should see a new entry:

```
Switch1#show users
     Line       User        Host(s)      Idle       Location
    0 con 0                  1.1.1.1      00:00:00
    1 vty 0     ben          1.1.1.1      00:00:00 1.1.1.1
*   2 vty 1     ben          idle         00:00:00 1.1.1.1

   Interface   User        Mode         Idle       Peer Address
```

Notice that the subsequent VTY number increased by 1. The thing to note here is that IOS allows multiple Telnet or SSH sessions simultaneously, and you can individually identify each session. This isn't particularly exciting, but keeping this information in mind will help you when reconfiguring Telnet and SSH in a moment. By the way, the maximum number of simultaneous sessions is limited by the number of available VTY lines, and this number varies by device. I'll show you how to get that information shortly.

18.2   *Reconfiguring the VTY lines*

One of the goals of this chapter is to enable SSH so that you can eventually disable insecure Telnet access. Before you can do either of these things, however, you have to understand how the VTY lines are currently configured.

> **Try it now**
>
> On Switch1 issue a `show run | s line vty 0`.

You should see the following:

```
Switch1#show run | s line vty 0
line vty 0 4
 login local
 transport input telnet
```

Let's break this configuration section down line by line:

- `line vty 0 4`—This represents a range of VTY numbers, 0 through 4 inclusive. You can use the inline help to get the maximum number of VTY lines. Enter ? instead of 4 and IOS will give you the highest VTY line number.
- `login local`—This tells IOS to require a locally configured username and password of anyone who connects to any of the VTY lines.
- `transport input telnet`—This enables Telnet access to the switch.

18.2.1   *Enabling SSH and disabling Telnet access*

Next, you'll enable SSH and disable Telnet using a single command. Even though you're Telnetted into Switch1, disabling Telnet won't affect your current sessions.

> **Try it now**
>
> Issue the following commands to enable SSH and disable Telnet:
>
> ```
> line vty 0 4
> transport input ssh
> ```

Now that you've disabled Telnet, you'll need a way to SSH into Switch1 from Switch1. Fortunately, Cisco thought of this too and included an SSH client with IOS.

> **Try it now**
>
> From Switch1, SSH into Switch1 using the following command. Replace ben with the username you configured earlier:
>
> ssh -l ben 1.1.1.1
>
> Once you're in, execute a show users.

You should get prompted for a password, just as when using Telnet:

```
Switch1#ssh -l ben 1.1.1.1
Password:
Switch1#show users
    Line        User        Host(s)      Idle       Location
   0 con 0                  1.1.1.1      00:00:00
   1 vty 0      ben         1.1.1.1      00:00:00 1.1.1.1
   2 vty 1      ben         1.1.1.1      00:00:00 1.1.1.1
*  3 vty 2      ben         idle         00:00:00 1.1.1.1

    Interface   User        Mode         Idle       Peer Address
```

Notice that the existing Telnet sessions are unaffected. Disabling Telnet in the running configuration doesn't boot out connected users. This safety net can help prevent you from accidentally locking yourself out!

Also notice that there isn't any discernible difference between the SSH session connected to VTY line 2 and the two Telnet sessions on lines 0 and 1. If you want to see just the SSH sessions, you'll have to run a different command.

> **Try it now**
>
> Execute a show ssh.

You should see the following:

```
Switch1#show ssh
Connection  Version  Mode  Encryption    Hmac       State            Username
2           1.99     IN    aes128-cbc    hmac-sha1  Session started       ben
2           1.99     OUT   aes128-cbc    hmac-sha1  Session started       ben
%No SSHv1 server connections running.
```

The first column lists 2, which refers to the VTY line number. The last column, of course, shows the username.

I had you open two Telnet sessions to ensure that you didn't accidentally lock your-self out. Now that you've disabled Telnet access and verified SSH is working, you can safely close all your Telnet sessions.

Try it now

Exit your SSH session by entering `exit`.

Then enter `exit` twice to close your two Telnet sessions.

Using the built-in SSH client, connect back in to Switch1:

`ssh -1 ben 1.1.1.1`

Finally, verify that the other Telnet sessions are gone:

`show users`

You should successfully connect and see both Telnet sessions gone:

```
Switch1#ssh -1 ben 1.1.1.1
Password:

Switch1#show users
    Line         User        Host(s)       Idle        Location
    0 con 0                   1.1.1.1       00:00:00
*   1 vty 0      ben          idle          00:00:00 1.1.1.1

    Interface    User         Mode          Idle        Peer Address
```

18.2.2 *Restricting SSH access using access lists*

If a privileged username and password get out, there's an increased risk of some hood-lum—inside or outside the organization—using it to log into your Cisco devices and wreaking havoc. To add an additional layer of security, you should consider restricting management access to those IP addresses that you and other authorized administra-tors are likely to use.

For the next lab, you'll restrict SSH access to the following subnets and IP addresses:

- *The VLAN1 subnet*—192.168.1.0/24
- *Switch1's loopback*—1.1.1.1
- *Switch2's loopback*—2.2.2.2

In chapter 9 you learned how to use access lists to block traffic to individual interfaces. Although you can use this method to control remote access to your Cisco devices, it's a lot of work because you'd have to apply an access list to every interface where some-one might connect. This is also risky, especially in a production environment, because a single misconfigured ACL entry could take down the whole network.

Instead of applying an ACL directly to a bunch of interfaces, you can apply an ACL directly to the VTY lines. Not only is this simpler, but it's also safe to do in a production environment. If you make a mistake, the worst that will happen is that you'll block subsequent SSH sessions. But your existing sessions will be unaffected.

Try it now

Create a new extended IP address access list called Management:

```
ip access-list extended Management
permit ip 192.168.1.0 0.0.0.255 any
permit ip host 1.1.1.1 any
permit ip host 2.2.2.2 any
```

Apply the access list to the VTY lines:

```
line vty 0 4
access-class Management in
```

The destination portion of each ACL entry—any—allows the specified source addresses to SSH to any interface IP address on Switch1. This is nice because as long as you know one of the active IP addresses of a Cisco device, you can SSH directly to it.

Try it now

From Switch2, attempt to SSH to Switch1's loopback address:

```
ssh -l ben 1.1.1.1
```

Even if you configured everything correctly, you may not be able to connect:

```
Switch2#ssh -l ben 1.1.1.1
% Connection refused by remote host
```

Remember that the only source addresses allowed are 1.1.1.1 and 2.2.2.2. Switch2 has multiple IP addresses, and apparently it's not using the IP address of its loopback1 interface, 2.2.2.2. To fix this, you have to explicitly tell it to use this interface's IP address.

Try it now

On Switch2, execute the following global configuration command:

```
ip ssh source-interface loopback 1
```

Attempt to SSH to Switch1 again:

```
ssh -l ben 1.1.1.1
```

You should now be able to connect:

```
Switch2#ssh -l ben 1.1.1.1
Password:

Switch1#
```

18.3   *Securing the console port*

As your final task on Switch1, you'll secure the serial console port to require a username and password. Compared to securing the VTY lines, this configuration is almost offensively simple.

> **Try it now**
>
> Execute the following global configuration commands on Switch1:
>
> ```
> line con 0
> login local
> ```

For the most part, I've been silent about *how* you've been connecting to your devices. If you followed the lab setup, you used the console port to log in and install the initial configurations. If you've been using Telnet or SSH to connect to your devices, you may not be in a position to test the console port. If you have the console port connected to Switch1, go ahead and follow the "Try it now." Otherwise, don't worry because you'll take care of this during the hands-on lab.

> **Try it now**
>
> Connect to the console port of Switch1 as you did during the lab setup and log in using the credentials you configured earlier in the chapter.
>
> Follow this with a show users.

You should see the following:

```
Switch1 con0 is now available

Press RETURN to get started.

User Access Verification

Username: ben
Password:
Switch1#show users
    Line       User       Host(s)      Idle       Location
*   0 con 0    ben        idle         00:00:00

  Interface    User       Mode         Idle       Peer Address
```

Instead of a VTY line, you have a con 0, indicating you're connected to the console port.

18.4 Commands used in this chapter

Refer to table 18.1 to complete the hands-on lab.

Table 18.1 Commands used in this chapter

Command	Configuration mode	Description
username ben privilege 15 secret cisco	Global	Creates a privileged user with the username "ben" and encrypted password "cisco"
telnet 1.1.1.1	N/A	Telnets to 1.1.1.1 using the IOS Telnet client
show users	N/A	Displays users connected to the VTY lines and console port
line vty 0 4	Global	Enters VTY line configuration mode for lines 0 through 4, inclusive
transport input ssh	VTY line	Enables SSH and implicitly disables Telnet
access-class Management in	VTY line	Applies the access list named "Management" to the selected VTY lines
ssh -l ben 1.1.1.1	N/A	Establishes an SSH session to 1.1.1.1 using the IOS SSH client
show ssh	N/A	Displays users connected via SSH to a VTY line
ip ssh source-interface loopback 1	Global	Configures the source address used by the IOS SSH client
line con 0	Global	Enters line console configuration mode
login local	Line console	Requires a local username and password to log in via the console port

18.5 Hands-on lab

For today's hands-on lab, you'll secure Switch2 and Router1. Perform the following steps on both devices:

1 Configure a username and password.
2 Enable SSH and disable Telnet access. Ensure you can connect via SSH.
3 Secure the console and ensure you can connect to it as well.
4 Save your configurations on Switch1, Switch2, and Router1.

Facilitating troubleshooting using logging and debugging

When configuring a Cisco network from scratch, you can get things up and running flawlessly provided that you've configured everything properly. But chances are that in your day-to-day work you won't get to build a network from scratch. You'll inherit an existing network, and it will likely have some minor misconfigurations. In the worst case, it may even be broken. But even if your network isn't broken by a misconfiguration, routers and switches do eventually wear out. Ports stop working, IOS images become corrupted, and power supplies fail.

The bottom line is that you'll eventually encounter various problems that appear to be network-related. Here are some examples:

- A computer can't get a DHCP-assigned IP address.
- A user can't access network resources.
- A switch is missing a VLAN.
- An IP route is missing from a group of routers.

Some will obviously be related to a configuration issue on a router or switch, whereas others will be more ambiguous. Before you can begin troubleshooting the network, you have to determine whether the cause of the problem resides somewhere in your Cisco network or elsewhere. To do that, you'll use two tools: debugging commands and the logging buffer.

Debugging commands are IOS commands that generate detailed messages about what a specific technology is doing at that moment. Most network folks refer to these messages as *debugs*. IOS can display these messages to the terminal console or write them to the *logging buffer*. The logging buffer is a spot in RAM that holds the output of various events, such as an interface going down, a new OSPF adjacency, and, of course, debug messages.

This chapter will show you how to use logging and debugging to gather detailed information about some of the technologies you've configured throughout the book. The idea is to help you collect enough information to either begin troubleshooting on your own or enlist the help of a colleague or vendor.

To be clear, troubleshooting every technology you've learned is beyond the scope of this book. I won't cover every possible debug, and I won't interpret all of the debugging messages. There also won't be much in the way of "Try it now" exercises. If you do want to learn in-depth troubleshooting, you'll find some training resources in the last chapter of the book.

Before you begin, I offer this word of caution: do not enable debugs in a production environment without getting appropriate permission. Turning on debugs creates additional load on the CPU, and although most debugs are safe, some can overwhelm a router or switch to the point that it stops forwarding traffic. I'll warn you about the riskier debug commands, but don't perform any of the commands in this chapter in a production environment unless the network is already down. Let's get started!

19.1 *Configuring the logging buffer*

By default, IOS stores all debug messages in the logging buffer, which stores up to 4,096 bytes by default. Once the log becomes full, IOS overwrites the oldest events first. The defaults notwithstanding, it's a good idea to verify that the logging buffer is configured properly.

Try it now

Choose a router or switch and execute the following command on it:

```
show logging
```

You should see something similar to the following:

```
Syslog logging: enabled (0 messages dropped, 0 messages rate-limited, 0
    flushes, 0 overruns, xml disabled, filtering disabled)

No Active Message Discriminator.


No Inactive Message Discriminator.

    Console logging: level debugging, 58 messages logged, xml disabled,
                filtering disabled
```

```
       Monitor logging: level debugging, 0 messages logged, xml disabled,
                        filtering disabled
       Buffer logging:  level debugging, 8 messages logged, xml disabled,
                        filtering disabled
       Exception Logging: size (4096 bytes)
       Count and timestamp logging messages: disabled
       File logging: disabled
       Persistent logging: disabled

   No active filter modules.

       Trap logging: level informational, 62 message lines logged
           Logging Source-Interface:        VRF Name:

   Log Buffer (4096 bytes):
```

Notice that `Console logging` and `Buffer logging` are set to the `debugging` level. This means that once you enable debugs, IOS will display any debug messages to the terminal console and write them to the logging buffer. Also, notice that the logging buffer is 4,096 bytes. This roughly translates to over 50 lines, which is plenty in most cases. But just in case, let's double it to 8,192 bytes.

> **Try it now**
>
> Execute the following global configuration commands to configure IOS to send debug outputs to the logging buffer:
>
> `logging buffered debugging`
>
> Increase the size of the buffer to 8192 bytes:
>
> `logging buffered 8192`
>
> Optionally, you can clear the log to make it easier to read. Execute the following command at the enable prompt:
>
> `clear logging`

By the way, once the logging buffer fills up, IOS will just overwrite the oldest events. It won't stop logging, so don't fret too much about the size. Once you've done all that, you're ready to start debugging!

19.2 Debug commands

In most cases you can use the IOS inline help feature to figure out which debugs you need to turn on. But as you'll see, some debug commands aren't intuitive or easy to find. Your best bet is to search the internet for the command you're looking for. In the following pages, I'll give you some examples of how to enable and use various debugs, so you can see how it's done.

19.2.1 Debugging Port Security

In this first example, Executive-PC1 can't access any network resources. After verifying that the PC has physical connectivity, you check to make sure Port Security isn't blocking the PC's MAC address:

```
Switch2#show port-security
Secure Port  MaxSecureAddr  CurrentAddr  SecurityViolation  Security Action
               (Count)        (Count)        (Count)
-------------------------------------------------------------------------------
    Fa0/21            1              1              172           Restrict
-------------------------------------------------------------------------------
Total Addresses in System (excluding one mac per port)     : 0
Max Addresses limit in System (excluding one mac per port) : 6144
```

It appears that Port Security is blocking something, but it's not clear whether it's Executive-PC1 or another device. To get more information, you need to turn on debugging for Port Security.

> **Try it now**
>
> Enable Port Security debugs by issuing the following command at an enable prompt:
>
> `debug port-security`
>
> Leave the debug running for about a minute; then turn it off:
>
> `undebug all`
>
> Finally, view the log buffer:
>
> `show logging`

You'll see the following:

```
*Mar  2 19:49:26.156: PSECURE: psecure_packet_enqueue: psecure receives
      a packet: addr = 0800.2759.d9fd, swidb = Fa0/21, vlan = 700,
      linktype = NullPak
*Mar  2 19:49:26.156: PSECURE: Read:197, Write:198
*Mar  2 19:49:26.156: PSECURE: swidb = FastEthernet0/21 mac_addr =
      0800.2759.d9fd vlanid = 700
*Mar  2 19:49:26.156: PSECURE: Violation/duplicate detected upon receiving
      0800.2759.d9fd on vlan 700: port_num_addrs 1 port_max_addrs
      1 vlan_addr_ct 1: vlan_addr_max 1 total_addrs 0: max_total_addrs 6144
*Mar  2 19:49:26.156: PSECURE: Security violation, TrapCount:197
```

Although not without some cryptic elements, this output is fairly straightforward. `Violation/duplicate detected upon receiving 0800.2759.d9fd on vlan 700` gives you the MAC address that Port Security is blocking and even what VLAN it's on. Armed with this information, you can determine whether that MAC address belongs to Executive-PC1 or another machine. You can then adjust Port Security to allow it (refer to chapter 5 for more details).

19.2.2 *Debugging DHCP*

In this example, Executive-PC1 isn't receiving a DHCP-assigned IP address from Switch2. To get to the bottom of it, you enable the DHCP server debugs. A word of warning: this debug can generate a lot of output depending on how many DHCP clients are using the server. Do not run this in a production environment unless you're doing real troubleshooting!

Try it now
Clear the logging buffer:

```
clear logging
```

Debug DHCP server events:

```
debug ip dhcp server events
```

Wait about 10 seconds; then turn the debug off:

```
undebug all
```

View the logging buffer:

```
show logging
```

Here's an excerpt from the output:

```
*Mar  2 20:03:36.744: DHCPD: subnet [172.31.70.1,172.31.70.254]
         in address pool Executives is empty.
*Mar  2 20:03:36.744: DHCPD: Sending notification of ASSIGNMENT FAILURE:
*Mar  2 20:03:36.744:    DHCPD: htype 1 chaddr 0800.2759.d9fd
*Mar  2 20:03:36.744:    DHCPD: remote id 020a0000ac1f46fe0c000000
*Mar  2 20:03:36.744:    DHCPD: interface = Vlan700
*Mar  2 20:03:36.744:    DHCPD: class id 4d53465420352e30
*Mar  2 20:03:36.744:    DHCPD: out_vlan_id 0
*Mar  2 20:03:36.744: DHCPD: Sending notification of ASSIGNMENT_FAILURE:
*Mar  2 20:03:36.744:    DHCPD: due to: POOL EXHAUSTED
*Mar  2 20:03:36.744:    DHCPD: htype 1 chaddr 0800.2759.d9fd
*Mar  2 20:03:36.744:    DHCPD: remote id 020a0000ac1f46fe0c000000
*Mar  2 20:03:36.744:    DHCPD: interface = Vlan700
*Mar  2 20:03:36.744:    DHCPD: class id 4d53465420352e30
*Mar  2 20:03:36.744:    DHCPD: out_vlan_id 0
```

You'll sometimes have to sift through murky output like this to find the cause. In this case, the two lines indicating pool Executives is empty and POOL EXHAUSTED are the ones with the valuable information. Executive-PC1 isn't able to get an IP address because there are no addresses available for assignment in the pool!

It's worth noting that show commands can give you much of the same information a debug gives you. For example, the show ip dhcp pool command would tell you that the DHCP pool has no available addresses. But it wouldn't tell you the specific MAC address of the PC requesting a DHCP-assigned IP address, nor would it give you a timestamp of when that request occurred. Only debugging can give you a nearly real-time stream of what IOS is doing under the hood.

19.2.3 *Debugging the VLAN Trunking Protocol*

Most debugging commands are fairly obvious, but some require you to dig a bit to find them. The debug commands for the VLAN Trunking Protocol (VTP) fall into this category.

In this example, Switch1 is a VTP server and Switch2 is a VTP client, and Switch2 isn't receiving a certain VLAN from Switch1. The command to debug VTP events is nested under a different set of debug commands that isn't so intuitive.

> **Try it now**
>
> Issue the following command to enable debugging for VTP events:
>
> ```
> debug sw-vlan vtp events
> ```
>
> Getting the output isn't as speedy as for the previous debugs. You may have to wait up to five minutes for the VTP server to send an advertisement. Once you've given it some time, turn off the debug and check the log:
>
> ```
> undebug all
> show logging
> ```

You'll see the following:

```
*Mar  1 00:38:07.833: VTP LOG RUNTIME: Summary packet received,
        domain = cisco, rev = 11, followers = 1, length 77, trunk Fa0/24

*Mar  1 00:38:07.833: VTP LOG RUNTIME: Summary packet rev 11 greater than
        domain cisco rev 10

*Mar  1 00:38:07.833: VTP LOG RUNTIME: Domain cisco currently not in
        updating state

*Mar  1 00:38:07.833: VTP LOG RUNTIME: pdu len 77, #tlvs 1

*Mar  1 00:38:07.833: VTP LOG RUNTIME: Subset packet received, domain =
        cisco, rev = 11, seq = 1, length = 348

*Mar  1 00:38:07.833: VTP LOG RUNTIME: MD5 digest failing
calculated = B0 21 87 A1 4F 00 0C F4 14 7C C5 68 C6 84 A2 60
transmitted = B8 96 82 DE 39 52 A7 F7 6E 9C 60 EF 16 E4 77 23
```

This one is a bit more difficult to decipher. As a rule, whenever you encounter an unfamiliar debug and aren't sure what to make of it, look for words that have a negative connotation. The last item in the log says MD5 digest failing, which means the VTP passwords on the client and server don't match. That's not obvious unless you're familiar with the inner workings of VTP, but it doesn't need to be. Most of the time you can copy and paste the error into your favorite search engine and get a quick answer on what it means.

19.2.4 Debugging IP routing

For the final example, I'm going to show you how to track changes to the IP routing table. As you recall from chapter 16, dynamic routing protocols such as OSPF and EIGRP automatically install the best route to a network in the IP routing table. If a WAN connection between routers goes down, it can cause network performance problems, especially if the connection repeatedly goes down and comes back up. IP routing table debugs can tell you exactly when such events take place.

Take a look at the OSPF routes in the IP routing table on Switch1:

```
Switch1#show ip route ospf
Codes: L - local, C - connected, S - static, R - RIP, M - mobile, B - BGP
       D - EIGRP, EX - EIGRP external, O - OSPF, IA - OSPF inter area
       N1 - OSPF NSSA external type 1, N2 - OSPF NSSA external type 2
       E1 - OSPF external type 1, E2 - OSPF external type 2
       i - IS-IS, su - IS-IS summary, L1 - IS-IS level-1, L2 - IS-IS level-2
       ia - IS-IS inter area, * - candidate default, U - per-user static route
       o - ODR, P - periodic downloaded static route, H - NHRP, l - LISP
       + - replicated route, % - next hop override

Gateway of last resort is not set

      2.0.0.0/32 is subnetted, 1 subnets
O        2.2.2.2 [110/2] via 10.0.99.2, 03:51:43, FastEthernet0/24
      10.0.0.0/8 is variably subnetted, 5 subnets, 2 masks
O        10.0.21.0/30 [110/2] via 10.0.99.2, 03:51:43, FastEthernet0/24
                      [110/2] via 10.0.12.2, 03:51:53, Vlan999
      172.31.0.0/16 is variably subnetted, 3 subnets, 2 masks
O        172.31.70.0/24 [110/2] via 10.0.99.2, 03:51:43, FastEthernet0/24
```

Notice that the 2.2.2.2 network is reachable out of the FastEthernet0/24 interface with 10.0.99.2 (Switch2) as the next hop. To see what happens behind the scenes when this link goes down, you can enable debugs for the IP routing table.

> **Try it now**
> On a router or layer-3 switch, enable IP routing debugs:
>
> ```
> debug ip routing
> ```

Watch what happens when the link to Switch2—FastEthernet0/24—goes down:

```
Switch1#debug ip routing
IP routing debugging is on
Switch1#
00:20:19: %LINEPROTO-5-UPDOWN: Line protocol on Interface FastEthernet0/24,
    changed state to down
00:20:20: %LINK-3-UPDOWN: Interface FastEthernet0/24, changed state to down
```

```
*Mar  1 00:20:20.232: is_up: FastEthernet0/24 0 state: 0 sub state: 1 line: 0
00:20:20: %OSPF-5-ADJCHG: Process 1, Nbr 2.2.2.2 on FastEthernet0/24 from
     FULL to DOWN, Neighbor Down: Interface down or detached
*Mar  1 00:20:20.232: RT: interface FastEthernet0/24 removed from
     routing table
*Mar  1 00:20:20.232: RT: del 10.0.99.0 via 0.0.0.0, connected metric [0/0]
*Mar  1 00:20:20.232: RT: delete subnet route to 10.0.99.0/30
*Mar  1 00:20:20.232: RT: del 10.0.99.1 via 0.0.0.0, connected metric [0/0]
*Mar  1 00:20:20.232: RT: delete subnet route to 10.0.99.1/32
*Mar  1 00:20:23.688: RT: updating ospf 2.2.2.2/32 (0x0):
    via 10.0.12.2 Vl999

*Mar  1 00:20:23.688: RT: closer admin distance for 2.2.2.2, flushing 1 routes
*Mar  1 00:20:23.688: RT: add 2.2.2.2/32 via 10.0.12.2, ospf metric [110/3]
*Mar  1 00:20:23.688: RT: updating ospf 172.31.70.0/24 (0x0):
    via 10.0.12.2 Vl999

*Mar  1 00:20:23.688: RT: closer admin distance for 172.31.70.0,
     flushing 1 routes
*Mar  1 00:20:23.688: RT: add 172.31.70.0/24 via 10.0.12.2, ospf metric
     [110/3]
*Mar  1 00:20:23.688: RT: del 10.0.21.0 via 10.0.99.2, ospf metric [110/2]
```

Switch1 removes the 10.0.99.0/30 subnet from its IP routing table, as indicated by the `delete subnet route to 10.0.99.0/30` entry. Following that, Switch2 updates the route for 2.2.2.2/32 to use a different path via 10.0.12.2.

Keep in mind that the output of an IP routing debug probably won't make much sense unless you're looking at a network diagram. What's important is that you know how to enable the debug and view its output should you ever need it.

19.3 Logging severity levels

At the beginning of the chapter I told you that by default IOS stores all debugging messages in the logging buffer. But you may have noticed that IOS also writes several non-debugging messages to the log as well.

> **Try it now**
>
> Pick a switch or router and reboot it. Don't save the running configuration!
>
> ```
> reload
> Proceed with reload? [confirm]
> 00:03:06: %SYS-5-RELOAD: Reload requested by admin on console. Reload
> Reason: Reload command.
> ```
>
> When it comes back up, view the logging buffer:
>
> ```
> show logging
> ```

You may see a dozen or more messages like these:

```
*Mar  1 00:00:33.546: %LINEPROTO-5-UPDOWN: Line protocol on Interface Vlan1,
    changed state to down
```

```
*Mar  1 00:00:35.508: %SPANTREE-5-EXTENDED_SYSID: Extended SysId enabled for
    type vlan
*Mar  1 00:00:37.295: %DC-4-FILE_OPEN_WARNING: Not able to open flash:/
    dc_profile_dir/dc_default_profiles.txt
*Mar  1 00:00:37.295: %DC-6-DEFAULT_INIT_INFO: Default Profiles DB not
    loaded.
00:00:38: %SYS-6-CLOCKUPDATE: System clock has been updated from 00:00:38 UTC
    Mon Mar 1 1993 to 20:00:38 EST Sun Feb 28 1993, configured from console
    by console.
00:00:39: %LINEPROTO-5-UPDOWN: Line protocol on Interface FastEthernet0/24,
    changed state to down
00:00:39: %LINEPROTO-5-UPDOWN: Line protocol on Interface Vlan600, changed
    state to down
00:00:39: %LINEPROTO-5-UPDOWN: Line protocol on Interface Vlan999, changed
    state to down
00:00:39: %SYS-5-CONFIG_I: Configured from memory by console
```

Keep in mind that debugs are off, and the logging buffer gets cleared when you reboot, so these aren't debug messages. Most of these messages are notifications. The term *notifications* refers to one of eight *logging severity levels,* or *logging levels* for short. To see what they are, follow the next "Try it now."

Try it now
View the inline help by tying the global configuration command `logging buffered ?`.

IOS displays the relevant inline help as follows:

```
Switch1(config)#logging buffered ?
  <0-7>               Logging severity level
  <4096-2147483647>   Logging buffer size
  alerts              Immediate action needed         (severity=1)
  critical            Critical conditions             (severity=2)
  debugging           Debugging messages              (severity=7)
  discriminator       Establish MD-Buffer association
  emergencies         System is unusable              (severity=0)
  errors              Error conditions                (severity=3)
  filtered            Enable filtered logging
  informational       Informational messages          (severity=6)
  notifications       Normal but significant conditions (severity=5)
  warnings            Warning conditions              (severity=4)
  xml                 Enable logging in XML to XML logging buffer
  <cr>
```

The eight logging levels are numbered in ascending order from most important to least important. For example, `emergencies` has a severity level of 0, whereas `notifications` has a severity level of 5. The highest level of 7 is for debugging. What's important to note is that each logging level implicitly includes all levels below it. For example, when you set the logging level to level 7, debugging, IOS will still log messages with a lower severity level.

Try it now

Pick a router or switch and configure the logging severity level to level 4, `warnings`:

```
logging buffered warnings
```

Save your running configuration and reload:

```
write memory
reload
```

Finally, view the logging buffer:

```
show logging
```

You should see much less output:

```
*Mar  1 00:00:37.337: %DC-4-FILE_OPEN_WARNING: Not able to open flash:/
    dc_profile_dir/dc_default_profiles.txt
00:00:42: %LINK-3-UPDOWN: Interface FastEthernet0/12, changed state to up
```

Notice that each entry has a modulus (%) followed by capital letters, a dash, and a number. The number indicates the severity level. For example, the `%LINK-3-UPDOWN` event has a severity level of 3, `errors`.

19.4 *Configuring syslogging*

The logging buffer is a nice tool, but it has a major drawback: it's stored in RAM, which means it's limited in size and it gets cleared when the device reboots or powers off. When you need to check the logs across multiple devices, logging into each one and viewing the logging buffer can become a tedious, time-consuming process. To make your life easier, you can configure your Cisco devices to send logs to a syslog server.

Configuring a syslog server is well beyond the scope of this book, but most paid network monitoring tools include one. There are also free offerings, Kiwi being one of the more popular ones. The syslog server sits on the network and continually receives logs from devices that are configured to send them. Just like with the logging buffer, you specify logging severity levels to control what types of logging messages IOS sends to the syslog server.

To configure a router or switch to send its logs to a syslog server, you need two things:

- The IP address of the syslog server
- The logging severity level

Try it now

Choose a router or switch and configure it to send logs to the syslog server at the IP address 1.2.3.4:

```
logging host 1.2.3.4
00:27:11: %SYS-6-LOGGINGHOST_STARTSTOP: Logging to host 1.2.3.4 port 514
started - CLI
```

(continued)

Set the logging trap level to 7, `debugging`:

```
logging trap debugging
```

Verify your configuration with a `show logging`.

Starting about 20 lines into the output, you should see the following:

```
Trap logging: level debugging, 29 message lines logged
        Logging to 1.2.3.4  (udp port 514, audit disabled,
            link up),
            2 message lines logged,
            0 message lines rate-limited,
            0 message lines dropped-by-MD,
            xml disabled, sequence number disabled
            filtering disabled
        Logging Source-Interface:       VRF Name:
```

Enabling syslogging doesn't stop IOS from logging to the logging buffer. For consistency, it's a good idea to maintain the same logging level for both the logging buffer and the syslog.

19.5   *Commands used in this chapter*

For the most part, logging and debugging commands are intuitive. Table 19.1 lists the ones you saw in this chapter. As always, use the inline help to locate specific debug commands as the need arises.

Table 19.1   Commands used in this chapter

Command	Configuration mode	Description
show logging	N/A	Displays logging settings and the contents of the logging buffer
logging buffered debugging	Global	Sets the logging severity level of the logging buffer to 7
logging buffered 8192	Global	Sets the size of the logging buffer to 8,192 bytes
clear logging	N/A	Clears the contents of the logging buffer
debug port-security	N/A	Enables debugging for Port Security
undebug all	N/A	Disables all debugs
debug sw-vlan vtp events	N/A	Enables debugging for VTP events
debug ip routing	N/A	Enables debugging of the IP routing table
reload	N/A	Reboots the device

Table 19.1 Commands used in this chapter

Command	Configuration mode	Description
`logging buffered warnings`	Global	Sets the logging severity level of the logging buffer to 4
`logging host 1.2.3.4`	Global	Sends logs to the syslog server at 1.2.3.4
`logging trap debugging`	Global	Sets the logging severity level of the syslog to 7

19.6 *Hands-on lab*

You can use the command `undebug all` to turn off all debugs. But for some inconceivable reason, Cisco has made it possible to turn on all debugs simultaneously using the `debug all` command. In this hands-on lab, you'll explore the consequences of having too much debugging going at once.

Perform the following on your lab router or switch. Do not perform any of these commands on production equipment!

1 Enable debugging to the console by issuing the command `logging console debugging`. This will cause IOS to dump all debug output to the terminal console so you can view it in real time.

2 Execute the `debug all` command. What happens?

3 Quickly issue an `undebug all` and observe how long it takes for the debug messages to stop.

4 Suppose you have a switch configured as a DHCP server, but clients aren't receiving IP addresses from it. What debug commands might help you figure out what's going on?

Recovering from disaster 20

In your career as a Cisco network administrator, you're going to encounter some situations where large portions of the network—or the whole network—inexplicably stop working. In the last chapter, you learned some troubleshooting techniques to deal with specific technologies that aren't functioning.

But when you're dealing with a disaster scenario, you may not have the luxury of performing in-depth troubleshooting. You need to get the network up and running again, as fast as you can! The goal of recovering from disaster isn't to get everything back to exactly the way it was; it's to get everything working as best you can with what you have. To put it in health terms, you're not trying to win a fitness competition; you're just trying to get your vital signs within the normal range.

Having said that, the exercises in this chapter are for you to use only as necessary when the needs of your organization demand that you do whatever it takes to get the network up and running. This is one of the last chapters of the book, and the exercises in this chapter are to be used as a last resort.

Here are the basic steps you'll follow to recover from a disaster:

1 Narrow the problem to a set of IOS devices. It's unlikely that all or even most of your network devices would malfunction at the same time. Chances are it's just one or a few that are causing the problem.

2 Reload the devices one by one. Although we IT folks often frown upon the "reboot first" troubleshooting advice, it's sometimes warranted. In this case, we're assuming your organization has told you to do whatever it takes to get the network back up.

3 If the problem persists, you may have to delete the startup configuration of one or more devices and reconfigure them from scratch. This is the most painful and least desirable option, but as a Cisco network administrator, it's one you need to be prepared for.

Let's get started!

20.1 Narrow the scope to a subset of devices

Whenever you're dealing with a large-scale network outage, there's one troubleshooting step you must perform no matter how many people are screaming in your ear to fix the network. You must narrow the problem to a set of IOS devices. For example, if everyone in an office has lost all network connectivity, you'll need to consider every switch everyone's connected to, as well as every router in that office. On the other hand, if the network outage is confined to a department or section of the office, you may be able to narrow the problem to one or two switches.

If the network outage affects multiple offices simultaneously, chances are slim that the issue lies in a specific group of routers and switches. It's much more likely that there's an issue with the WAN connections among your different sites. In that case, there's not much you can do other than contact your carrier and perform old-school troubleshooting with them.

A word of caution, though: if you're not able to narrow the problem to a subset of devices, don't proceed with the rest of the steps. The worst thing you can do is to start messing with devices at random. Making sweeping changes in the hopes of getting the network up and running will inevitably make the problem worse or cause a new one that will come back to bite you later.

20.2 Reloading the device

Once you've narrowed the problem to a subset of devices (or, if you're fortunate, just one device), the next step is to *reload* it, which is Cisco parlance for rebooting it.

Reloading a switch or router isn't unlike rebooting a computer. It's a catchall, "try this first" technique that has a reputation for working much of the time. Some technology purists don't like the idea of rebooting as a first step. But in an organization with a crippling network outage, you don't have time to follow a scientific troubleshooting process. Getting the network working is what's most important.

A reload does one very useful thing: it gets your device back to the startup configuration. If you (or someone else) have changed anything in the running configuration without saving it, a reload will reverse that change and could even fix the problem. A reload can also flush the ARP and MAC address tables, clear Port Security entries, reset routing protocols, reestablish trunks and EtherChannels, and clear out a host of other things—any of which could fix the problem.

Going back to my earlier word of caution, it's important to remember that the effects of a reload can stretch beyond the device you're reloading, at least momentarily.

Hence, it's possible that reloading a switch or router will cause the network problem to get worse before things settle down again. For example, if you were to reload an OSPF router, other OSPF routers connected to it would momentarily have to reroute their traffic down a different path. If no other path was available, those routers would have no choice but to drop the traffic.

Try it now

Reload any device or switch in your lab using the following enable command:

```
Reload
```

The device will ask you for a confirmation and will then immediately reboot:

```
Router1#reload
Proceed with reload? [confirm]
```

You should immediately see output indicating a pending reload:

```
*Nov 12 03:14:34.142: %SYS-5-RELOAD: Reload requested by admin on console.
    Reload Reason: Reload Command.
```

20.2.1 Scheduling a reload

In the case of a network problem that can wait until everyone has gone home (including you), you have the option of scheduling a reload to occur later. You can schedule a reload to occur either at a specific time or after a specified number of minutes. This is especially handy if your organization requires you to postpone the reload until some unholy hour when you'd rather be sleeping.

Try it now

On any device in your lab, schedule a reload to occur in 15 minutes from now:

```
Reload in 15
```

Once again, you'll be prompted for a confirmation:

```
Switch2#reload in 15
Reload scheduled for 22:01:04 UTC Fri Nov 11 2016 (in 15 minutes) by admin on
    console
Proceed with reload? [confirm]
Switch2#
Nov 11 21:46:06.073: %SYS-5-SCHEDULED_RELOAD: Reload requested for 22:01:04
    UTC Fri Nov 11 2016 at 21:46:04 UTC Fri Nov 11 2016 by admin on console.
```

You can specify the reload time in minutes or in both hours and minutes. For example, if you wanted to reload the device in 1 hour, 15 minutes, you'd issue the command `reload in 1:15`. As an aside, using the `reload in` command can keep you from locking yourself out when making changes on a remote device. For example, if you're working on a router in an office that you're not in physical proximity to, you can schedule a reload for a few minutes out and then make your changes. If your changes cause you to lose connectivity, you have to wait a few minutes for the router to reload. Once it reloads, it'll forget your changes, and then you can then connect back and try again.

But what if your changes *do* work? In that case, you need to cancel or abort the reload.

Try it now

On the same device on which you scheduled a reload, use the following command to cancel the reload:

```
Cancel reload
```

IOS will immediately halt the countdown and won't reload the device:

```
Switch2#reload cancel


***
*** --- SHUTDOWN ABORTED ---
***

Nov 11 21:46:38.721: %SYS-5-SCHEDULED_RELOAD_CANCELLED:  Scheduled reload
    cancelled at 21:46:38 UTC Fri Nov 11 2016
```

If you're reasonably certain you know which device is causing the problem, and a reload doesn't fix it, it may indicate that the problem is in the startup configuration, which a reload won't fix.

For this reason, it's a good idea to keep copies of your working startup configurations. If one of your IOS devices isn't working properly even after a reload, you can compare the startup configuration on the device to your copy. Remember that when a router or switch boots, IOS copies the startup configuration into the running configuration, so after a reboot, both should be identical. If you find any discrepancies between the running configuration and your backup, you can fix them and hopefully solve the problem.

But if you don't have a good backup of the startup configuration, then you have what I call the nuclear option—deleting the startup configuration.

20.3 *Deleting the startup configuration*

Deleting the startup configuration on an IOS device means that you must reconfigure the device from scratch. This isn't something you just do willy-nilly. Before venturing down this path of effectively starting over, you should be convinced that it would take longer to untangle the messed-up configuration than it would to start from scratch. In other words, this isn't for the faint of heart!

Deleting the startup configuration is the easy part, and the process is the same for both routers and switches. If you followed the lab setup guide and have done all the exercises in this book, you have a pretty good idea of what starting from scratch entails. I won't rehash all of that here. Just keep in mind that deleting the startup configuration means almost nothing will work until you configure it.

Try it now

Choose a device on which to delete the startup configuration. To be on the safe side, you'll take a backup of the configuration. Display the device's startup configuration by issuing the following enable mode command:

```
show startup
```

Copy the entire contents and paste it into your favorite text editor.

Delete the startup configuration using the following enable mode command:

```
Delete nvram:startup-config
```

After entering the command, IOS will prompt you for the filename and a confirmation. Press Enter twice.

You should see the following:

```
Router1#delete nvram:startup-config
Delete filename [startup-config]?
Delete nvram:startup-config? [confirm]
[OK]
```

Non-volatile Random Access Memory (NVRAM) is where IOS devices store the startup configuration as well as the VLAN database. The preceding command doesn't delete everything in NVRAM, just the startup configuration file. Because IOS uses the running configuration for its minute-by-minute operations, deleting the startup configuration has no effect until you reload the device.

Once you reload the device, it will have no management IP address. That means the only way to access it is via the serial console, as you did in the lab setup.

Try it now

Referring to the lab setup appendix as needed, connect your computer to the serial console of the device from which you just deleted the startup configuration.

Reload the device using the `reload` command.

Once it comes back up, you should be able to get into enable mode without a password:

```
Router>enable
Router#
```

Notice that the old hostname of Router1 is gone, and now the prompt just reads `Router`. At this point, you're free to reconfigure the router from scratch.

20.4 Resetting the password

Another interesting problem crops up more often than you might think: not being able to log into a device because you don't know the password. It's not a disaster, but it can get in the way of fixing an actual disaster if there ever is one. The process for resetting the password is different for routers and switches, but in both cases you must use the serial console (as you did in the lab setup) to reset it.

Personally, I've never had to reset a password because I forgot it. But I have acquired secondhand devices that had a password set, which prevented me from logging in. This is the most likely scenario you'll run into: you acquire a device from someone else and don't know the password.

It's important to note that resetting the password in the way I'm about to show you wipes out the startup configuration. As a rule, you shouldn't perform these steps on a production device that's working properly. This is just for two extremes: the devices you don't care about and the devices you must get into right away!

The process for resetting the password differs slightly on routers and switches. In both cases, you must get into *Read-only Memory Monitor (ROMMON) mode*. ROMMON mode allows you to bypass the normal boot process so that the device doesn't read from the startup configuration but instead drops you into a default startup configuration. From there, you have free rein to make any changes you want, including creating usernames and passwords. After you make your changes, you'll save the new startup configuration, overwriting the old one and finally rebooting.

The difference between resetting the password on a router and a switch is that you have to push the Mode button on the front of the switch to get it into ROMMON mode, whereas on the router you have to send a special *break* command using your terminal emulation program. Given that you'll have to connect to the serial console of the switch anyway, pushing the lone button on the front of the switch shouldn't be a big deal. In fact, it's much easier to get into ROMMON on a switch than a router, so let's start with the hardest task first.

20.4.1 Resetting the password on a router

The first step is to reboot the router, which in this case will involve toggling the power switch or just pulling the power and plugging it back in. Again, because you'll be rebooting and wiping out the configuration, you'll need to connect to the serial console of the router before starting.

> **Try it now**
> With a serial console connected to the router of your choice, reboot the router by power-cycling it. Watch the boot process carefully.

You should see the normal boot output:

```
System Bootstrap, Version 12.3(8r)T8, RELEASE SOFTWARE (fc1)
Technical Support: http://www.cisco.com/techsupport
Copyright (c) 2004 by cisco Systems, Inc.
PLD version 0x10
GIO ASIC version 0x127
c1841 processor with 393216 Kbytes of main memory
Main memory is configured to 64 bit mode with parity disabled
```

You'll need to interrupt the boot process by sending a *break* signal from your terminal emulation program. Not all terminal emulators can do this, but PuTTY can. Refer to figure 20.1 to send a break signal to the router.

Try it now

Send a break signal from your terminal emulator. In the PuTTY menu, select Special Command and Break.

You should see what looks like an error, followed by a prompt:

```
*** Address Error (Load/Fetch) Exception ***
Access address = 0x1

PC = 0x1, Cause = 0x10, Status Reg = 0x3041e803
rommon 1 >
```

Figure 20.1   Sending a *break* signal using PuTTY

If you see the `rommon` prompt, then you've successfully interrupted the boot process and gotten into ROMMON mode! The next step is to change the *configuration register* to ignore the startup configuration. The configuration register controls several things about the router's operation, including whether it reads the startup configuration or ignores it.

Try it now

At the `rommon` prompt, type `confreg 0x2142` and press Enter.

After issuing the command, you should see a message telling you to reboot:

```
rommon 1 > confreg 0x2142
You must reset or power cycle for new config to take effect
```

Type `reset` and press Enter:

```
rommon 2 > reset
```

The router will reboot, and if all went well, after several moments you should see the following:

```
        --- System Configuration Dialog ---
Would you like to enter the initial configuration dialog? [yes/no]:
```

At this point, you can answer no to the initial configuration dialog to get to the usual IOS prompt or yes to let IOS guide you through some basic configuration settings. Regardless of which you choose, you're not finished yet!

> **Try it now**
>
> Get into global configuration mode and create a username and password:
>
> ```
> Router(config)#username ben privilege 15 secret cisco
> ```
>
> Change the enable password:
>
> ```
> Router(config)#enable secret cisco
> ```
>
> Feel free to make any other changes you like, such as setting the hostname. Before you wrap up, change the configuration register to 0x2102:
>
> ```
> Router(config)#config-register 0x2102
> ```
>
> This will tell ROMMON to install the startup configuration (which you're about to save) when it boots up.
>
> Finally, save the running configuration and reload the router:
>
> ```
> Write memory
> Reload
> ```

The order of operations here is important. You must save the configuration *after* changing the configuration register back. If all went well, the router will boot into IOS with the changes you just made.

20.4.2 Resetting the password on a switch

The process for resetting the password on a switch is almost identical to that of the router, except for how you get into ROMMON mode.

> **Try it now**
>
> Power cycle the switch, and during the boot process, press the Mode button on the front of the switch. The switch should drop you into ROMMON mode. The steps from this point on are the same as for the router, so I'll just summarize them here.
>
> In ROMMON, change the configuration register to 0x2142 using the command `confreg 0x2142`.

(continued)

Reboot the switch.

When it boots up, make your changes, set the configuration register back to 0x2102 using the global configuration command `config-register 0x2102`.

Save the running configuration, and then reboot the switch to enjoy your new configuration!

20.5   *Commands used in this chapter*

In a disaster scenario, your focus is going to be on getting things up and running again, so there are a limited number of commands at your disposal. Table 20.1 lists those commands and when to use them.

Table 20.1   Commands used in this chapter

Function	Command	Configuration mode	Description
Reloading the device	`Reload in 15`	N/A	Schedules a reload 15 minutes from now
Reloading the device	`Reload cancel`	N/A	Cancels a scheduled reload
Deleting the startup configuration	`Delete nvram:startup-config`	N/A	Deletes the startup configuration from NVRAM
Resetting the password	`confreg 0x2142`	ROMMON	Configures ROMMON to ignore the startup configuration
Resetting the password	`config-register 0x2102`	Global	Configures ROMMON to load the startup configuration at boot time

Performance and
health checklist

In this chapter, I'll give you a checklist of performance and health items that may come in handy when you're blindsided with a vague complaint about the network being slow. Even if the complaint comes from just one user, you'd be remiss not to tentatively investigate. This checklist will give you some clues as to whether you need to eliminate the network as a problem or investigate further. I emphasize that this checklist is not a troubleshooting guide. It's only going to tell you if there's a problem—not necessarily what that problem is or how to fix it.

In addition to providing a checklist, I'll show you how to check each item. Some of this you've seen before, and some of it will be new. Keep in mind that you may have to work through this checklist on multiple devices in your network. It's rare that a network problem will manifest itself in an obvious way on every router and switch. By the way, all the IOS commands I show you in this chapter, with one exception, will work on both routers and switches. I'll point out that exception when we get to it.

Here's the checklist:

- Is the CPU being overloaded?
- What's the system uptime?
- Is there a damaged network cable or jack?
- Are ping times unusually high or inconsistent?
- Are routes flapping?

21.1 *Is the CPU being overloaded?*

What constitutes normal CPU usage varies based on the device, what role it plays in your network, and how busy your network is overall. The command `show processes cpu history` will display three graphs showing historical CPU usage for the last 60 seconds, 60 minutes, and 72 hours:

```
Switch1#show processes cpu history
```

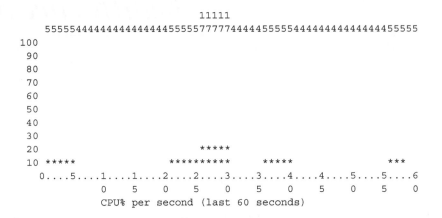

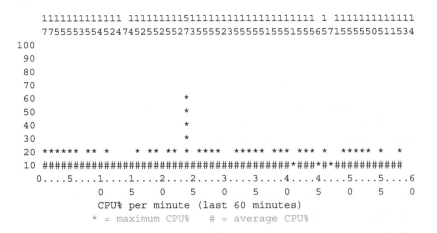

```
    564545555354545
    512522004969548
100
 90
 80
 70
 60 ** *       * * *
 50 ** * **** *** *
 40 ***************
 30 ***************
 20 ***************
 10 ###############

    0....5....1....1....2....2....3....3....4....4....5....5....6....6....7.
    .

          0   5   0   5   0   5   0   5   0   5   0   5   0
              CPU% per hour (last 72 hours)
            * = maximum CPU%   # = average CPU%
```

In the last two graphs, the hash or pound sign (#) indicates the average CPU usage. On Switch1, it's consistently 10% or less for the past hour. Second-by-second fluctuations in CPU usage are normal, but what you want to look for is a high average CPU usage. If you see a sustained average CPU usage above 80%, it could indicate a problem.

Notice that on the 72-hour graph, the data stops prior to the 15-hour mark. This indicates the switch was turned off until about 15 hours ago.

21.2 What's the system uptime?

Generally, routers and switches should always be on. If one reboots unexpectedly, it's almost always either human error or a device problem. You can figure out when the device last rebooted by using the show version command:

```
Switch1#show version
Cisco IOS Software, C3560 Software (C3560-IPSERVICESK9-M), Version
    15.0(2)SE5, RELEASE SOFTWARE (fc1)
Technical Support: http://www.cisco.com/techsupport
Copyright (c) 1986-2013 by Cisco Systems, Inc.
Compiled Fri 25-Oct-13 13:18 by prod_rel_team

ROM: Bootstrap program is C3560 boot loader
BOOTLDR: C3560 Boot Loader (C3560-HBOOT-M) Version 12.2(44)SE6, RELEASE
    SOFTWARE (fc1)

Switch1 uptime is 14 hours, 43 minutes
System returned to ROM by power-on
System image file is "flash:/c3560-ipservicesk9-mz.150-2.SE5.bin"
```

Switch1 rebooted almost 15 hours ago, which agrees perfectly with what the CPU graph shows. One thing that's misleading, however, is the output System returned to ROM by power-on. This does not necessarily mean that someone pulled the power plug on the switch. IOS will display this message even if you do a soft reload using the `reload` command.

21.3   *Is there a damaged network cable or jack?*

If only one user is complaining about the network, you may have a physical connectivity problem somewhere between the switch and the user. The command `show interfaces counters errors` is a reliable way of pinpointing such problems. The only downside is that it won't give you any useful information on a router:

```
Switch1#show interfaces counters errors

Port      Align-Err   FCS-Err   Xmit-Err    Rcv-Err   UnderSize   OutDiscards
Fa0/1            0         0           0          0           0             0
Fa0/2            0         0           0          0           0             0
Fa0/3            0         0           0          0           0             0
Fa0/4            0         0           0          0           0             0

...

Port   Single-Col   Multi-Col   Late-Col   Excess-Col   Carri-Sen   Runts   Giants
Fa0/1           0           0          0            0           0       0        0
Fa0/2           0           0          0            0           0       0        0
Fa0/3           0           0          0            0           0       0        0
Fa0/4           0           0          0            0           0       0        0
```

If you run this command on one of your switches, you'll see many more lines of text. I've truncated the output here. You don't need to know what each of these items means. You just need to know that ideally they should all be 0. If any of them aren't zero, it doesn't necessarily indicate a problem, but any nonzero values should stay the same. If you see any of the numbers steadily increasing, you have a physical connectivity problem such as a damaged or defective cable, an improper punch-down to the patch panel or network jack, or even the wrong type of network cable.

21.4   *Are ping times unusually high or inconsistent?*

High ping times, especially over a WAN connection, can indicate a physical connectivity problem or a heavily loaded link. A ping response time nearing 100 ms doesn't necessarily indicate a problem, but it does warrant further investigation. Inconsistent ping times can indicate a device, link, or routing protocol going up and down. Having a graph of ping times can be tremendously helpful in spotting patterns.

My favorite tool for graphing ping times on the fly is Colasoft Ping Tool (colasoft .com). Figure 21.1 illustrates what a series of normal, consistent pings looks like.

Visually, the graph isn't very interesting. It's mostly flat, with some spikes here and there. Most of the ping response times are 1 millisecond (ms), which is fantastic. Keep in mind that the figure illustrates ping times in my lab network, so the graph looks better than what you'd see in a real network.

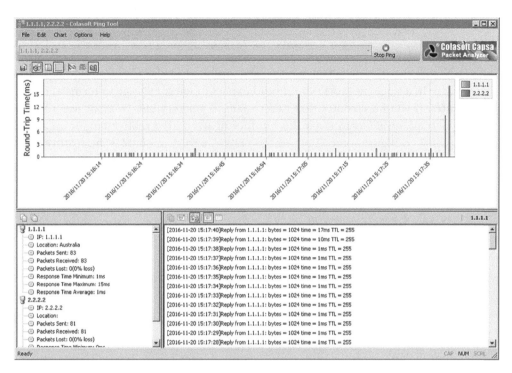

Figure 21.1   Colasoft Ping Tool showing a series of pings

21.5   *Are routes flapping?*

An IP route going down and coming up or flapping without explanation always requires investigation. The easiest way to check for this is to run a show ip route:

```
Switch1#show ip route

Codes: L - local, C - connected, S - static, R - RIP, M - mobile, B - BGP
       D - EIGRP, EX - EIGRP external, O - OSPF, IA - OSPF inter area
       N1 - OSPF NSSA external type 1, N2 - OSPF NSSA external type 2
       E1 - OSPF external type 1, E2 - OSPF external type 2
       i - IS-IS, su - IS-IS summary, L1 - IS-IS level-1, L2 - IS-IS level-2
       ia - IS-IS inter area, * - candidate default, U - per-user static
    route
       o - ODR, P - periodic downloaded static route, H - NHRP, l - LISP
       + - replicated route, % - next hop override

Gateway of last resort is not set

     1.0.0.0/32 is subnetted, 1 subnets
C       1.1.1.1 is directly connected, Loopback1
     2.0.0.0/32 is subnetted, 1 subnets
O       2.2.2.2 [110/2] via 10.0.99.2, 00:10:17, FastEthernet0/24
     10.0.0.0/8 is variably subnetted, 2 subnets, 2 masks
C       10.0.99.0/30 is directly connected, FastEthernet0/24
```

```
L         10.0.99.1/32 is directly connected, FastEthernet0/24
      172.31.0.0/24 is subnetted, 1 subnets
O         172.31.70.0 [110/2] via 10.0.99.2, 00:10:17, FastEthernet0/24
```

Notice that the two OSPF routes were installed in the routing table only 10 minutes ago. In a stable network, you should expect to see routes age in terms of days, not minutes. If you have routes that never seem to get very old, you can use a feature called *route table profiling* to track the number of IP routing table changes on a device. The global configuration command `ip route profile` enables the feature.

Once you issue this command, IOS will inspect the routing table every five seconds and record the number of changes. You can view the number of changes with a `show ip route profile`:

```
Switch1#show ip route profile
IP routing table change statistics:
Frequency of changes in a 5 second sampling interval
-------------------------------------------------------------
Change/   Fwd-path  Prefix   Nexthop   Pathcount  Prefix
interval  change    add      change    change     refresh
-------------------------------------------------------------
0         251       251      260       260        260
1         0         0        0         0          0
2         9         9        0         0          0
3         0         0        0         0          0
4         0         0        0         0          0
5         0         0        0         0          0
10        0         0        0         0          0
```

I must admit that I still have difficulty remembering how to interpret this table, so I'll keep it simple. In a stable network, the numbers in the 0 row should increase every five seconds. The 0 indicates the number of changes to the IP routing table that have occurred within the last five seconds. In a stable network, you should have no changes, hence the 0. The numbers in the other rows should not increase. If they do, routes are flapping and you'll need to investigate.

21.6   *Commands in this chapter*

Refer to the commands in table 21.1 to complete the hands-on lab exercises.

Table 21.1   Commands used in this chapter

Command	Configuration mode	Description
show processes cpu history	N/A	Displays historical CPU usage
show version	N/A	Displays device uptime
show interfaces counters errors	N/A	Displays interface errors
show ip route	N/A	Displays the IP routing table

Table 21.1 Commands used in this chapter

Command	Configuration mode	Description
ip route profile	Global	Enables IP routing table profiling
show ip route profile	N/A	Displays the number of changes to the IP routing table

21.7 Hands-on lab

As you read through this checklist, you may notice a theme: what's normal depends on your network. As you get time, answer the following questions to create a baseline for each of your devices so you have a better idea of what normal looks like for your network. Be sure to do this when the network is humming along smoothly and nobody's complaining.

Here are some things to record:

- What's the average CPU usage for the past 24 hours?
- What are the average ping times to network resources (servers) from different offices?
- Are there any ports that always seem to have errors?
- What's the typical age of routes?
- Are there any routers or switches that have been up for a surprisingly long or short time?

It can take some time to compile this information, so don't feel like you have to do this in one sitting. You may never need it, but having it available can make performing a differential diagnosis that much easier.

Next steps

As your month of lunches draws to a close, you should have a pretty good idea of whether you want to continue developing your Cisco networking skills. In this chapter, I'll give you some learning resources so you can keep the momentum going.

22.1 *Certification resources*

If you're serious about a career in Cisco networking, the next logical step is getting Cisco-certified. Cisco offers different certification tracks that focus on different technologies, and the most popular track has historically been the Routing and Switching track. The Cisco Certified Entry Networking Technician (CCENT) and Cisco Certified Network Associate (CCNA) are the two entry-level certifications, but many recruiters and hiring managers haven't even heard of the CCENT. My advice is that if you're going to go the certification route, shoot for your CCNA to start with.

Certification gives you three things:

- A solid foundation of network theory
- Practice in advanced configuration and troubleshooting
- More money

A certification often makes the difference between getting an interview and hearing "Do you know anyone else who might be a good fit?" Many years ago, I sat in an office next to a technical recruiter, and this is exactly how it works. Few places will take you seriously as a full-time Cisco network administrator if you don't have a certification.

Certification isn't free. The cost of the CCNA exam is about $300 USD, and it's non-refundable. To pass, you'll need solid training and lots of practice. Pluralsight.com has a wealth of training for all levels of Cisco certification, ranging from entry level to expert and everything in between.

22.2 Cisco's Virtual Internet Routing Lab

In chapter 1, I advised against using Cisco's Virtual Internet Routing Lab (VIRL) for the labs in this book because it doesn't give you the same experience you get when working with physical gear. This may sound trivial, but if you're going to focus on Cisco networking in your career, you should know how to work with physical routers and switches. A coworker once told me a story about his brother's unusual job interview experience. The person conducting the interview sat him down in front of a Cisco router and asked him to configure it. Strangely enough, the position wasn't even for a network administrator! You can imagine how much more a prospective employer might ask of you if you interview for a network administrator position.

Having said that, you'll want to practice with several routers and switches to get a feel for what it's like to configure and troubleshoot a larger network. Setting up and operating such a network using physical Cisco gear is cost-prohibitive, not to mention noisy. If you're ready to take the plunge and set up VIRL, check out Brandon Carroll's Pluralsight course, Using Cisco VIRL for CCENT and CCNA Studies (https://www.pluralsight.com/courses/cisco-virl-ccent-ccna-studies).

22.3 Troubleshooting end-user connectivity

In this book, you've learned how to configure Cisco routers and switches, as well as perform a bit of troubleshooting. But to be a well-rounded network administrator, you'll also want to learn how to perform some network troubleshooting from an end user's workstation. This is especially important if you don't have permission to touch Cisco devices at work but still want to nurture your network administration skills.

My Pluralsight course, Practical Networking (https://www.pluralsight.com/courses/practical-networking), gives you a practical, hands-on understanding of how to troubleshoot network-related issues from the end user's workstation. If you combine this knowledge with what you've learned in this book, you'll get a better understanding of how your desktops and servers interact with your routers and switches.

22.4 Never the end

These resources should give you enough to start with, whether you want to delve into full-time network administration or just want to tinker around with routers and switches on the side. For now, you should have enough of a foundation to be comfortable performing the most common basic administration tasks. How far you go from here is up to you!

index

Symbols

? (question mark) 41, 94
. (dot character) 188
* (asterisk character) 245
# (hash sign) 32, 42

A

access lists, restricting SSH access with 248–250
Access Mode VLAN setting 136
access-class Management in command 251
access-group command 121
ACE (access control entry) 117
ACLs (access control lists)
    applying to interfaces 120–122
    applying to subinterfaces 194–195
    applying to SVIs 126–127
    creating 117–120
    replacing 124–125
action 116
active port 163
addresses
    DHCP, configuring devices to request 106–107
    IP
        assigning 99–114
        blocking traffic between 116–120
    MAC
        overview 66–67
        sticky 70–72
addressing devices, across broadcast domains 18
Administrative Mode 136–137
Advanced Enterprise Services (ADVENTERPRISE)
    package 39
Advanced IP Services (IPSERVICES) package 39

aging time parameter 67–69
Alternate DNS Server field 101
area parameter 226
ARP (Address Resolution Protocol) 20–21, 185
AS (autonomous system) number 216
attacks, flooding MAC 60–63
auto-cross 134
auto-MDIX feature 134
autonegotiation, duplex and speed 55–56

B

backbone area 226
backup port 163
banner command 42
bindings 110
BLK status 163
bookmarks 10
bouncing 56, 137
break command 269
break signal 270
bridging loops, using STP to protect against
    159–170
    PortFast 168–170
    Rapid Spanning Tree 166–168
broadcast domains 14–18
    addressing devices across 18
    and MAC address tables 15–16
    connecting
        overview 18
        using routers 21–24
    limiting size of 17
    traversing using default gateways 24–28

C

cables, StackWise 133
CAM (content addressable memory) table 15
Cancel reload command 267
Capability column 241
carriage return 35
Catalyst 3550 134
CCENT (Cisco Certified Entry Networking
    Technician) 1
CCNA (Cisco Certified Network Administrator) 1
CDP (Cisco Discovery Protocol) 235–236
certification resources 280–281
channel-group 1 mode active command 182
channel-group 1 mode on command 182
channels
    dynamic
        configuring using LACP 173–177
        overview 172–173
    static 172–173
        creating 177–179
        overview 172–173
    to optimize network performance
        load-balancing methods 179–183
        overview 171–178
Cisco devices, securing 243–251
    creating privileged user accounts 244–246
    reconfiguring VTY lines 246
    securing console ports 250–251
    testing privileged user accounts 244–246
Cisco DHCP servers, configuring 100–103
    lease time 102
    options 101–102
    scopes 101
    subnets 102–103
    VLANs 102–103
Cisco IOS 30–45
    compared with Cisco NX-OS 6–7
    defined 30–31
    frequently used commands 45
    logging into Cisco devices 31–32
    no command 44–45
    packages, identifying 38–39
    running configurations
        changing 41, 43
        viewing 39–41
    show command 32–37
    startup configurations, saving 43
    using different versions of 6
    versions
        identifying 38–39
        numbers 38
Cisco networks
    broadcast domains 14–18
        addressing devices across 18

    and MAC address tables 15–16
    connecting 18, 21–24
    limiting size of 17
    traversing using default gateways 24–28
    Ethernet frames 12–14
    IP addresses 18–21
        and ARP 20–21
        determining location using 18–19
        versus MAC addresses 20
    MAC addresses 10–11
    overview 8–29
    routers
        managing 29
        overview 9–10
    switches
        managing 29
        overview 9–10
Cisco NX-OS, compared with Cisco IOS 6–7
clear logging command 262
CLI (command-line interface) 30
Colasoft Ping Tool 276
commands, frequently used 45
configuration register 270
configurations
    router-on-a-stick 185–186
    running
        changing 41–43
        viewing 39–41
    startup
        deleting 267–269
        saving 43
configure terminal command 45
connected networks 209
connected status 47
console ports, securing 250–251
content addressable memory table. See CAM
copy running-config startup-config command 45
CPU, overloading 274–275
CurrentAddr column 63

D

damaged jacks and network cables 276
Data Link layer 185
databases, VLANs 76–77
debug ip routing command 258, 262
debug port-security command 262
debug sw-vlan vtp events command 262
debugging
    commands 254–259
    DHCP 256–257
    IP routing 258–259
    Port Security 255
    VTP 257–258
decapsulates 26

Default Gateway field 89, 101
default gateways
    configuring 95–98, 204
    to traverse broadcast domains 24–28
default-gateway command 104
default-router command 103
Delete nvram:startup-config command 268
deny action 117
description keyword 188
Destination host unreachable message 194
destination IP address 117
Destination unreachable message 195
devices
    configuring to request DHCP addresses
        106–107
    moving 66–69
        aging time parameter 67–69
        MAC addresses 66–67
    moving to new switches 141–142
    narrowing scope to subset 265
    reloading 265–267
    tracking 232–242
        CDP 235–236
        obtaining IP addresses 233
        obtaining MAC addresses 233, 236, 239
        scenarios 232–233
        steps 233
        tracing to last hop 233
        tracing to last hop with traceroute 234–235,
            238–239
        viewing MAC address tables 236–241
    unauthorized, preventing 69–73
        by making Port Security maximally secure 70
        using sticky MAC addresses 70–72
DHCP (Dynamic Host Configuration Protocol)
    addresses, configuring devices to request
        106–107
    assignment, excluding IP addresses from
        104–106
    debugging 256–257
    leases, viewing 110–111
    overview 99–100
    pools
        associating with VLANs 108–109
        configuring 103–104
        creating for Executives subnets 205–212
        creating second 109–110
    to assign IP addresses 99–114
DHCP Discover message 106, 112
DHCP exhaustion 102
DHCP Offer message 107
disabled status 47
disabling
    ports 52–54
    Telnet access 246–248

domain name 102
domains, broadcast 14–18
    addressing devices across 18
    and MAC address tables 15–16
    connecting 18, 21–24
    limiting size of 17
    traversing using default gateways 24–28
dot character 188
DTP (Dynamic Trunking Protocol)
    configuring to automatically negotiate
        trunk 136–138
    configuring VLANs using 135–136
    overview 172
DUAL (Diffusing Update Algorithm) 220
duplex
    and autonegotiation 55–56
    changing 57
    overview 55
Duplex column 55
dynamic auto setting 136
dynamic desirable setting 136–137
dynamic port channels
    configuring using LACP 173–177
    overview 172–173
dynamic routing protocols 213–231
    configuring EIGRP 216–225
        choosing best path 221–224
        overview 225
        routing around link failures 224
    OSPF 225–230
    router IDs
        configuring loopback interfaces 215–216
        overview 214–216

E

egressing frames 161
EIGRP (Enhanced Interior Gateway Routing Pro-
        tocol), configuring 216–225
    choosing best path 221–224
    overview 225
    routing around link failures 224
enabling
    IP routing 93
    ports 49–52
    SSH 246–248
    VTP pruning 153–157
end-users, troubleshooting connectivity 281
environments
    choosing for labs 3–4
    recommended for labs 5–6
    virtual 4–5
EPT (extended page tables) 5
EtherChannel Misconfiguration Guard 177–178
Ethernet frames 12–14, 91–92

exclude command 35, 37
exit command 86
extended IP access list 117

F

failures, STP and 163–165
FastEthernet 34, 37, 51
filtering output
    excluding lines 37
    including lines 36–37
flapping
    overview 56, 137
    routes 277–278
flooding
    attacks, MAC 60–63
    overview 13–14
forward delay timer 165
frames, Ethernet 12–14
full duplex 55
FWD state 163

G

gateways, default
    configuring 95–98, 204
    to traverse broadcast domains 24–28
GigabitEthernet 34, 37
global configuration mode 41, 58, 94
greater-than sign 32
GUI (graphical user interface) 30

H

half duplex 55
hardcoding 55

I

implicit deny rule 119–120
in keyword 121
inbound traffic 121
include command 35
ingressing frames 161
Inter-Switch Link. See ISL
inter-VLAN routing 184
interface command 50
interface configuration mode commands 58
Interface loopback0 command 230
interface range command 51–52, 54
interface vlan 600 command 98
interfaces
    applying ACLs to 120–122
    assigning IP addresses to 201–202
    loopback, configuring 215–216

unused, finding 53–54
interfaces trunk command 137
interrupt 13
inventorying VLANs 76–78
    databases 76–77
    default 78
    determining number of 78
    planning new 78
IOS (Internetwork Operating System) 5, 93
IP access control lists, securing networks with
        115–131
    blocking IP-to-IP traffic 116–120
    blocking IP-to-subnet traffic 122–127
    blocking subnet-to-subnet traffic 127–130
    by applying ACLs to interfaces 120–122
IP addresses 18–21
    and ARP 20–21
    assigning
        excluding from 104–106
        using DHCP 99–114
    obtaining 233
    to determine location 18–19, 23
    transit
        assigning to physical interfaces 201–202
        assigning to subinterfaces 202–203
        assigning to SVIs 202–203
    versus MAC addresses 20
IP Base (IPBASE) package 39
ip dhcp excluded-address command 105
IP helper-address command 112–113
ip helper-address interface command 112
IP packet 28
ip route profile command 278–279
IP routing
    debugging 258–259
    enabling 93
IP routing tables
    interpreting 192–194
    manually directing traffic with 197–212
        configuring default gateways 204
        configuring transit subnets 200–203
        connecting Router1 to Switch2 199–200
        creating DHCP pools for Executives
            subnets 205–212
        removing trunk link between switches 203
IP-to-subnet traffic, blocking 122–127
    applying ACLs to SVIs 126–127
    replacing ACLs 124–125
    wildcard masks 123–124
ipconfig 24, 110
ISL (Inter-Switch Link) 142

J

jacks, damaged 276

L

labs
 Cisco IOS versions 6
 environments
  choosing 3–4
  recommendations 5–6
  virtual 4–5
 live networks 5
 overview 3–6
 production networks 5
LACP (Link Aggregation Control Protocol)
 configuring dynamic port channels with
  173–177
 overview 173
LAN (local area network) 11
last hop
 tracing devices to 233
 tracing with traceroute 234–235, 238–239
lease time 102
leases, DHCP 110–111
Line column 245
line con 0 command 251
lines
 excluding 37
 including 36–37
link failures, STP and 163–165
links, routing around failures 224
live networks, for labs 5
load-balancing methods 179–182
local user account 243
location, determining using IP addresses 18–19, 23
logging buffered ? command 260
logging buffered 8192 command 262
logging buffered debugging command 262
logging buffered warnings command 263
logging buffers, configuring 253–254
logging in, to Cisco devices 31–32
logging severity levels 259–261
logging trap debugging command 263
login local command 251
loopback interfaces, configuring 215–216
loops, using STP to protect against 159–170
 PortFast 168–170
 Rapid Spanning Tree 166–168

M

MAC (media access control) 59, 66–67, 86, 91
 address tables, and broadcast domains 15–16
 flood attacks, preventing 60–63
 obtaining 233, 236, 239
 overview 10–11
 sticky 70–72
 tables, viewing 236–241

 versus IP addresses 20
masks, wildcard 123–124
MaxSecureAddr column 63
Mbps (megabits per second) 54
misconfigurations 252
modulus 261
Monoprint 20–21
multi-VLAN access port 85

N

Name column, in VLAN databases 77
name Executives command 86
negotiation 135
neighbors 216
network cables, damaged 276
network command 226
network interface card. *See* NIC
network settings, Executive-PC1 101
network statement 219
networks
 broadcast domains 14–18
  addressing devices across 18
  and MAC address tables 15–16
  connecting 18, 21–24
  limiting size of 17
  traversing using default gateways 24–28
 Ethernet frames 12–14
 IP addresses 18–21
  and ARP 20–21
  determining location using 18–19
  versus MAC addresses 20
 live, for labs 5
 MAC addresses 10–11
 overview 8–29
 performance checklist 273–279
  damaged jacks 276
  damaged network cables 276
  flapping routes 277–278
  overloaded CPU 274–275
  ping times 276
  system uptime 275–276
 production, for labs 5
 routers
  managing 29
  overview 9–10
 securing with IP access control lists 115–131
  blocking IP-to-IP traffic 116–120
  blocking IP-to-subnet traffic 122–127
  blocking subnet-to-subnet traffic 127–130
  by applying to interfaces 120–122
 switches 9–10
 using port channels to optimize
  performance 171–183
next hop 206

NIC (network interface card) 3, 10, 47, 168
no command 44–45
no interface port-channel 1 command 182
no switchport command 201, 212
non-Cisco DHCP 111–113
notconnect state 53–54, 57
notifications 260
NVRAM (non-volatile RAM) 43, 268
NX-OS (Nexus Operating System) 7

O

Operational Mode 136–137
OSI (Open Systems Interconnect) model 92, 185
OSPF (Open Shortest Path First) 225–230
OUI (organizationally unique identifier) 11
output, filtering
    excluding lines 37
    including lines 36–37
overloading CPU 274–275

P

P-to-IP traffic, blocking 116–120
packages, identifying 38–39
PAgP (Port Aggregation Protocol) 173
parameters, aging time 67–69
password keyword 244
passwords, resetting 269–271
    on routers 269–271
    on switches 271
permit action 120
ping command 97–98
ping failure 126
ping times 276
Ping Tool, Colasoft 276
pipe character 36–37
PoE (Power over Ethernet) 65
Port Aggregation Protocol. *See* PAgP
port channels
    dynamic
        configuring using LACP 173–177
        overview 172–173
    optimize network performance
        load-balancing methods 179–182
        overview 171–183
    static 172–173
        creating 177–179
        overview 172–173
Port column 47
port group 171
Port Security feature 59–74
    debugging 255
    maximum configuration of 70
    minimum configuration of 60–64

preventing MAC flood attacks 60–63
    violation modes 64
moving devices while using 66–69
    aging time parameter 67–69
    MAC addresses 66–67
preventing unauthorized devices 69–73
    by making maximally secure 70
    using sticky media access control
        addresses 70–72
testing 65–66
port-channel load-balance src-mac command 183
Port-channel1 interface 175
PortFast 168–170
ports
    configuration, checking 81
    disabling 52–54
    enabling 49–52
    securing using Port Security feature 59–74
    speed 54–57
        autonegotiation and 55–56
        changing 56–57
        overview 54–55
    status, viewing 47–49
Ports column, in VLAN databases 77
pound sign 275
Preferred DNS Server field 101
privileged user accounts, creating and
        testing 244–246
production networks, for labs 5
pruning, enabling VTP 153–157
PSTN (public switched telephone network) 184
PuTTY 31, 244, 270

R

RAM (random access memory) 39
recovering 264–272
    deleting startup configuration 267–269
    narrowing scope to subset of devices 265
    reloading devices 265–267
    resetting passwords 269–271
        on routers 269–271
        on switches 271
reload command 43, 45, 262, 268
reload in command 266
Remaining Age column 72
restrict violation mode 64
ROMMON (Read-only Memory Monitor)
        mode 269
rommon prompt 270
route table profiling 278
routed interface 201
router eigrp 7 command 216, 230
Router ospf 1 command 230
router-on-a-stick configuration 185–186

Router1
  connecting 186–187
  connecting to Switch2 199–200
routers
  creating scalable networks by connecting with
    switches 184–196
    applying ACLs to subinterfaces 194–195
    configuring subinterfaces 187–192
    connecting Router1 186–187
    interpreting IP routing tables 192–194
    router-on-a-stick configuration 185–186
  enabling IP routing 93
  managing 29
  overview 9–10
  resetting passwords on 269–271
  to connect broadcast domains 21–24
    determining location using IP addresses 23
    subnets 23–24
routes, flapping 277–278
Routing Descriptor Blocks section 228
Routing for Networks section 219
routing protocols 213–231
  configuring EIGRP 216–225
    choosing best path 221–224
    overview 225
    routing around link failures 224
  OSPF 225–230
  router IDs
    configuring loopback interfaces 215–216
    overview 214–216
routing tables, IP
  interpreting 192–194
  manually directing traffic with 197–212
RSTP (Rapid Spanning Tree Protocol) 166–168
rule 117
running configurations
  changing 41–43
  viewing 39–41

S

scalable networks, by connecting routers and
  switches 184–196
  applying ACLs to subinterfaces 194–195
  configuring subinterfaces 187–192
  connecting Router1 186–187
  interpreting IP routing tables 192–194
  router-on-a-stick configuration 185–186
scopes, when configuring DHCP 101
secret keyword 244
Secure Shell. *See* SSH
security
  Cisco devices 243–251
    creating privileged user accounts 244–246

reconfiguring VTY lines 246
    testing privileged user accounts 244–246
  console ports 250–251
  minimum configuration of 60–64
    preventing MAC flood attacks 60–63
    violation modes 64
  moving devices while using 66–69
    aging time parameter 67–69
    MAC addresses 66–67
  ports 59–74
  preventing unauthorized devices 69–73
    by making maximally secure 70
    using sticky MAC addresses 70–72
  testing 65–66
SecurityViolation column 63
sequence number 118
servers, configuring Switch1 as VTP 148–149
show ? command 45
show arp command 236
show cdp neighbors command 235, 242
show command
  filtering output from 35–37
    excluding lines 37
    including lines 36–37
  overview 32–37
show etherchannel load-balance command 182
show etherchannel summary command 174, 182
show interfaces counters errors command 276,
  278
show interfaces pruning command 157
show interfaces status command 48–49
show interfaces trunk command 141, 153, 155,
  157
show ip dhcp binding command 110
show ip dhcp pool command 256
show ip eigrp neighbor command 230
show ip interface brief command 35–36, 187, 216
show ip ospf neighbor command 230
show ip protocols command 230
show ip route command 98, 193, 206, 277–278
show logging command 253, 262
show mac address-table command 236, 242
show port-security command 64, 74
show port-security interface fa0/1 command 74
show processes cpu history command 274, 278
show run interface fa0/1 command 74
show running-config command 45
show spanning-tree vlan 700 command 161
show ssh command 247, 251
show startup-config command 45
show users command 245, 251
show version command 45, 275, 278
show vlan brief command 76, 86
show vlan command 151

show vtp status command 148–149, 157
shutdown command 50
shutdown violation mode 64
slash notation 202
spanning-tree mode rapid-pvst command 170
spanning-tree portfast command 170
speed, of ports 54–57
    autonegotiation and 55–56
    changing 56–57
    overview 54–55
SSH (Secure Shell)
    enabling 246–248
    restricting access using access lists 248–250
ssh command 31
StackWise 133
startup configurations
    deleting 267–269
    saving 43
startup-config file 43
static access port 81–84, 86
static port channels 172–173
    creating 177–179
    overview 172–173
Status column
    in VLAN databases 77
    overview 47
STP (Spanning Tree Protocol)
    link failures and 163–165
    to protect against bridging loops 159–170
        PortFast 168–170
        Rapid Spanning Tree 166–168
    understanding 161–165
subinterfaces
    applying ACLs to 194–195
    assigning IP addresses to 202–203
    configuring 187–192
subnet address 88
subnet mask 23–24
subnets
    blocking traffic between 127–130
    Executives, creating DHCP pools for 205–212
    overview 23–24
    VLANs and 88–91
    when configuring DHCP 102–103
SVIs (switched virtual interfaces) 92, 154, 186
    applying ACLs to 126–127
    assigning IP addresses to 202–203
    configuring 93–95
    creating 93–95
    defined 93–95
    VLANs with 87–98
        choosing subnets 88–91
        configuring default gateways 95–98
        routers 91–93
        switches 91–93

switch ports 46–58
    disabling 52–54
    duplex 54–57
        autonegotiation and 55–56
        changing 57
        overview 55
    enabling 49–52
    speed 54–57
        autonegotiation and 55–56
        changing 56–57
        overview 54–55
    status of, viewing 47–49
Switch1
    configuring as VTP server 148–149
    creating new VLANs on 150–153
Switch2
    configuring 138–141
    configuring as VTP client 149–150
    connecting to Router1 199–200
switches
    connecting new 133–134
    connecting using trunk links 132–145
        changing trunk encapsulation 142–144
        configuring Switch2 138–141
        connecting new switches 133–134
        moving devices to new switches 141–142
        VLAN trunk links 134–138
    creating scalable networks by connecting with
        routers 184–196
        applying ACLs to subinterfaces 194–195
        configuring subinterfaces 187–192
        connecting Router1 186–187
        interpreting IP routing tables 192–194
        router-on-a-stick configuration 185–186
    enabling IP routing 93
    managing 29
    new
        configuring on VLANs 139–141
        moving devices to 141–142
    overview 9–10
    removing trunk links between 203
    resetting passwords on 271
switchport access vlan 700 command 86, 142
switchport mode access command 83–84, 86, 136,
    142
switchport port-security command 63, 74
switchport port-security mac-address sticky
    command 74
switchport port-security maximum 5 command 73
switchport port-security violation restrict
    command 73
switchport port-security violation shutdown
    command 73
switchport voice vlan 20 command 85–86

syslogging, configuring 261–262
system uptime 275–276

T

tables
  MAC address 15–16
  MAC, viewing 236–241
telnet command 31, 251
Telnet, disabling access 139, 246–248
terminal monitor command 65
testing
  connectivity between VLANs 97–98
  Port Security feature 65–66
  privileged user accounts 244–246
traceroute 222, 224, 234–235, 238–239
tracing, to last hop with traceroute 234–235,
    238–239
traffic, manually directing with IP routing
    tables 197–212
  configuring default gateways 204
  configuring transit subnets 200–203
  connecting Router1 to Switch2 199–200
  creating DHCP pools for Executives
    subnets 205–212
  removing trunk link between switches 203
transit subnets, configuring 200–203
  assigning transit IP addresses to physical
    interfaces 201–202
  assigning transit IP addresses to
    subinterfaces 202–203
  assigning transit IP addresses to SVIs 202–203
transport input ssh command 251
traversing broadcast domains, using default
    gateways 24–28
troubleshooting 252–263
  configuring logging buffers 253–254
  configuring syslogging 261–262
  debugging
    commands 254–259
    DHCP 256–257
    IP routing 258–259
    Port Security 255
    VTP 257–258
  end-user connectivity 281
  logging severity levels 259–261
trunk
  encapsulation, changing 142–144
trunk links
  connecting switches using 132–145
    changing trunk encapsulation 142–144
    configuring Switch2 138–141
    connecting new switches 133–134
    moving devices to new switches 141–142
    VLAN trunk links 134–138
  removing between switches 203

trunks
  configuring DTP to automatically
    negotiate 136–138

U

undebug all command 262
user accounts, privileged 244–246

V

versions
  identifying 38–39
  numbers 38
violation modes 64
VIRL (Virtual Internet Routing Lab) 5, 281
VLAN column, in VLAN databases 77
VLANs (virtual LANs) 75–86, 134–138
  assigning 80–84
    checking port configuration 81
    setting access 81–83
    setting access mode 83–84
  associating with DHCP pools 108–109
  configuring 135–136
  configuring automatically using VTP 146–158
  configuring DTP, to automatically negotiate
    trunk 136–138
  configuring on new switches 139–141
  creating 78–80
  creating new on Switch1 150–153
  databases 76–77
    Name column 77
    Ports column 77
    Status column 77
    VLAN column 77
  defined 75–76
  inventorying 76–78
    default 78
    determining number of 78
    planning new 78
    VLAN database 76–77
  new
    planning 78
    using 85–86
  SVIs with 87–98
    choosing subnets 88–91
    configuring default gateways 95–98
    routers 91–93
    switches 91–93
  testing connectivity between 97–98
  voice 84–85
  when configuring DHCP 102–103
voice VLANs 84–85
VPNs (virtual private networks) 197
VT-x (virtualization extensions) 5

VTP (VLAN Trunking Protocol)
  automatically configuring VLANs using
    146–158
  configuring Switch1 as server 148–149
  configuring Switch2 as client 149–150
  creating new VLANs on Switch1 150–153
  debugging 257–258
  enabling pruning 153–157
  warnings 147–148
vtp mode client command 157
vtp mode server command 157

vtp password MoL command 157
vtp pruning command 154, 157
VTY (Virtual TeletYpe) lines, reconfiguring 246
  disabling Telnet access 246–248
  enabling SSH 246–248
  restricting SSH access using access lists 248–250

W

WAN (wide area network) 184
wildcard masks 123–124